Iran Without Borders

Iran Without Borders

Towards a Critique of the Postcolonial Nation

HAMID DABASHI

VERSO
London • New York

First published by Verso 2016
© Hamid Dabashi 2016

Figure 1 (p. 7): Flood Gallery Fine Art Center Collection, Asheville, NC; from Hamid Dabashi, *In Search of Lost Causes: Fragmented Allegories of an Iranian Revolution* (Asheville, NC: Black Mountain Press, 2013). Reprinted with the kind permission of the publisher.
Figure 2 (p. 61): Nicky Nodjoumi, *Caught on the Way* (2008–09), oil on canvas, 96 in. x 120 in. Courtesy of the artist and Taymour Grahne Gallery, New York.
Figure 3 (p. 70): "Slavs and Tatars," *Molla Nasreddin: The Magazine that Would've Could've Should've* (Bruges: Christoph Keller Editions, 2011).
Figure 5 (p. 140): Azadeh Akhlaghi, "Sohrab Shahid-Saless—1 July 1998—Chicago" (2012—Print on Photo Paper—9 Editions + 1AP—247 cm × 110 cm). From "By an Eyewitness" (series). Reprinted with the kind permission of Azadeh Akhlaghi.
Figure 6 (p. 155): Photograph available online at panoramio.com/photo/52868351.
Figure 7 (p. 215): Reprinted with the kind permission of Amir Naderi.

1 3 5 7 9 10 8 6 4 2

Verso
UK: 6 Meard Street, London W1F 0EG
US: 20 Jay Street, Suite 1010, Brooklyn, NY 11201
versobooks.com

Verso is the imprint of New Left Books

ISBN-13: 978-1-78478-068-5 (HB)
ISBN-13: 978-1-78478-069-2 (US EBK)
ISBN-13: 978-1-78478-070-8 (UK EBK)

British Library Cataloguing in Publication Data
A catalogue record for this book is available from the British Library

Library of Congress Cataloging-in-Publication Data

Names: Dabashi, Hamid, 1951- author.
Title: Iran without borders : towards a critique of the postcolonial nation / Hamid Dabashi.
Description: Brooklyn, NY : Verso, 2016.
Identifiers: LCCN 2016008724 | ISBN 9781784780685 (hardback)
Subjects: LCSH: Iran—Civilization. | Iran—Intellectual life. | BISAC: HISTORY / Middle East / General.
Classification: LCC DS266 .D238 2016 | DDC 955--dc23
LC record available at http://lccn.loc.gov/2016008724

Typeset in Sabon by MJ&N Gavan, Truro, Cornwall
Printed in the US by Maple Press

For
Alejandra Gómez Colorado
and
Moisés Garduño García
Iranians beyond borders

Contents

Introduction

I succeeded:
I registered myself—
I adorned my name
Within an Identity Card,
And now my existence
Has a number:
Thus Hooray and Long Live Number 678
Issued from the Fifth District
Residence of Tehran!
Now I am totally at ease:
The kind bosom of the Motherland,
The pacifier of the Glorious Historical Heritage,
The lullaby of Civilization and Culture,
And all the jingling of the jingle bells of Law!

Forough Farrokhzad,
"Oh Bejeweled Land" (1964)

My father, Khodadad Dabashi, worked for the railroad. In Ahvaz, where I was born and raised, the Iranian national railroad—extending from Khorramshahr in the south to Tehran in the north and then turned east to Mashhad in the northeastern province of Khorasan—had a major station, where my father worked since before I was born, in mid June 1951, until his death in the summer of 1970. He made a meager but steady salary which, upon receipt, he handed entirely to my mother, who would immediately give him his monthly stipend for his one bottle of Russian vodka and one pack of cigarettes. The supply would ordinarily last him only three weeks of the month, during which he was a staunch anticolonial national-ist. But on the first day of the fourth week of the month when he ran out of his vodka and cigarette supply, signs of his ardent Nasserite socialism began to appear, building to a crescendo before his next paycheck and stipend about a week later, when once again Mosaddegh would resurface and Nasser subside.

I grew up in a household that was entirely matriarchal in its nature and disposition. My mother, Zahra Parviz Motlaq (Dabashi) was the boss. What she said, we all did. My father was the cook. He would come home from work, immediately report to our small kitchen, turn on his radio to Basra station, start listening to the legendary Egyptian singer Umm Kalthum, pour himself a shot of his vodka, light his cigarette, and begin cooking for us. His anticolonial nationalism and Third World socialism dovetailed somewhat miraculously with my moth-er's Shi'i piety. She never drank (except on very rare nocturnal occasions with my dad, when she thought my younger brother Aziz and I were asleep). She prayed fastidiously five times a day, fasted during the month of Ramadan, and led us in pilgrimage to Qom and Mashhad with the free train tickets my father received as part of his benefits. My father never prayed or fasted—except one summer when we were in Qom, when suddenly he stood up and prayed for about an hour, for the entire duration of which my mother could not stop laughing.

There was a blind Molla—we called him Molla Javad—who was among the regular retinue of my mother's Shi'i piety. Molla Javad would come to our home once a month, initially to answer my mother's juridical questions and concerns—ranging from the proper ritual purity mandates of a Muslim woman, to laws of alms and religious taxes. This would usually last about ten to fifteen minutes. Then he would start chanting songs (*rozeh-khani*, as we say in Persian) in praise of Imam Hossein and his seventy-two valiant supporters in the famous Battle of Karbala in the year 680 of the Common Era—the most sacrosanct traumatic event on the Shi'i calendar. My mother took advantage of Molla Javad's blindness, quietly attending to her household chores while asking him her juridical concerns. But when he began singing in praise of Seyyed al-Shohada my mother sat down in our living room and cried for a few minutes. When the *rozeh* was over, she quietly returned to her chores and Molla Javad began addressing me, my younger brother Aziz, and my cousin Hossein (if he happened to be there)—alternating between warning us against the sinful hazards of masturbation and teaching us about the virtues of Ayatollah Khomeini and his revolutionary zeal.

If the day that Molla Javad had come to our home for his monthly ritual happened to be a Friday, soon after his preaching he would get into an argument with my father—and the nature of their political debate entirely depended on whether my father was in his (first three weeks of the month) anticolonial nationalist mood, or (final week of the month) socialist mood. Either way, a heated discussion would ensue, Molla Javad would denounce both Mosaddegh and Nasser, and praise Ayatollah Khomeini, as my father quietly sipped his vodka, puffed on his cigarette, and found a judicious way to concur with Molla Javad on one thing: that the British were bastards.

In between my father's alternating anticolonial nationalism and Third World socialism, on one side, and Molla Javad's militant Islamism, competing for the gracious, patient, and quiet gaze of my mother's Shi'i pietism, the spectrum of my childhood's politics was extended into my adult life as I left my hometown for Tehran to go to college. In the mid 1970s I left Iran altogether for the United States, and watched the unfolding of the Iranian revolution of 1977–79 from afar. The socialist Tudeh Party was the most significant representation of Third World socialism in twentieth-century Iranian history, while Mohammad Mosaddegh's championing of the nationalization of the oil industry against British colonial domination exemplified the anticolonial nationalism of the same era. But Ayatollah Khomeini's militant Islamism ultimately outmaneuvered its rivals, stealing their thunder and triumphantly establishing an Islamic Republic in Iran.

Multiple Ideologies and One Nation

These three political cultures percolating around me were not just dominant in my childhood world, but in fact defined the geopolitics of the entire region, from the Indian subcontinent, through Iran and Central Asia, all the way to the Arab world and North Africa. Examined closely, these three simultaneous, competing, alternating ideologies were identifiable as the byproduct of some two hundred years of confrontation and contestation with European imperialism.

However, they may all be traced back to one singularly significant public intellectual, Seyyed Jamal al-Din al-Afghani (1838–97), who may in fact have been an Iranian Shi'i—a master at disguising himself in multiple and varied identities. He had been and he remained an authentic revolutionary—an anticolonial nationalist, a Third World socialist, and a militant Islamist all at the same time—by means of never being culturally authentic to any identity politics. My task in this book is to bring to life that world beyond identity politics, so different from the simplistic depiction presented in the daily news, in which Iranian society consists of the tyrannical Islamic ruling regime against the secular, liberal, urban elites. In fact, no ruling regime could ever make an exclusive claim over the idea of "Iran" as a nation, a people, a public sphere, a cultural effervescence still awaiting its political fulfillment.

When a State Fails to Represent

But what exactly is that difference? How do we make a distinction between an Islamic Republic trying to rule a country and the people, the nation, the political constituency it claims but fails completely to represent or conveniently rule? A false and falsifying binary has for the longest time dominated the Iranian political narrative, asserting that the ruling regime is "Islamic/Islamist" while the majority of people—or the sizable educated and urban component of it—is actually "secular." The active formation of a self-described platoon of "religious intellectuals," who mostly endorsed the Islamic Republic initially and then began to find fault with it, had generated its nemesis in the form of "secular intellectuals." This binary became a self-fulfilling prophecy, and leading representatives of these two camps soon began to recruit the younger generation of adherents, and before long a foggy air of suspension and supposition divided the political culture between the dominant Islamists and resistant secularists. A principal task of this book is to dismantle that false binary, and propose what you will see me repeatedly invoke as the "cosmopolitan worldliness" characterizing the modus operandi of Iranian culture, from its own imperial background to its subsequent postcolonial character, as well as the future rediscovery of its origins beyond its current fictive frontiers—borders manufactured through colonial domination and consolidated by means of multiple ideological narratives.

The Iranian Revolution of 1977–79 was in fact the historic rendezvous of all of these three ideologies, rooted in the Third World socialism of the Tudeh Party in the 1940s (which would be picked up by the Marxist guerilla uprisings of the Cherik-ha-ye Fada'i Khalq in the 1970s), the anticolonial nationalism of Mohammad Mosaddegh in the 1950s, and the Islamist uprising of Ayatollah Khomeini in the 1960s.

As the defeated and outmaneuvered nationalists and social-ists had lost their moral and intellectual grip on the society at large to the militant Islamists, they had now gathered under the false flag of "secularism"—a term with no historical roots in Iranian political parlance, and yet made veritable pre-cisely in its concocted, untranslatable Persian transliteration: "sekular."

In June 2009, a rigged presidential election resulted in a massive social uprising code-named the "Green Movement," which shook the ruling regime to its foundations. Superficially, the Green Movement was just questioning the accuracy of the electoral vote-count, as millions of protestors strongly believed the election had been rigged; but at a deeper and more trou-bling level for the regime, it was giving air and momentum to something more deeply repressed. What the Green Movement proved beyond any shadow of doubt was that the Islamic Republic had failed to manufacture a *Homo Islamicus*, and that the defiant spirit of Iran's cosmopolitan political culture (which included but was not reducible to militant Islamism) had resurfaced in triumph.

As late as during the preparatory stages of the revolution of 1977–79, the fact of this transnational disposition within Iranian political culture found itself displayed on a global stage. The wide range of revolutionary posters, produced within and outside Iran by militant students, and thus by far the most public face of the revolution, revealed the regional and global solidarity of these students with every progressive revolutionary movement around the globe, including those marked by International Labor Day (1 May) and International Women's Day (8 March), and the Palestinian national libera-tion movement.

Though the historical context of these particular revolu-tionary posters ranged from the 1950s through the 1960s, the origin of the political universalism they represented went all

Figure 1: Iranian revolutionary posters from the 1950s to the 1970s.

the way back to the late eighteenth century, the rise of a vast and multivariate travel literature. The extraordinary work of an astonishing range of expatriate public intellectuals ultimately paved the way for the Constitutional Revolution of 1906–11, in the preparatory stages of which a knowledge of the French Revolution of 1789 and the European revolutions of 1848—soon to be followed by the Russian Revolution of 1917—was critical.

Nation as Cosmopolis
The cosmopolitan disposition of Iranian culture is deeply rooted in its cultural history. Scarcely was any significant cultural development in nineteenth- or twentieth-century Iran initiated inside the country. The first Persian newspaper, *Kaghaz-e Akhbar*, was published using a printing machine that a young student had brought with him back from London; the first Iranian films, such as Abdolhossein Sepanta's *Lor Girl: The Iran of Yesterday and the Iran of Today* (1932), were made in India; the first major Persian novels, such as *Siyahatnameh-ye Ibrahim Beig* ("Ibrahim Beig's Travelogue"), by Haji Zeyn al-Abedin Maraghei (1839–1910), were written in Cairo or Berlin; and the country's most significant periodicals were edited in London, Paris, Berlin, Cairo, and Calcutta. Sadeq Hedayat, the founding father of twentieth-century fiction in Iran, published his masterpiece, *The Blind*

Owl (1937) in Mumbai, while Istanbul was the major cosmopolitan city to which Iranian intellectuals were attracted throughout the nineteenth century. Mosaddegh, Nehru, and Nasser were interrelated figures within the same anticolonial nationalist movement. Meanwhile, Faiz Ahmad Faiz from Pakistan, Nazem Hekmet from Turkey, Vladimir Mayakovsky from Russia, Pablo Neruda representing the whole Latin American continent, Langston Hughes from the United States, and Mahmoud Darwish from Palestine and thus the larger Arab world, were all influences upon the poetry of the Iranian rebel poet Ahmad Shamlou. This cosmopolitan culture culminated in the 1977–79 revolution, but militant Islamism launched a succession of brutal mass executions in prisons, university purges, cultural revolutions, and diversionary propaganda outside the country to denigrate and dismiss its competitors. Its own "religious intellectuals" began to oppose it in terms that were indigenous to its militant hegemony, and the more they opposed it the more they paradoxically consolidated its enduring power. The Green Movement of 2009 was the return of this repressed opposition. In the following pages I document the return of the repressed over the last two centuries, with its deeper roots in the furthest reaches of Iranian history.

My principal argument is very simple: the sudden decline and final demise of the Qajar dynasty (1785–1925), beginning early in the nineteenth century, conditioned the eventual rise of a public sphere that accommodated the emergence of the Iranian public intellectuals—journalists, essayists, poets, scholars; and then later novelists, dramatists, artists, and filmmakers—of the country's nascent postcolonial nationhood. From the very beginning, that process was perforce was cosmopolitan, non-sectarian, non-denominational, gender and class conscious, and above all transnational and worldly in its character and culture. This cosmopolitan culture was articulated by public intellectuals who had left their homeland either physically or emotionally, or both, and had adumbrated the terms of their country's future from outside its fictive frontiers. In short, the production of Iranian "national identity," I contend, was always already a transnational and postnational process.

This cosmopolitan worldliness was the *urtext* from which various ideological formations took shape. This urtext was composed of old imperial memories now finding a new normative habitat. Iranian intellectuals were being born into a public space they had never known outside the royal court. Two opposite developments were taking place: as the architects of this cosmopolitan worldliness worked through their prose and poetry, and their visual and performing arts, their crudest manifestations coagulated around ideological formations that effectively eclipsed that cosmopolitanism, as they channeled their efforts into the political mobilization of the emerging masses. Those mobilizations had their historic role to play, and finally arrived at a head-on collision in the course of the 1977–79 revolution, which succeeded in toppling the monarchy. But just before it could succeed in establishing a free and democratic republic, the revolution was hijacked by militant Islamists who were far more vicious and violent than all of the others combined. It took them more than three decades to redefine Iranian political culture in exclusively Islamist terms, but they have consistently failed to address challenges of public discontent, the women's rights movement, labor unrest, and student protest. All of these finally culminated in the Green Movement, in its bid to claim public space. Whether isolated or concerted, these were manifestations of a defiant cosmopolitan culture that the militant and besieged Islamists wished to deny; but the harder they denied it, the stronger it became.

Iran Beyond Borders

In the following pages I intend to offer a layered genealogy of this cosmopolitan culture—a perspective that categorically dispenses with the Eurocentric notion of "modernity." In this genealogy, which I will follow chronologically from the late eighteenth to the early twenty-first century, I map out an alternative view of Iranian history and its geographical and cultural vicinities, in which Islamism and secularism form a false and irrelevant binary, while "tradition versus modernity" is an even more falsifying choice. The three ideological formations of Islamism, socialism, and anticolonial nationalism were only the transient, politically expedient manifestations of this cosmopolitan worldliness. Meanwhile, its more sporadic but nonetheless consistent expressions included social movements from the Constitutional Revolution, the nationalization of the oil industry in the 1950s, and the Iranian Revolution of 1977–79, all the way to the Green Movement of 2009, as well generations of labor, women's, and student movements.

In dismantling the European project of modernity on its colonial edges, and overcoming the colonial modernity it has historically occasioned, my intention is to map out the trajectory of a cosmopolitan worldliness rooted in a nation's history of struggles for liberty, rather than one imported or imposed by European colonialism.

Although it was the decline and fall of the Qajar dynasty in the nineteenth century that finally set the stage for the emergence of Iran from its last imperial curve, we can begin from any number of earlier critical points in history when contemporary Iranians began to fathom their position in a world defined by imperial exchanges between their ruling dynasties and the emerging world powers. Much of the history of contemporary Iran in terms of its fading boundaries can in fact be traced back to the fateful moment when the last grand imperial order of the realm, in the form of the Safavid dynasty

(1501–1736), established Shi'ism as the official state religion of its empire, and began to face both the challenges of the Ottomans and the increasing interest of European powers in the region. Though that interest was primarily strategic (to combat the Ottomans), its commercial underpinning pulled the Safavids inexorably towards the expanding horizons of global capitalism.

The Safavids emerged from the deepest corners of Persian and Islamic history, and traced their origins to a mystical order over which their eponymous founder Shaykh Safi al-Din Abu Ishaq Ardabili (1252–1334) had presided. Safavid court historians traced the genealogy of the family to Imam Musa al-Kazem (745–99), the Seventh of the Twelfth Imami Shi'ites, though subsequent historians have questioned this genealogy. By 1500 Shah Ismail (1487–1524), at the age of thirteen, had established himself at the head of a band of ardent devotees who called themselves "red-headed" (*qezelbash*) because of a red bandana they sported on their turbans. In about two years he had conquered much territory in northwestern Iran, declaring himself the king and establishing Shi'ism as the new official creed of the realm. From Azerbaijan, Ismael first moved south towards Iraq and Khuzestan, and from there advanced towards the northwest, heading for Khorasan. His military conquests and territorial gains were tantamount to the eradication of his Sunni nemesis, and the establishment and spread of Shi'ism as his preferred creed. The Safavid consolidation of Shi'ism as their state religion provided a solid ideological basis for their legitimacy. Though this objective was achieved with much cruelty towards the Sunni populations of Iran, through Shi'ism the Safavids laid the groundwork for the subsequent establishment of territorial integrity in Iran as a postcolonial nation-state. For theirs was the very last grand imperial design on the model of the Persianate imperium, though no longer predicated on the ideological premises of Persian literature (which now perforce emigrated to India), but decidedly on the scholasticism of Shi'ism. But that Shi'ism itself was and remained an already transnational proposition, by virtue of the fact that significant territories in the Ottoman Empire—from Iraq to Lebanon—and then down to the Arabian Peninsula and deep into the Indian subcontinent, also remained Shi'i. The most sacred sites of Shi'ism, in Karbala, as well as its highest seats of learning, in Najaf, were in Iraq, which changed hands between the Safavids and the Ottomans before emerging as a postcolonial nation-state.

A key factor in the geopolitics of the region in this crucial period was the location of the Safavid territories between the Mughal and Ottoman empires—with which the Safavids enjoyed a friendly and a hostile relationship, respectively. Shah Ismail's conquests in Khorasan also benefited the Mughal emperor Zahir-ud-din Muhammad Babur (1483–1530), and thus a firm solidarity emerged between the Safavids and the Mughals against their common Turkic enemies in Central Asia. By 1514 Shah Ismail had to face Sultan Selim I (1465–1520), the Ottoman emperor, who fought the Safavid monarch in the famous Battle of Chaldiran, dealing him a heavy blow with his superior and mechanized army, equipped with artillery. After the Battle of Chaldiran, Shah Ismail did not fight any major battles, but Tabriz was eventually retrieved back into his territory. When Ismail died, in 1524, he had spent twenty-four years of his young life ruling over his realm. He was chiefly responsible for consolidating Shi'ism as the state religion, in clear contradistinction to the Sunnism of the Ottomans. In the Ottoman, Safavid, and Mughal empires, Muslims had already started to sense their historic affiliations spreading tentatively into a world beyond their familiar geography, as Europeans had found their territories to be of immediate and enduring interest.

The religious and political rivalry between the Ottomans and the Safavids made the latter a natural ally of the European powers. The result was the extension of a trans-imperial domain that spread from Mughal India through the Safavid realms and beyond the Ottomans into Europe. During the reign of Tahmasb I (1514–76), when relations with the Ottomans were much improved, and Safavid control over Georgia and Armenia expanded, Sultan Suleiman's son, Şehzade Bayezid (1525–61), spent some time at the Safavid court. This improved relationship consolidated both empires along their shared border and crafted a remissive space between the two territories in which much commercial and cultural exchange took place.

A critical development in this period was the opening of trade relations between the Safavid court and the British, particularly facilitated by a British merchant named Anthony Jenkinson (1529–1611), who had explored Muscovy and Russia on behalf of the Muscovy Company and the English crown. British merchants like him came to the Safavid court bringing gifts to Shah Tahmasb from Queen Elizabeth I (1533–1603), seeking lucrative trade cooperation between the two countries. The Muscovy Company was chartered in 1555, and held a monopoly on trade between England and Muscovy through the seventeenth and eighteenth centuries.

The British had their rivals, however. The Portuguese had a strong presence in the Persian Gulf during the Safavid period, and by 1506 had secured complete control over the island of Hormuz, with almost full power over all of the coastal regions. By 1519, even Bahrain had been captured from the Safavids—though in 1600 it was brought back under their control. By 1602 Shah Abbas had turned his attention to his western territories, trying to regain control of the area from Tabriz to Baghdad, and by 1622 he had conquered Baghdad and performed his ritual duties at the sacred Shi'i sites. Now he was poised to deal with the Persian Gulf theater more effectively. In 1602, Philip III sent a mission to Shah Abbas, which reached agreement on shared control of the Persian Gulf between the Portuguese and the Safavids. In 1614 Shah Abbas sent a mission to Spain to negotiate closer ties with Philip III in return for his collaboration with the Portuguese in the Persian Gulf. But soon Shah Abbas found a better partnership—with the British in the Persian Gulf area and beyond—and altogether abandoned the Spaniards. Iran was by now fully immersed in high-power global trade and politics. But something altogether new was now affecting Iranian political culture: non-territorial imperial projects emanating from Europe were now deeply involved in the mapping out of new historical realities.

The East India Company fleet began actively to challenge the Portuguese and the Spaniards in the Persian Gulf, and Shah Abbas shifted his allegiance away from them and towards the British. Ultimately, however, a cat-and-mouse game commenced between the Safavids, the British, and the Portuguese–Spanish alliance, that radically transformed the geopolitics of the region. These developments coincided with the construction of hundreds of caravan stations that facilitated internal Safavid trade. These transformative developments occurred during the travels of the Shirley brothers, Sir Anthony (1565–1635) and Sir Robert (ca. 1581–1628), two British traders who sought to facilitate a more profitable relationship between the Safavids and the British. The brothers and their entourage helped Shah Abbas to modernize his army, and for a time Robert Shirley acted as Shah Abbas's ambassador to the courts of Europe. Iran was now being propelled forcefully beyond its domestic and regional frames of references, into the arena of global politics. The result was catalytic: domestic, regional, and global factors (both economic and political) were combining to generate a radically new global topography, in which power oscillated between the dying and the rising empires, and the fate of newly imagined nation-states remained deeply uncertain.

Rethinking the Borromean Ring

A critical rethinking of the unit of the nation-state as the site of our knowledge-production—a rethinking that is central to the argument of this book—has now assumed a renewed urgency.

In a major intervention in the Marxist theory of capital and the political cultures it enables, Kojin Karatani, in *The Structure of World History* (2014), has proposed a shift in the axis of analysis away from *modes of production* towards *modes of exchange*. This strategic move, he suggests, relieves our critical thinking of analytical entrapment within the nation-state (both the state and the nation), whose evident failure to disappear or even weaken under economic crisis has led Marxists to posit a "relative autonomy of the ideological superstructure." The increased importance thereby accorded to the superstructure has in turn resulted in the weakening of our reading of the economic infrastructure, the abandoning of any systematic attempt to understand the relation between the two, and, a fortiori, a passive acceptance of the status quo. Karatani thus shoots a spinning arrow through the Borromean ring of capital–nation–state by replacing modes of production with modes of exchange. Karatani's radical proposal is exceptionally important for my argument in this book.

Through an historical examination of the Borromean ring of capital–nation–state, Karatani's concern is primarily the varied forms of the global operation of capitalism. His examination also opens the way for a rethinking of the operative instrumentality of the postcolonial nation-state in the operation of capital. The importance of Karatani's thesis does not necessarily reside in a return to a totalizing narrative of global history. He sets in motion a kind of critical thinking that enables a more dynamic reading of the postcolonial nation-state, far beyond the frontier fictions that have now been thoroughly fetishized. I find this move critical for the kinds of postnational perspectives I wish to bring to bear here on modern Iranian history.

Labor Migration and Cosmopolitanism

A solid example of this critical thinking beyond the current frontier fictions should make the project informing this book more evident.

Early in February 2014, there was a report that "an Arab-Iranian poet and human rights activist, Hashem Shaabani [had] been executed for being an 'enemy of God' and threatening national security." Hashem Shaabani and his fellow defendants were all charged with "separatist terrorism." In subsequent reports Shaabani was identified as "a member of the Arabic-speaking Ahvazi ethnic minority."

Much confusion and disinformation clouded the circumstances in which such violations of civil liberties were perpetrated in Iran and its violent neighborhood. I was born and raised in the city of Ahvaz. The term "Arabic-speaking Ahvazi ethnic minority" is a misnomer. Not all Ahvazis are Arabs, and not all Iranian Arabs live in Ahvaz. Ahvaz is a major cosmopolitan city in southern Iran, the capital of the oil-rich Khuzestan province, which attracts labor migrants from all over the southern provinces, as well as from elsewhere in Iran and the wider region. The nature of urbanization and labor migration in Ahvaz and other major Iranian cities has created a mosaic of ethnicized communities brought together by the force and necessity of labor, and not by the various rampant fantasies of bourgeois nationalism.

My own father came to Ahvaz as a laborer for the Iranian national railroad from Bushehr, my mother's family from

Dezful. Neither of them were Arabs. There is no "indigenous" population in any part of a vastly multifaceted and multi-cultural society. All urbanizations are the result of steady labor migration. From Azerbaijan and Khorasan in the north to Isfahan and Yazd in the center, and down to the coastal regions of the Persian Gulf, labor migrants regularly come to Ahvaz in search of work. As the capital of Khuzestan, Ahvaz belongs to all of them, and thus the term "Arabic-speaking Ahvazi ethnic minority" is categorically flawed. While Ahvaz has a major Arab population, not all Ahvazis are Arabs, as indeed not all Tehranis are "Persians," or even Persian-speaking. A significant wave of labor migration to Tehran has consisted of workers from Azerbaijan, who continue to speak their native Turkic language, just as some Ahvazis who are Arabs speak Arabic. All forms of manufactured ethnicized identity among the Iranian Arabs, Kurds, or Azaris categorically disregard the centrality of labor migration in the formation of cosmopoli-tan urbanism in cities extending from Ahvaz or Shiraz in the south to Tehran and Mashhad in the north. As in all its other fantasies, bourgeois nationalism (Persian, Arabic, Turkish, or whatever) uses, abuses, and dispenses with labor when manu-facturing its ideologies.

Whether or not Mr. Shaabani was a separatist, separa-tist movements have existed not just among Arab Iranians in Khuzestan province, but also among Kurds in Kurdistan, Azaris in Azerbaijan, and Baluchis in Baluchistan. Before bour-geois nationalism appropriates and abuses their legitimate causes, the sustained and ugly history of racism against these violently ethnicized communities gives them every legitimate reason to nurse ambitions of separation from the central gov-ernment, and at times even take up arms to defend that cause. Calling these separatists "terrorists" without ever addressing the institutionalized forms of racism against the communi-ties concerned has only exacerbated such feelings, as has the obliviousness of the central government towards the dire social and economic malaise that has affected them. Separatist sentiments around Iran rightly identify to a sustained history of "Persian racism" against systematically ethnicized minorities. Persian racism against Arabs is echoed in Arab racism against Persians—a prolonged bourgeois binary that has dialectically sustained itself for generations within colonized minds mimicking European ethnic nationalism.

The histories of both Persian and Arab bourgeois nationalism are solidly predicated on a sustained genealogy of racist bigotry, partaking in its European prototype. Today, legitimate criticism of the Islamic Republic easily degenerates into a nasty Islamophobia among a wide spectrum of Iranian bourgeois liberalism that fancies itself "secular." There is a very porous line between that Islamophobia and a rabid anti-Arab racism, astonishingly shared by a significant portion of the selfsame constituency for whom a delusional notion of "Cyrus the Great" is the ahistorical panacea of an entire history of imperial nostalgia. This racism is not limited to the history of the Islamic Republic, but extends well into the Pahlavi period, and before it to the Qajar dynasty, when leading Iranian intellectuals ranging from Mirza Aqa Khan Kermani (1954–97) back to Sadeq Hedayat (1903–51) harbored the most pernicious anti-Arab racism. They categorically attributed what they saw as Iranian backwardness to Islam, tainted by its association with Arab fanaticism and stupidity, and thus began to celebrate a lopsided reading of pre-Islamic Iranian history chiefly informed by the exertions of their own racist imaginations.

The feeling, alas, has been mutual. Arab bourgeois nationalism has reciprocated in kind. As Joseph Massad has demonstrated in his study of Arab sexuality, *Desiring Arabs* (2007), the colonial construction of Arab modernity was very much predicated on the production of "the Persian" as a sexual pervert. Even today, a leading Arab scholar like

Leila Ahmad, in her classical study *Woman and Gender in Islam* (1993), considers the source of polygamy to have been the selfsame Persians. In other words, the construction of Arab Eurocentric (bourgeois) modernity has yet to decide whether this "Persian" other is a model of sexual perversion for being an unbridled homosexual or a promiscuous philanderer. Evidently, the answer is both: had it not been for these Persians, Arabs would presumably all have been properly heterosexual and monogamous, observing a corresponding Christian morality and Victorian ethics!

The height of this Arab–Persian binary was during the Iran–Iraq war (1980–88), when Saddam Hussein had managed to recruit the leading Egyptian filmmaker Salah Abu Seif to make a film about the Battle of al-Qadisiyyah, a decisive confrontation between the invading Muslim army and the Sassanid Empire, which he thought useful in his propaganda machinery mobilizing Arab sentiments against Iranians. The full dimensions of the carnage that this bourgeois nationalism has wreaked on both sides of the divide are unfathomable.

Like millions of other Ahvazis, I am a product of the multicultural fact of that magnificent city. Our province, and by extension the entire northern and southern shores of the Persian Gulf, stands at the confluence of four cultural forces: Iranian from the north, Arab from the west, Indian from the east, and African from the south. The false and falsifying Arab–Persian divide has, above all, categorically ignored and dismissed the strong and enduring Indian and African presence in the region.

The construction of the complementary modes of Arab and Persian bourgeois xenophobia has historically entailed their manufacturing each other as mere obstacles to their sublime achievement of white-identified, Eurocentric modernity; consequently, what they both simultaneously conceal is their mutual fear of *the African* and *the Indian*, both of which are conspicuously absent from their identically racist identity politics. The whitewashed bourgeois nationalism of both Arab and Persian vintages is so deeply afraid of being "colored" by the factual evidence of history that, their mutual antagonism notwithstanding, they converge in their representation of African and Indian components of the region.

The Zanj Rebellion of 869–83 is among the earliest indications we have of a massive slave revolt in and around Basra, at the tip of the Persian Gulf. The origin of my own last name (meaning "bilingual") is just one small indication of a profound Indian influence in southern Iran, extending all the way from the Persian Gulf to the Arabian Sea and the Indian Ocean. From the ninth-century Zanj Rebellion to the massive contemporary labor migration of workers from Asia and Africa to the rich and thriving Gulf states of the UAE, Qatar, and Bahrain, the presence of African and Asian laborers has been systematically concealed in order to manufacture a whitewashed bourgeois nationalism of both Arab and Persian varieties.

Defending the term "Arab Gulf," a dear Egyptian friend once told me that a man he knew had concluded on the basis of his research that "all people living on the northern shore of the Persian Gulf spoke Arabic," which, to the degree that it may be true, is balanced by the fact that as many on the southern shore also speak Persian—two imperial languages that for millennia were the lingua francas of successive empires. What this obscures is the more compelling fact that, today, languages ranging from Hindi and Malayalam to Hausa and Swahili are in reality equally if not more audible in the region, if we were only to listen more carefully.

To the silly choice between Arab or Persian Gulf, I always respond, only half-jokingly, that we should call it by its real name: "the American Gulf." The navigational and maritime imperial realities of the region are far more accurate reflections of who and what we are in that region than the cultural identities "Arab" and "Persian." Shatt al-Arab, Persian Gulf, Arabian Sea, Indian Ocean—these names are how history has opted to identify the varied and interconnected waters of the region. During the Shah's time, we were told to call the Shatt al-Arab Arvand Rud, but we could not; for us it was the Shatt al-Arab, pouring into the Persian Gulf, pouring into the Arabian Sea, pouring into the Indian Ocean. This reflects a fair and even distribution of water between people, if we are able to disregard the fact that Africans are left out of the equation—except when they appear as "pirates."

The history of the region—in both its emotive and economic realities—speaks a different language. Arguments against divisive separatist movements that will only help empires to divide and rule more effectively need not be abandoned to the bogus jingoism of a Tehran- or Riyadh-centered racism, but simply reflect the factual evidence that there is no pure anything. In our robust veins runs the blood of God knows how many sailors from what distant shores. As the late Iranian poet Sohrab Sepehri once put it:

> I am from Kashan
> My lineage may reach a plant in India,
> A relic from the soil of Sialk,
> Or perhaps a prostitute in Bukhara.

Merely to criticize the pervasiveness of this brand of bourgeois nationalism is not sufficient. What is necessary is the retrieval and cultivation of other collective memories that empirically override it. Consider the fact that my generation of Iranians grew up on the poetry of Mahmoud Darwish, Ahmad Shamlou, Faiz Ahmad Faiz, Aimé Césaire, Nâzim Hikmet, Pablo Neruda, and Vladimir Mayakovsky, almost entirely oblivious or indifferent to their Arab, Iranian, Pakistani,

Turkish, African, Latin American, or Russian origins. These poets formed a liberating space out of their emotive universe, and in reading their work we did not think we had crossed any borders. Quite to the contrary: we were freed by their poetry into a recognition of who and what we were. Against persistent colonial and imperial machinations instigating separatist movements to pursue their divide-and-rule strategy, these poets defied the postcolonial fiction of nation-states, bringing nations closer to each other in the poetics of their resistance to tyranny and injustice. This sense of transnational solidarity was by no means limited to the realm of poetry, but extended well into politics. Consider the monumental figures of Nehru, Mosaddegh, Nasser, and Lumumba—champions of the anti-imperial struggles of people from Asia and Africa long before the ferocious fiction of the Arab–Persian divide, or even worse, that of the Sunni–Shi'i conflict, had divided them in order to rule them more effectively.

There is scarcely anything more terrorizing than the murder of a poet. Hashem Shaabani joined Said Soltanpour and a whole pantheon of martyr poets—going all the way back to Mirzadeh Eshghi and Farrokhi Yazdi in both the Islamic Republic and the Pahlavi regimes—dreaming a better world for their people, and it is the historic task of such people precisely to interpret those dreams in liberatory and increasingly universal terms. Arab and Persian bourgeois nationalism represent the diametrical opposite of such emancipatory imperatives.

A New Regime of Knowledge

A central argument I advanced in *The Arab Spring: The End of Postcolonialism* (2012) was that, in the aftermath of these groundbreaking revolutions, we are in dire need of *a new regime of knowledge*—echoing the cry of the many millions of people around the Arab and Muslim world that "People

Demand the Overthrow of the Regime." That "regime," I argued, was not just the political order. Equally essential was the cultivation of a new way of thinking about a region of the world hitherto both scrutinized and brutalized under the colonial construct "Middle East." These ancient and modern state formations need as much to be epistemically emancipated as politically liberated. This new regime of knowledge will have to arise from a creative and critical combination of what we already know in order to challenge the boundaries of what we have so far not even dared to imagine, let alone think. A mythic combination of love and hatred, fear and fantasy, fury and daring, has hitherto informed our received conception of modern nation-states and their real or imagined ancient pedigree. Iranians are a particularly proud people, their confidence about their past compensating for a sense of grievance about their modern history—always thinking they have been given less credit than they deserve, that modernity has handed them the short end of the historical stick. An imperial imaginary informs their contemporary measures of a modern nation-state. The dismantling of that comforting connivance between fact and fantasy rubs people the wrong way, and the shimmering sight of a future in which contemporary nation-states are faded and folded into more complicated pasts and amorphous futures is a particularly daunting prospect.

Consequently, this book pursues a critique of the postcolonial nation geared towards revealing these hidden layers of historical formation. The idea of the "nation" in Iran is today trapped within its manufactured postcolonial borders. I wish to open those borders widely, and to locate the nation within the transnational public sphere, where it was first and most saliently conceived. Nations like Iran, Turkey, India, Pakistan, and Egypt are the contemporary descendants of a succession of remote empires, and remain very much conscious of their imperial heritage. The empires collapsed under the influence of their own inner tensions and contradictions, as well as the militant onslaught of a hegemonic European imperialism. The result has been the fetishized formation of postcolonial nation-states like India, Pakistan, Iran, Turkey, and Egypt. In their current incarnations, all of these nations have been formed on the transnational bourgeois public (and parapublic) spheres extending from Europe to its widespread colonial claims, and yet forcefully framed within the fictive frontiers of postcolonial nation-states. In the following pages I wish to use the example of Iran to expose the larger transnational public sphere within which all of these nations have been formed.

There is a politics of emancipation that sets the postcolonial nation free from its colonial entrapment within a false consciousness characterized by a flawed ethnic nationalism that invariably collapses into sectarian provincialism of the worst kind—all of which are the extended shadows of a fateful encounter with European colonialism. Today, not only Iran and the Arab world, but in fact the entire region extending from India to Turkey, Egypt, and by extension North Africa, are trapped within such manufactured ethnic identity politics and sectarian hatred, both of which are conducive to the bourgeois foregrounding of globalized neoliberalism. My contention in mapping out the contours of Iran beyond its current borders, and articulating the idea of the nation beyond its postcolonial registers, is to liberate the nation from the false epistemic and political foregrounding of ethnic nationalism, sectarian provincialism, and thus to restore the cosmopolitan worldliness out of which these nations were formed in the first place.

With the dramatic events unfolding in Iran and the Arab world, we are in dire need of radically new perspectives on what is taking place before our eyes. Old ideas, national boundaries, clichéd tropes, outdated ideologies, fetishized maps, and arrested academic writings, participate in a shared failure to come to terms with what we read in the headlines. A new regime of knowledge is needed that is morally imaginative and politically provocative, while intellectually matching the popular demand for the overthrow of the regime. Such changes in the modes and manners of knowledge-production will not happen overnight, or be achieved by any single author, perspective, or text. Collectively, and beyond frontier fictions that have limited our truth, we stand at the threshold of more liberatory ways of thinking about our world.

I believe that academic and popular writing about Iran, or any other nation-state in its neighborhood for that matter, has today hit a plateau. Scholars and journalists, experts and casual observers, have all been narrating the story of Iran within established and cliché-ridden narratives, taking the current political boundaries of the postcolonial nation-state as their abiding frame of reference. The kinds of insights that this mode of narrative can produce have long been exhausted, and have saturated its epistemic limitations. In this book I offer a radically different frame of reference, in effect trespassing beyond the postcolonial frontier fictions, and offering an empirically based alternative vision of the postcolonial nation-states in this and similar regions. In narrating the story of Iran over the last two hundred years and more, I will seek to speak in terms that go beyond fetishized borders and frontier fictions, and yet are idiomatic of the lived experiences of peoples and their movements in this period.

This book is intended for the widest possible readership in the English-speaking world—one that is critically aware of the changing world, and thus deeply in need of more liberatory thinking about its vital issues. It is intended as an example of critical thinking about the future of postcolonial nation-states beyond their current fictive frontiers, and into the geopolitics of their lived experiences and transnational realities. Academic disciplines, in particular, have long since hit their analytical and epistemic buffers, and remain confined by departmental and narrative cul-de-sacs that have produced enclosed communities with little to no public relevance, particularly in a rapidly and profoundly changing world. The answer to this limitation, of course, is not loose journalistic and amateurish writing, but a form of critical thinking that, while recognizing the narrative potency of the various disciplines, can nevertheless creatively cross between them, keeping its theoretical eye firmly on the ball of lived experience, including that of the mobilizing forces that are poised to change our world. A strategy of multiple archives, incorporating hard economic and political facts as well as the effervescence of the visual and performing arts, needs to come together to inform the sites of our understanding of this moment in history, when postcolonial nation-sates are remapping the geography of their liberation.

The order of my narrative will be chronological, though I will occasionally pause for a moment of meditative (what they call "theoretical") reflection, so I may draw your attention to a larger frame of reference, or else for what I call a "poetic implosion" within the story.

The book begins with events early in the 1800s, when the Perso-Russian wars and subsequent loss of significant Qajar territories to the Russians in the Caucuses made for a rude awakening of Iran to the new geopolitics of its environment. Chapter 1 contains a close reading of *Tohfat al-Alam* ("Gift of the World") (1788–1804), by Mir Abd al-Latif Khan Shushtari (1758–1805), a travelogue written by a notable Iranian of his generation while he lived in India, in which we witness one of the earliest encounters of Iranians with European colonial modernity. Between the Caucuses and the Indian subcontinent, I will map out this geopolitics as the emerging horizons of a world that would redefine Persian political culture. The imperial rivalries between the Russians, the British, and the French was definitive of the colonial circumstances that ushered Iran into its geopolitical context, and it was precisely in this context that its political culture assumed a necessarily cosmopolitan character.

Chapter 2 shifts focus to the 1850s, taking a close look at such leading public intellectuals as Mirza Aqa Khan Kermani (1854–97), Zeyn al-Abedin Maragheh'i (1839–1910), Mirza Aqa Tabrizi (fl. 1870s), and Seyyed Jamal al-Din al-Afghani (1838–97). These were peripatetic intellectuals, navigating a geography of liberation that connected their homeland to a wider frame of political imagination. They produced critical thoughts that liberated their people from the overpowering burden of their received cultures. The purpose of this chapter is to allow the new political idiom of cosmopolitan worldliness to come back to life and inform our reading of the emerging postcolonial nations. As I examine the court-initiated reforms of the Qajar premiers Amir Kabir (1807–52) and Mirza Hossein Khan Sepahsalar (1828–81), I will also consider the rise of the Babi Movement (1844–52), the last major revolutionary uprising of the nineteenth century emerging from Shi'i millenarian proclivities, so massive and far-reaching that it shook the foundations of the Qajar dynasty and implicated its neighboring Ottoman domains. The combined effect of the revolutionary ideas generated by expatriate intellectuals from Calcutta to Cairo to Istanbul, and of those led by revolutionaries inside the Qajar domains, was the radical transformation of the emerging political culture in a decidedly cosmopolitan direction.

Chapter 3 examines such crucial early twentieth-century periodicals as *Qanun* (London), *Habl al-Matin* (Calcutta), *Sur-Israfil* (Tehran), *Kaveh* (Berlin), and *Iranshahr* (Berlin), which were instrumental in facilitating the formation of a transnational public sphere, and thereby eventually directing the spirits of the French and Russian revolutions towards the making of the Constitutional Revolution, and prompting the emergence of the first left, liberal, and Islamist political ideologies. The success of the Constitutional Revolution during this period in transforming an absolutist monarchy into a constitutional monarchy, and in laying the basis for the founding of the Tudeh Party during World War II, was the most potent manifestation of this environment. Active rivalry between the Russians and the British, whose later counterpart was that between the Soviet Union and the United States, pushed Iran into the transnational context of a political parlance in which from its prose to its politics had to speak a worldly speech.

Chapter 4 moves to the 1950s, looking at the impact of the Indian anticolonial movement on the rise of Mohammad Mosaddegh, thus linking Nehru, Nasser, and Mosaddegh together in the project of constructing a liberation geography that still informs the geopolitics of the region. The chapter also discusses the contribution of a number of world-renowned poets—Faiz Ahmad Faiz from Pakistan, Ahmad Shamlou from Iran, Pablo Neruda from Chile, Vladimir Mayakovsky from Russia, Nâzim Hikmet from Turkey, and Mahmoud Darwish from Palestine—to this renewed solidarity in the global South. The anticolonial nationalism that motivated Mohammad Mosaddegh's nationalization of the Iranian oil industry and the fateful confrontation with British Petroleum (BP) was very much informed by this environment. The CIA-sponsored coup of 1953 dampened this mood, but failed to derail it.

Chapter 5 addresses the 1960s, detailing the contours of a full-blown cosmopolitan culture. This is the period when Forough Farrokhzad went to Italy, Ali Shari'ati went to Paris, Jalal Al-e-Ahmad traveled around the world, and when Frantz Fanon, Algeria, and Cuba entered the Iranian political consciousness. As Brecht, Chekhov, Ibsen, and Miller were translated into Persian, Bahram Beiza'i, Akbar Radi, and Gholam Hossein Saedi emerged as the leading dramatists of their generation. The Nimaic revolution in poetry was in full swing at this time; Iranian cinema was blooming; and the post-1953 coup blues were transforming themselves in creative and defiant ways. The chapter argues that Khomeini's 1963 uprising was as much against the Pahlavi monarchy as it was against the cosmopolitan worldliness of this era, which he considered "secular" and "Western," and thus inimical to his Islamist ideology.

Chapter 6 addresses the crucial decade of the 1970s, marking the rise of the Cherik-ha-ye Fada'i Khalq rural and urban guerilla movement, during the height of worldly cosmopolitanism in prose, poetry, and cinema, which ultimately resulted in the 1977–79 revolution that embodied it all in its preparatory stages. The chapter pays particular attention to the poetry of Sohrab Sepehri, who provided the poetic metaphysics underlying this worldly cosmopolitanism. As Ayatollah Khomeini and his militant lieutenants moved quickly to claim the entirety of the revolution for themselves, the spirit of cosmopolitan worldliness they sought to suppress fled underground and across fictive frontiers, awaiting future resurrection.

Chapter 7 discusses the 1980s, when two opposite developments occurred: Islamism took over inside Iran, seeking to destroy cosmopolitan culture, while visual and performing arts (cinema in particular) became that culture's embodiment, carrying it around the world. Amir Naderi, Sia Armajani, Manouchehr Yektai, Nikzad Nodjoumi, Ardeshir Mohassess, Shirin Neshat, and scores of other Iranian artists took over the mission of carrying the torch of their denied worldliness into the wider world. The Islamists were left helpless, and proceeded to generate their own opposition in the form of religious intellectuals, and thus to try to limit the domain of contestation to their own game. But the robust body of Iranian visual and performing arts denied them that strategy, framing Iranian cosmopolitan worldliness for the whole world to see.

Chapter 8 concentrates on the Green Movement of 2009, demonstrating how it brought that repressed and denied cosmopolitan culture back to the public sphere with such unparalleled political potency that the Islamic Republic may never recover from its aftershocks.

My conclusion argues that it is impossible to imagine Iran except in its immediate and distant environments. Iranian Arabs, Kurds, Azaris, those living by the Caspian Sea, or in the province of Khorasan, are all as much part of Iran as they are integral to their surrounding cultures and environments. This cosmopolitanism can at times degenerate into separatist movements on the part of Arabs, Kurds, Turks, and Baluchis, precisely because they have been systematically disenfranchised under both the Pahlavis and the Islamic Republic—both of which, by virtue of their monarchical Persianism and clerical Islamism, respectively, were in categorical denial of that very cosmopolitanism. A distorted history of the nation has, as a result, yielded to lopsided subnational sentiments and a prevalence of false consciousness, and thus to stunted ideological ambition, robbing people of their worldly and enabling cosmopolitanism. But the enduring phenomenon of a transnational public sphere that embraces and enables that cosmopolitanism is the most persistent indication of Iran as a nation living and breathing beyond its borders.

CHAPTER I

Craving for India

I was craving for India.

Mir Seyyed Abd al-Latif Shushtari (1788)

The opening of Iran's horizons towards a changing world began many centuries ago. In what today we call Iran, the Safavid dynasty (1501–1722) unified a vast area stretching from India to the Ottoman territories, forming a Shi'i empire. The Safavids oversaw a flourishing of art, architecture, industry, and commerce, as well as a vast body of scholastic learning. Under pressure from their Russian and Ottoman neighbors, the Safavids finally collapsed in response to a tribal Afghan uprising, giving rise to the triumphalist figure of Nader Shah (r. 1736–47), who defeated the Afghans, secured much of the Safavid border, and founded his own Afsharid dynasty(1736–96). After a short interval in which power was held by the Zands (1750–94), finally the Qajars (1785–1925) came to power. The Constitutional Revolution (1906–11) marked the end of the Qajar absolutist monarchy, eventually leading to their final demise and the rise of the Pahlavis (1926–79), whose rule collapsed in turn under a popular revolution (1977–79) that resulted in an Islamic Republic (1979 to the present).

This skeletal narrative is only there to be disabled, for all these dynastic claims to legitimacy and political domination have always been consistently challenged by revolutionary uprisings by the combined energies of the impoverished peasantry and the urban poor. Centralizing dynasties and centrifugal uprisings have driven the momentum of power-play in Iranian and many other similar histories. Massive urbanization under the Safavids was crudely interrupted and reversed by tribal solidarity under the Afsharids and Zands, and a sudden thrust for colonial power under the Qajars ushered Iran into the heart of this tumultuous age. The Iranian urban population grew steadily, while guilds and merchants in bazaars and foreign trade began systematically to incorporate Iran into the regional and global economy. Mosques and royal courts remained the major sites of power struggles, with the bazaar eventually coming to political terms with its emerging power. Foreign trade by colonial powers became an increasing force beginning with the Safavids and culminating with the Qajars, threatening the interests of local and regional merchants and forcing an uneasy alliance between them and the clergy. After the Safavids came to power, Shi'ism became the official state religion, but many Sunni enclaves persisted, joining Iranian Jews, Christians (Armenians), and Zoroastrians in thriving or suffering with the fate of the nation as a whole. Such tribal affinities as those of the Lors and the Bakhtiyari remained a constant force into the twentieth century.

Exposure to foreign ideas from the late eighteenth century became definitive of Iranian political culture. Travel narratives soon emerged as a particularly popular genre. Diplomats, merchants, and students traveled abroad, wrote books and magazine articles, bringing news of the wider world to their compatriots. With the arrival of the printing press, in the early nineteenth century, newspapers, books, and periodicals became widely available. Translations of texts from European languages (English and French, in particular) encouraged the simplification of Persian prose, making it ready to reach far beyond its traditional home in royal courts, to be read by an emerging literate public, and for far more radical purposes. Iran and Iranians were exiting a world over which they had a high degree of control, and entering one that increasingly lay beyond it.

Nader Shah Goes to India

The details of these historical developments lead us towards the dynamic force of Iranian social and intellectual history, far beyond its current frontiers. In the post-Safavid period, the history of Iranian territorial disintegration under colonial pressure began to unfold. Nader Shah (1688–1747) emerged as a military leader during the reign of Shah Tahmasb II, by way of helping him consolidate Safavid control of greater Khorasan and Afghanistan. But the main menace to the Safavid dynasty was the Afghan invasion and occupation of Isfahan. In the decisive battle of Murcheh Khvort, on November 12, 1729, Nader helped the Safavid monarch deliver a severe defeat to the combined forces of the Afghans and the Ottomans. Nader spent the next three years expelling the Ottomans and the Russians from other Safavid territories in the north and west, and in 1732 he deposed Tahmasb II. Installing his infant son Abbas III on the throne, Nader began to rule the Safavid realm in his name. While still engaged in battle against the Ottomans and the Russians in 1736, Nader dismantled the Safavid dynasty altogether and declared himself king.

The most significant event in the reign of Nader Shah was his invasion and occupation of India. At the Battle of Karnal, on February 13, 1739, Nader dealt a decisive defeat to the defending Indian army, and entered Delhi in triumph. This victory of Nader's soon gave new ideas to the East India Company. As his fame grew in Europe, he inadvertently paved the way for the British colonization of the subcontinent. "By his famous invasion of India," observed Karl Marx in an editorial he published in *New York Daily Tribune* on February 14, 1857, Nader had "contributed much to that disorganization of the declining Mogul empire, which opened the way for the rise of the British power in India."[1]

Half a century after Nader's invasion of India, with the British now firmly entrenched in that country's commercial and political grid, an Iranian merchant spent a major portion of his life in India, setting down his impressions and observations of what he saw and thought in what is now a major textual source attesting to the first encounter of an Iranian with European colonial modernity. *Tohfat al-Alam/ Gift of the World* (1788–1804), by Mir Abd al-Latif Khan Shushtari (1758–1805), the travelogue he wrote while he lived in India, is one of the earliest accounts of a native Iranian leaving his homeland and encountering European colonialism at first-hand in a neighboring country, now in the full grip of the British commercial and political snare.[2] Between the Caucasus and the Indian subcontinent we can now map out the emerging horizons of a world that would redefine Persian political culture. Imperial rivalries between the Russians, the British, and the French were definitive of the emerging colonial circumstances that brought Iran and its environs face to face with its geopolitical context, and it was precisely in this context that their political culture assumed a necessarily cosmopolitan character.

Shushtari's text is among the earliest extant accounts of an Iranian's encounter with European institutions of (colonial) modernity. He was a man of unusual intelligence with a particular penchant for observing and recording for posterity what he thought were new and groundbreaking ideas concerning social formations, political prowess, and cultural

---

1 Karl Marx, "The War against Persia," in Karl Marx and Frederich Engels, *On Colonialism: Articles from the New York Tribune and Other Writings* (New York: International Publishers, 1972), p. 97.

2 For a critical edition of this travelogue, see Mir Abd al-Latif Khan Shushtari, *Tohfat al-Alam* ("Gift of the World"), ed. S. Movahhed (Tehran: Tahuri, 1363/1994).

effervescence. In India he had discovered the Europeans and their achievements. They mesmerized him, and he wanted his fellow Iranian countrymen to know what he had learned. His travelogue was written during the Qajar period, by an Iranian—but far away from Iran, at a time when European colonialism in India provided the young traveler with an unusual opportunity to reimagine his homeland within a new world order, and while outside its borders; his native country became a homeland by virtue of the distant gaze he was thereby afforded.

Shushtari was born to a learned clerical family and received a solid scholastic education in Iran and Iraq. But he soon abandoned the course of his higher education, opting to live the life of a lay businessman traveling to India and getting to know the world far beyond his ancestors' juridical imagination. What is critical about his observations about Europe is that he never actually traveled to any European country, and all his impressions were indirect products of his experiences in India, now in the full grip of British commercial and political colonialism. About one hundred years before the rise of the Constitutional Revolution in Iran, Shushtari wrote of constitutional rights, civil liberties, separation of clerical and political authority, and the institutional protection of individual citizens. At the time of his writing about these institutions, Qajar Iran was ruled by an absolutist monarchy —and thus his prose is decidedly not only informative but also inquisitive, transformative, and mobilizing.

Shushtari is entirely beholden to the British Empire. More than anything, he is drawn to the global power of the British, and tries to understand how that transcendental power has come about. His book provides a fascinating panorama of an emerging geography, central to which are the discovery of the New World and the emerging power of the United States. He traces the manifestations of this global power in the cosmopolitan worldliness of Europe's cities, its institutions of contemporary civilized life, city designs, urban landscape, and civic services. He is particularly drawn to the rise of European philosophers in the public domain, and the corresponding decline in the power of religious institutions in general, and of the church in particular. He is fascinated by the freedom of the press, which he connects to the rise of a new mode of historiography in which the historian is no longer intimidated by the power of the monarch, and does not write history to appease his patron. He leaves very little doubt that he wishes to see these institutions emerge in his homeland, too. His ideals are palpably English, while his observations are made in India. Between these two locations, he imagines his Iranian homeland.

In his travelogue, Shushtari scarcely writes about Iran. He is chiefly preoccupied with describing European achievements, and those of the British in particular, of whom he had a direct knowledge in India. Writing his book in a simple and accessible Persian prose, for the obvious benefit of his countrymen, he nevertheless placed Iran at the center of his thoughts when describing the institutions of a rich and diversified civil society. But it is British colonialism and the power of its globalized empire that most fascinate Shushtari, as well as the inventions and discoveries that have facilitated such economic and political prowess. He is completely in awe of the British, but his positive description of their political wisdom is obviously intended as a critique of the monarchical institutions of brute force and arbitrary rule operating at the time. His central proposition is that Europeans were able to move beyond those institutions by breaking away from papal authority, and thereafter developing institutions of civic and political authority independent of the Vatican. He tells his readers how the decline of papal power corresponded with the rise of the institutions of parliamentary democracy and rule of law. But he obviously has contemporary Iranian and Ottoman monarchs in mind, and when he gives full descriptions of the parliamentary debates that take place before the British king makes a definitive decision, there remains no doubt what future he envisions for his homeland. Shushtari's admiration for the British must be understood in the context of his critique of Muslim monarchies and his desire for the rise of institutions of liberal democracy in his homeland.

It is crucial to keep in mind that Shushtari devotes fourteen of his nineteen chapters to a full description of his hometown of Shushtar, relating its history, geography, and anthropology. It is after the first half of the book that he informs his readers how he decided to move from his hometown, initially to Basra in Iraq and then to India. He describes, upon his arrival in India, the colonial domination of the British over the country, giving him occasion to talk about the military, industrial, scientific, and civic institutions of Europe in general, and the United Kingdom in particular, that had facilitated this domination. If he refers to Copernicus and Newton, it is to talk about their scientific discoveries, which had facilitated the rise of European science and technology. He devotes a full chapter to the European military sciences and their world-conquering capabilities. The final chapters of the book are entirely dedicated to his description of India, its history, geography, and anthropology. He concludes the book with a description of the rise of Wahhabism and their attack on Karbala.

When we consider the structure of Shushtari's narrative, we see that his attention to the British in India is really in the context of his concern about his immediate region—initially Iran, but then also India, and ultimately the Ottoman territories to which he returns. In fact, the traveling narrative is a ruse—a way of finding an appropriate language to address the afflictions that have beset Iran and its environs.

The fact that he is in India when writing the book gives him an added authority; having seen beyond his homeland, he is able to open the horizons of his compatriots—and thereby by the virtue of that location constitute the very emotive universe of that homeland.

After Nader Shah's invasion of India, the subcontinent became a major point of interest and attraction for generations of Iranian merchants and intellectuals. Shushtari was neither the first nor the last Iranian intellectual to be drawn to India. The entire Mughal Empire was heavily under the influence of Persian poets and literati who had immigrated into the Mughal domain and helped to create a magnificent Persianate culture in its court. But Shushtari represents a particularly poignant turning point at which Iranians began to feel the fever of colonial modernity coming their way from India.

Haji the Traveler

With all its significance for subsequent generations of critical thinkers and public intellectuals, Shushtari's account of his journey to India pales in comparison with that of another towering Iranian writer of a slightly later period. Hajj Mohammad Ali Mahallati (1836–1925), popularly known as Hajj Sayyah ("Haji the Traveler") explored the world widely, becoming a harbinger and herald of a world far beyond his contemporaries' imagination. It is hard for us to appreciate the extraordinary significance of this generation of Iranian travelers, who left their homeland behind to produce travelogues incorporating a radically simplified Persian prose with which they addressed what they saw as the vast discrepancy between European societies and that of their homeland, and thereby instigating reform and revolt against the status quo.

Sayyah was born in 1836 and raised in a rural family in

Mahallat, near Qom in central Iran.[3] He began to travel beyond his hometown at a very young age, initially to Tehran and subsequently to Najaf and Karbala in Iraq, to pursue his scholastic studies. During the 1840s and 1850s, when Sayyah was in southern Iraq, seminarian students from around the Muslim world (from India to Indonesia) would gather and, in addition to their legal studies, engage in debates and conversations about the fate of the Muslim world, now increasingly in the grip of European colonial powers. The Ottoman Empire was proving unable to cope with these seismic changes, the dysfunctional Qajar was at the mercy of European colonial machinations, and the Mughals in India were overrun by the British. In 1859, at the age of only twenty-three, Sayyah, now fully cognizant of these changes, returned to Iran. Avoiding marital life, he abruptly left his homeland once again for the Caucasus, concocting on his way the fiction of his own death, and conveying the news back to his family so that he could travel freely. What was the source of this defiant will to travel the world? Wherefore the synergy?

Thus began Sayyah's lifelong travels around the world, and around his own homeland, engaging with the most progressive, radical, and critical movements of his time. He was neither from a wealthy family nor at the service of any prince or merchant, and thus he traveled and lived in dire poverty. In the Caucasus he managed to learn Armenian, Turkish, and Russian and, like all other young students of his time, was drawn to the revolutionary ideas promoted within Russian intellectual circles. From the Caucasus he traveled to Istanbul.

3   For a pioneering study of the significance of Hajj Sayyah and similar thinkers in the preparatory stages of the Constitutional Revolution of 1906–11, see Mohammad Reza Fashahi, *Gozareshi Kutah az Tahavvolat-e Fekri va Ijtima'i dar Jame'eh Feodali-ye Iran* ("A Short Account of the Social and Intellectual Movements in the Iranian Feudal Society") (Tehran: Gutenberg, 1354/1975), pp. 322–42.

Financing his journeys by teaching Persian and Arabic, he eventually arrived in Europe, learning English, French, and even some German on his way, before going to North America, from there boarding an American ship heading to China, Japan, Burma, Singapore, and India. In every city he visited, he went to see factories, public schools, and churches, and even managed to meet and converse with high dignitaries. In India he visited the Agha Khan Mahallati, the region's widely influential Ismaili leader. From there he finally returned to Iran, after an absence of almost sixteen years.[4]

Sayyah—a major advocate of the liberty of his nation and of the rule of law—was instrumental in preparing the way for the Constitutional Revolution. He returned to Iran in July 1877, during the reign of the Qajar monarch Nasser al-Din Shah, and began composing his travelogue as the mode of narrative that would best communicate his insights to others. His travels had turned him into a wise and learned man, deeply attracted to European and North American progress—though neither was spared from his critical judgment—and determined to bring about change in his own homeland. He used his travelogue to mount a scathing attack on the backwardness of his homeland, constantly contrasting its deficiencies with the achievements of Europe and the wider world; official corruption and tyranny troubled him deeply. After visiting Shiraz and Isfahan—as well as Mahallat, to attend to his mother—Sayyah eventually went to Tehran, where he received a royal audience with Nasser al-Din Shah, who had heard of his travels. Nasser al-Din Shah first had his official

---

4 For the original Persian account of Hajj Sayyah's travels, see his *Khaterat-e Hajj Sayyah ya Doreh-ye Khof va Vahshat* ("The Memoirs of Hajj Sayyah or the Period of Fear and Terror"), ed. Hamid Sayyah (Tehran: Ibn Sina, 1346/1967). For an English translation of his travelogue, see Hajj Sayyah, *An Iranian in Nineteenth-Century Europe: The Travel Diaries of Haj Sayyah, 1859–1877*, trans. Mehrbanoo Nasser Deyhim (Bethesda, MD: Ibex, 1998).

translators test Sayyah's command of French, English, and Russian, and then asked his opinion of what had changed in his realm while he had been away. Sayyah gave a candid response about the calamity of social and economic conditions. The Qajar king dismissed him, impressed by his knowledge and audacity.[5]

Sayyah continued to consort with progressive Iranians of his time, visiting the royal court on further occasions, and constantly speaking of the necessity of reform. He traveled extensively through Iran, learning more about his home-land and relentlessly speaking against the calamities that had befallen it. He eventually left Iran, passing again through Russia, and then through the Ottoman territories on the way back to Europe, from which he departed for his Hajj pilgrim-age before again returning to Iran. He had found a singular vocation for himself, traveling through and beyond Iran, learning of the social and cultural conditions of progress and applying them to his homeland. He eventually befriended the leading revolutionary activist of his time, Jamal al-Din al-Afghani (1838–97), which began to create trouble for him with Qajar officials. Al-Afghani's criticism of the Qajar mon-archy eventually resulted in his deportation from Iran. Sayyah came under increasing pressure from Qajar officials, eventu-ally suffering arrest and torture. At one point he even applied for an American passport, with which he intended to go to China. But he remained in Iran until Nasser al-Din Shah was assassinated, and the Constitutional Revolution commenced, in the course of which he remained intensely active until his dying day.

---

5 For more details, see Mohammad Reza Fashahi, *Az Gatha-ha ta Mashrutiyyat: Gozareshi Kutah az Tahavvolat-e Fekri va Ijtima'i dar Jame'eh Feodali Iran* ("From the Gathas to the Constitutional Revolution: A Brief Report on Social and Intellectual Developments in the Iranian Feudal Society") (Tehran: Gutenberg, 1975), pp. 324–6.

Shushtari and Sayyah were not the only figures writing accounts of their adventures around the globe who informed the emerging nationalist sentiments of their homeland. Many others joined them, traveling to the four corners of the world, expanding the imaginative geography of their compatriots. Even the ruling monarch, Nasser al-Din Shah Qajar, joined their ranks, not only traveling to Europe but writing an account of his observations. In 1873, the Qajar monarch traveled from Tehran to the north of his kingdom, from where he continued on his journey, through Russia, to Europe, where he visited Germany, Belgium, England, France, Italy, and Austria, returning via the Ottoman territories and the Caucasus.[6]

The wider world was encroaching on Iran, and Iran was rushing in reverse towards it. The Perso-Russian wars of the early nineteenth century were a rude awakening for the ruling Qajars and their reformist and revolutionary nemeses alike. Accounts of travel by critical thinkers like Shushtari and Sayyah brought Iran into the full light of day, its opening frontiers drawing it away from the ruins of its preceding imperial incarnations. The result was not the rise of any kind of Eurocentric "modernity," but the critical vortex of a colonial modernity, with all of its innate paradoxes and contradictions. The geopolitics of the region were opened up to the widening horizons of a world that would soon redefine Iranian political culture, and with it the region as a whole.

---

6   This account is published as Nasser al-Din Shah Qajar, *Safarnameh* ("Travelogue") (Isfahan: Mash'al, n.d.).

CHAPTER 2

Learning French and Russian

My name is Mirza Aqa Tabrizi. From early childhood I was
eager to learn French and Russian ... After serving in the Royal
Teachers College and diplomatic mission in Baghdad and
Istanbul I have been serving as the First Secretary in the French
Embassy.

Mirza Aqa Tabrizi (1863)

For Iran, the Constitutional Revolution of 1906–11 represented
a threshold onto the transnational public sphere paradoxically
made possible by expansive European colonialism. At the time
of the revolution, Iran was still ruled by a decadent, incompetent, and bewildered Qajar dynasty, though a sustained course
of court-initiated reforms ironically dovetailed with revolutionary uprisings such as the Babi Movement (1844–52) and
the Tobacco Revolt (1890) to facilitate the final demise of the
ruling dynasty. The British were still dominant in the region,
from India to Egypt, while the rise of the Young Turks within
the Ottoman Empire (1908) echoed the reformist inclinations
of the Qajar court. The wider world was thus encroaching upon
the emerging nation-states. The European revolutions of 1848,
the Japanese victory in the Russo-Japanese war of 1904–05, and
the Russian Revolution of 1905, followed by the cataclysmic
revolution of 1917, were all harbingers of a global political
upheaval announcing massive shifts in the global economic
infrastructure, from which no nation could exempt itself.

The opening of horizons towards a changing world that I
noted in Chapter 1 is impossible to imagine solely with sed-
entary thinkers. In this chapter I move to the 1850s and more

closely consider peripatetic intellectuals where the rise of a pioneering playwright like Mirza Aqa Tabrizi marks a particularly poignant national awareness of the world at large.

A National Awareness of the World

To understand the spirit of the nineteenth century in this region, it is necessary to recognize that the gradual formation of a "national consciousness" from the ruins of the preceding empires was very much contingent on the eventual formation of a territorial totality that shrunk and expanded under successive dynasties—some powerful and expansionist, others incompetent and deeply corrupt—and ultimately yielded to the overbearing European empires and their colonial extensions. The Afsharids were followed by the Zands (1750–94), whose two most important leaders, Karim Khan Zand (1750–79) and Lotf Ali Khan Zand (1789–94), very much continued the earlier Safavid struggle to maintain the territorial integrity of their realm while coming to terms with the expanded colonial and commercial interest of European powers in the Persian Gulf. Internecine tribal rivalries and wars continued apace internally, while Karim Khan tried to sustain the Safavids' commercial interactions with the British East India Company in Bushehr. At this time, the British, the Dutch, and the French were actively competing in the Persian Gulf, in a process that was integrating the Iranian national economy, polity, and society into their regional and global contexts.[1]

These commercial and cultural factors were expanded and exacerbated well into the next dynasty, in which changes initiated within the Qajar polity might be traced to the circle around the era's reformist champion, Mirza Taqi Khan Amir Kabir (1807–52). Amir Kabir was acutely aware of the

---

[1] For excellent accounts of Karim Khan Zand's reign, see John R. Perry, *Karim Khan Zand: A History of Iran, 1747–1779* (Chicago: University of Chicago Press, 1979).

changing world around the Qajar dynasty, and was determined to infuse that worldly awareness into a renewed conception of the nation from the heart of a retrograde dynasty. Amir Kabir was the visionary statesman of the most far-reaching reforms in Qajar history. Perhaps the most significant of his initiatives was the establishment of the Dar al-Fonun polytechnic, the first institution of higher learning in Iran founded on a European model. He launched *Vaqaye' Ettefaqiyeh*, a national newspaper that brought the emerging nation together around daily news from various provinces, as well as from other parts of the world, and Europe in particular. He began seriously to tackle financial corruption at the court, and tried to regulate the state finances and budget. He dispensed with aristocratic titles, banned the carrying of weapons in public, laid the foundation of a national police system, established a national postal network, radically reformed and modernized the military, and did as much as possible to regulate and control the clerical establishment. He also established the careful regulation of diplomatic missions—a task he accomplished with remarkable vision, integrating the Qajar dynasty politically with the wider world. Through Amir Kabir's deeply transformative reforms, the Qajar dynasty became fully and ever so gently publicly aware of the world at large. Iranians began to travel abroad, to the Ottoman territories as well as to Europe, and to write and publish their travelogues. These travelers included the Qajar monarch whom Amir Kabir served, Nasser al-Din Shah Qajar (1831–96).[2] Amir Kabir was not a radical revolutionary but a mild-mannered reformist, who was responsible for brutally crushing the most significant revolutionary uprising of his time—the Babi movement. But he represents the kind of court-initiated liberalism that paved the

---

2   Still the best study of Amir Kabir's premiership and reforms is by the late Iranian historian Fereydun Adamiyat, *Amir Kabir va Iran* ("Amir Kabir and Iran") (Tehran: Amir Kabir, 1944).

way for the integration of the emerging Iranian bourgeoisie into the larger commercial and political network of the wider world. Amir Kabir was perhaps the most significant reformist of the Qajar period, chiefly responsible for opening up the moral and imaginative borders of the nation into the world beyond.

Mirza Hossein Khan Sepahsalar (1828–81) actively continued with Amir Kabir's reforms, encouraging the king to travel abroad to see European societies (Russia, Austria, France, and the United Kingdom in particular) and facilitate similar changes to those he would witness in person. He regulated the Iranian cabinet system, tried to establish a national railroad, advanced the postal system, made a contribution to simplifying official Persian prose, continued with Amir Kabir's educational reform, employed European advisors to improve his national customs system, and undertook other bureaucratic transformations of the Qajar regime.[3]

Perhaps the most prominent Iranian scholar of these reforms initiated by Sepahsalar and other Qajar-era reformists was the eminent historian Fereydun Adamiyat (1920–2008), whose singular achievement was to articulate a liberal democratic aspiration for his homeland, for which he sought to generate a nineteenth-century genealogy. The struggles for freedom, the rule of law, institutions of civil liberty, and national sovereignty were the central aspects of the liberalism that Adamiyat identified among the Qajar reformists. In his extensive work in this field, Adamiyat was perhaps the most prominent liberal historian of his time, tracing Iranian liberalism to its European and Enlightenment origins without evincing the slightest concern for the colonial context of its reception. Nevertheless, national

---

3 An excellent study of Sepahsalar's reforms can be found in Fereydun Adamiyat, *Andisheh-ye Taraqi va Hukumat Qanun dar Asr Sepahsalar* ("The Idea of Progress and Rule of Law during the Time of Sepahsalar") (Tehran: Khwarazmi, 1977).

independence and state sovereignty were the focus of a principled anticolonial nationalism for Adamiyat. In effectively tracing the ideas of Sepahsalar and other reformists to Europe, Adamiyat placed the rise of Iranian liberal nationalism in the domain of its fateful encounter with European powers. He has been faulted for ignoring, or even denouncing, the more radical or indigenous (Islamic) revolutionary dimensions of this period, but he remains instrumental in our understanding of the liberal front of the expansion of the Iranian public sphere to incorporate European ideas and movements.

Revolutionaries Against Reformists

While these two prominent reformers were deeply entrenched at the royal court, the revolutionary episode driven by the Babi Movement (1844–52) points to a much wider and more popular domain of social changes. The Babi Movement (Jonbesh Bab) was the most widespread revolutionary uprising of the mid nineteenth century, which attracted a wide range of revolutionaries from the ranks of the merchant class, as well as from both the impoverished peasantry and the urban poor, shaking the Qajar dynasty to its foundations.[4] Its founder, Seyyed Ali Muhammad Shirazi (1819–50), who took the title "Bab"—meaning "Gate"—drew his initial inspiration from the revolutionary disposition of Shi'ism, before he and his followers took a completely new tack and announced the commencement of a whole new revelation.[5] The Shi'i clerical establishment joined forces with the Qajar monarchy to crush and destroy the movement. As a millenarian movement, Babism was deeply rooted in Shi'i Imamology and eschatology,

---

4 For an excellent study of the Babi movement, see Abbas Amanat, *Resurrection and Renewal: The Making of the Babi Movement in Iran, 1844–1850)* (Ithaca, NY: Cornell University Press, 1989).

5 For an understanding of the Babi movement in the context of Shi'ism, see my *Shi'ism: A Religion of Protest* (Cambridge, MA: Harvard University Press, 2011).

in which the charismatic figures of the infallible Imams have always been conducive to revolutionary uprisings. Bab and his followers updated and radicalized this tendency, pushing it to its logical and rhetorical conclusions, until they declared the emergence of a whole new revelatory dispensation. The eschatological claim resonated with the urban poor and the impoverished peasantry, who joined its ranks and endangered both the political and clerical foundation of the Qajar rule. What was peculiar about Babism, which was later further developed into Baha'ism, was its claim of a whole new revelation for the universal emancipation of humanity. It sought to overcome its roots in Shi'ism and proclaim the dawn of a new era, a new prophet, a new revealed text. The territorial domain of the Babi movement went far beyond that of the Qajar dynasty in Iran, extending well into the Ottoman Empire. Babi revolutionary activists like Tahereh Qorrat al-'Ayn (1814–52) freely navigated between the Ottoman and Qajar territories.

A number of leading Iranian public intellectuals emerged simultaneously with or soon after the Babi movement. Some openly joined and supported it, while others were encouraged by its revolutionary disposition and the public discourse it had occasioned and enabled. The ideas of Mirza Aqa Khan Kermani (1854–97)—ranging from literary criticism to iconoclastic historiography—radically altered the moral imagination of his generation. Zeyn al-Abedin Maragheh'i (1839–1910) was another major expatriate figure, living in Ottoman territories, whose fictional account of a return to Iran from abroad, *Safarnameh-ye Ebrahim Beig* ("Ebrahim Beig's Travelogue"), became a pioneering text of social criticism. Along with Mirza Aqa Tabrizi, who flourished in the 1870s, and Seyyed Jamal al-Din al-Afghani, who was active in the second half of the nineteenth century, these writers roamed throughout the Muslim world and Europe, looking to radicalize their fellow Muslims politically. These pioneering thinkers were peripatetic intellectuals, moving from one country and continent to another, navigating a geography of liberation that connected their homeland to a wider frame of political imagination in which environment they produced critical thoughts that liberated their people from the heavy and overpowering burden of their ancestral cultures. All these thinkers came together to craft a robust political idiom of cosmopolitan worldliness, to come back to life and inform a pathbreaking reading of the emerging postcolonial nations.

Transnational Nations

My central argument here is that colonial nation-states, including their political, cultural, and economic characteristics —and thus national identity as such—were all in fact transnational products. All were formed using the ideological predicate of a prefabricated national alterity: Persian national identity was formed in contradistinction from Arab identity, and vice versa, while the same relationship operated between Persians and Turks, between Persians and Afghans, between Afghans and Tajiks, and between Pakistanis and Indians. These categories were all colonial constructs transmuted into postcolonial terms. From the very commencement of the project of (Europeanized) capitalist modernity, the operation of capital has become increasingly transnational, and ultimately global. The formation of colonially defined nation-states, and then of postcolonial nationalism, relied upon a frontier fiction that had repressed the idea of the "nation" by reducing it to a unit of bookkeeping in the violent transnational operation of capital, with its perpetual reliance on the procurement of cheap raw materials and the exploitation and abuse of workers.

The aggressive formation of the postcolonial nation-state in much of the colonial world was predicated on the racialized European model of the concept that, at least since Immanuel

Kant, had fabricated national characteristics for Europeans. By 1764, the year of the publication of Kant's *Observations on the Feeling of the Beautiful and Sublime*, the racialized frontier fiction that was then wholeheartedly adopted by colonized minds in the production of postcolonial national identity was already at an advance stage. These identities included those of Turks, Persians, Arabs, Indians, among others. In this book Kant categorized Europeans according to their national characteristics, and distinguishes among them by their various feelings towards the sublime and the beautiful and towards the end of his treatises does the same with non-Europeans, dividing them along the lines of Persians, Arabs, Indians, American savages, Africans, and so on:

> If we cast a fleeting glance over the other parts of the world, we find the Arab the noblest man in the Orient, yet of a feeling that degenerates very much into the adventurous ... If the Arabs are, so to speak, the Spaniards of the Orient, similarly the Persians are the French of Asia. They are good poets, courteous and of fairly fine taste. They are not such strict followers of Islam, and they permit to their pleasure-prone disposition a tolerably mild interpretation of the Koran.[6]

From this premise I propose that the formation of the post-colonial state and the nation it feigns to represent is in fact constitutionally and cognitively colonial. But the resulting nations, in their actual formation, are positively transnational and cosmopolitan. All ideological claims to national identity are in fact deeply and irreversibly colonial—unless they are framed by their transnational origin and imperial pedigree, and today by a cosmopolitan disposition.

---

6 See Immanuel Kant, *Observations on the Feeling of the Beautiful and Sublime* (Oakland, CA: University of California Press, 1960), p. 109.

A Worldly Awareness of the Nation

Marking this transnational formation of national destiny, a number of towering public intellectuals and gifted literati now intervened to redefine what the emergence of Iran as a nation (*mellat*) was to mean—many of them doing so from outside the political boundaries of their country, and thus enabling a worldly awareness of their homeland. Chief among these pioneering public intellectuals was Mirza Aqa Khan Kermani (1854–97), who was born and raised in Kerman province, in central Iran, to a learned family rooted in scholastic traditions. He eventually emerged as the most influential proponent of radical change to the cultural fabric of his homeland. Kermani received a solid early education in Islamic scholasticism (law and theology), from which he later drew heavily in his scholarly writings. Early in his education, he became attracted to Sheykh Ahmad Ahsa'i, a leading theologian and philosopher of his time, and through him to the revolutionary Babi movement (1844–52). He eventually joined his close friend and comrade Shaykh Ahmad Ruhi, and together they left Kerman for Isfahan, from where they traveled to Tehran, Rasht, and then Istanbul, and from there to Baghdad and Damascus. In Istanbul they lived in grinding poverty, but managed to write some of the most iconoclastic and provocative literary and political tracts of their time, whose impact endured to influence the rise of the Constitutional Revolution. Kermani and two of his comrades, Shaykh Ahmad Ruhi and Khabir al-Molk, were finally arrested (on suspicion of plotting against the Qajar dynasty) and extradited to Tabriz in 1897, where they were executed by the Qajar authorities.[7] Central to Kermani's mission as a public intellectual, at once critical of both the clerical and monarchical orders, was to lead his nation into a

---

7 The best study of Mirza Aqa Khan Kermani, in Persian, is Fereydun Adamiyat, *Andisheh-ha-ye Mirza Aqa Khan Kermani* ("The Ideas of Mirza Aqa Khan Kermani") (Tehran: Khwarazmi, 1967).

renewed pact with its contemporary history, fully cognizant of the world around it.

Equally critical in pulling Iran into the wider world was Seyyed Jamal al-Din al-Afghani (1838–97), a revolutionary activist, Islamist ideologue, and major source of agitation in the Ottoman Empire and Qajar monarchy. Al-Afghani left an indelible mark on the early mobilization of Muslims against domestic tyranny and foreign domination. Though for political reasons—mainly that of winning wider Sunni acceptance in the larger Muslim world—he called himself "al-Afghani," he was in fact a Shi'i Iranian born and raised in Asadabad, near Hamadan. But his chameleon-like habit, wherever he went in the Muslim world, was to claim that he was from somewhere else within it. Following a standard early education in Qazvin, Tehran, and Najaf, he traveled at seventeen to British India, then to Arabia for his first Hajj pilgrimage. Following his return to Afghanistan, via Iran, he remained active in Afghan affairs for a couple of years. In Cairo he met his disciple, the eminent Egyptian reformer Mohammad Abdu. He then traveled to Paris, London, Munich, Moscow, and St. Petersburg. It was in Paris that he published *Al-Urwah al-Wuthqa* ("The Indissoluble Link"), an exceptionally important and widely read periodical promoting his ideas for radical reform in Muslim countries. Responding to invitation from the ruling monarch, Nasser al-Din Shah, he eventually returned to Iran, where one of his disciples ended up assassinating the Qajar patriarch. His ideas and agitations finally resulted in a revival of Islamist politics, and played a major role in such historic events as the Constitutional Revolution.[8]

---

8 For an excellent account of al-Afghani's adventure in the wider domain of Asian politics, see Pankaj Mishra, *From the Ruins of Empire: The Intellectuals Who Remade Asia* (New York: Farrar, Straus & Giroux, 2012).

Leading public intellectuals like Kermani and Afghani were now definitive of a transnational body politic that was engaged in modern nation-building. Equally important among these figures was Zeyn al-Abedin Maragheh'i (1840–1910). Born to a merchant family in Maragheh, he began working for his father at an early age, and soon moved to Ardabil. When a business venture went sour, he moved to Tbilisi, in Georgia, where he performed consular work for the Iranian community. In Crimea he worked as a trader, now looking towards Istanbul; in Yalta he grew close to the Russian royal family, even becoming a Russian citizen. Meanwhile, his preoccupation with his homeland only intensified. Eventually he returned to Istanbul, where he spent the rest of his days, and abandoned his Russian citizenship. He lived in that city for the rest of his life, working with many periodicals, including Calcutta's *Habl a-Matin*, and eventually wrote his masterpiece, *Seyahat-nameh Ebrahim Beig* ("Ebrahim Beig's Travelogue") (1903).

Seyahat-nameh Ebrahim Beig is the story of a young Iranian man born in Egypt to a prominent merchant family, who from his early youth develops a fascination for his homeland. He eventually leaves his home, his family, and the woman he loves in Cairo and, via Istanbul and the Caucasus, travels to Iran, where he encounters rampant poverty, corruption, indifference, and hopelessness. The book thus becomes a sharply critical account of life under the Qajar dynasty. Ebrahim Beig finally returns to Cairo, where he begins to write his travelogue; but he abandons the task in utter desperation, at which point his companion Yusuf Amu continues with the narrative. The second volume continues with Yusuf Amu's narrative, now describing the agony of Ebrahim Beig far away from his homeland. With every piece of news that comes from Iran, good or bad, his health is affected accordingly. He finally marries the woman he loves, but soon after he dies, a deeply broken and disappointed man. The third volume continues with Yusuf Amu's narrative, though this time in the form of a dream in which, guided by a wise figure not dissimilar to Beatrice in Dante's *Divine Comedy*, he travels to the other world, and in Paradise encounters Ebrahim Beig. Thus, Cairo, Iran and the region around it, and Paradise itself are incorporated into the narrative domain of Maraghe'i's pioneering work of fiction, in which the social conditions of Iran were communicated through a widely popular narrative.[9]

The Story of Ashraf Khan

Equally important in this crucial period, Mirza Aqa Tabrizi (fl. 1870s) was a pioneering figure in Persian drama, sometimes referred to as the creator of Iranian black comedy, and was chiefly responsible for initiating the genre of realistic drama in Persian. He was deeply rooted in the social and political predicament of his time, with a theatrical gift for staging the real as the absurd. Tabrizi was born and raised in Tabriz, where he learned French and Russian, and through these two languages was exposed to the wider regional and world context of his homeland. He soon began a teaching career that brought him into contact with Austrian teachers as a translator. Soon he embarked on diplomatic missions to Baghdad and Istanbul, where his exposure to the political environment of his homeland expanded. Upon his return to Iran, he began working as a secretary in the French embassy. The characters in his plays are real, though shallow and archetypal, drawn from the dramatic circumstances of his daily life, and political awareness. Historians of the period like Baqer Momeni suggest that he had no hope that any of his plays would actually be staged, so he felt free to write what he wanted for

---

9 For an English translation of the novel, see Zayn el-Abedin Maragheh'i, *The Travel Diary of Ebrahim Beg*, trans. James D. Clark (Santa Ana, CA: Mazda, 2006).

the very limited readership that would get to read his plays—and of course for posterity. His works were not published during the reign of Nasser al-Din Shah and Mozaffar al-Din Shah, but burst onto the Iranian literary scene soon after the Constitutional Revolution. Some of his other works were also published in Berlin, though they were attributed to another major reform intellectual, Mirza Malkam Khan Nazem al-Dowleh. A pioneering figure in the use of colloquial Persian in this new literary genre, he wrote prose that also thrives on a profoundly dark and pessimistic worldview. In his own introduction to his collection of plays, dated 1871, Tabrizi informs his readers that his inspiration for writing the plays was the work of Mirza Fath Ali Akhondzadeh, a pioneering figure in the reform movement of the nineteenth century, who had written his own plays originally in Turkish.[10]

A typical example of Tabrizi's drama is *The Story of Ashraf Khan* (1881), a play in four acts, with a number of color-ful characters. Ashraf Khan is the governor of Arabestan, a semi-fictive province roughly evoking the Khuzestan region in southern Iran. He has come to the capital city of Tehran in order to pay the taxes he has collected from his province over the preceding three years, and to obtain from the proper authorities a statement that he has done so faithfully, and thus to regain his status and position as governor and go back to Arabestan.

The play depicts the range and depth of corruption at the heart of the Qajar court. Everyone the provincial governor meets, from the doormen at the court to the prime minister, is milking him for money, implying that they have no concern whatsoever as to how he collects that money or at what cost to people under his rule, so long as they get their share of the wealth. The supreme thief is of course the king himself,

---

10   See Mirza Aqa Tabrizi, *Chahar Teatr* ("Four Plays"), ed. M. Baqer Momeni (Tehran: 1976), pp. 1–2.

followed by his prime minster and courtiers, down to the lowest-ranking members of his retinue. *The Story of Ashraf Khan* portrays the rampant corruption at the royal court, as Khan seeks to secure continued rule over his province. The moral of the story is that, while the governor is at the receiving end of the corrupt courtiers extracting bribes from him, he ultimately yields to their demands because he wants to maintain his position, and go back to plunder the people under his command more freely.

Certainly, the play is elementary in its composition, lacking character development, psychological depth, or social sophistication, and predictable in the evolution of its plot, the four acts repeating in linear and prosaic form the predicament of Governor Ashraf Khan and his retinue without any twists or turns. If we consider the date of the play, 1881, and recall that this is exactly when Anton Chekhov (1860–1904) began his career as a dramatist, we realize the utterly prosaic origin of Persian drama at this point in the nineteenth century. Be that as it may, this typical play of the period points to the budding dramatic sensibilities of Mirza Aqa Tabrizi's generation of playwrights—sensibilities that would eventually mature to anticipate much richer artistic pedigree. The significance of plays of this kind at this nascent stage of the genre in the country is in their treatment of the mostly social and political concerns that preoccupied their authors and limited audiences. It would not be until a few decades later that this and similar plays would published and staged. But their emergence in this period marks the dramatic rise of Iranian national consciousness within a transnational public sphere that included the rise of Persian drama.

The Worlds of Kiarostami, Mozart, and Nodjoumi

Let us now fast-forward to examine a consequence of these early developments in Iranian performing arts, so we can see the two ends of a transnational creative spectrum at the same time. There is a long distance—in time and style—between Mirza Aqa Tabrizi in the late nineteenth century and Abbas Kiarostami in the late twentieth; but the collected confidence and creative audacity of contemporary Iranian artists on the global stage today is the unfolding legacy of those distant forbears. The distance between Mirza Aqa Tabrizi's earliest dramatic experiments and Abbas Kiarostami's mature and confident turn, later in his career, from Iranian cinema to European opera, marks the layered expansion of the Iranian literary and visual public sphere in this critical span of time.

There was nothing strange or surprising when leading Iranian filmmaker Abbas Kiarostami was invited to direct a new production of Mozart's *Così fan tutte* at the Aix-en-Provence Festival, in its summer 2008 season. As one observer put it at the time:

> In 1940, the Bolshoi Theatre in Moscow invited Sergei Eisenstein to stage Richard Wagner's *Die Walküre*. Since then, Ingmar Bergman, Andrei Tarkovsky, Baz Luhrmann, Luchino Visconti, Roman Polanski, Francis Ford Coppola, William Friedkin, and Woody Allen have all turned their considerable talents to opera. Later this month, Anthony Minghella's *Madame Butterfly* will return to London after a successful spell in New York. The Chinese film director Zhang Yimou will stage a production of the opera *Turandot* at the Bird's Nest Olympic Stadium in Beijing this autumn.[11]

By 2008 the idea had in fact become a commonplace, and the news that a leading Iranian filmmaker would try his hand in a different but related medium had become quite intriguing. But the idea did attract its share of skeptical optimism:

---

11 See Bianca Bonomi, "Cosi fan Kiarostami," *National*, June 7, 2009, available at thenational.ae.

Importing celebrated cinema directors is one of the riskier tactics favored by opera managements today. Although it generates plenty of initial press and audience interest, the odds on solid success are long, not least because the process of rehearsing singers and collaborating with conductors is so different from working behind a camera. Yet I can see that the prospect of Abbas Kiarostami's take on *Così fan tutte* would be intriguing. The films of this Iranian master are illuminated by qualities that could be described as Mozartian—an interest in human foible, a subtle and elliptical grace, a visual sensibility (he trained as an artist and practices as a stills photographer) marked by clarity and understatement.[12]

From staging, production, and performance perspectives, the proposition was still considered quite curious by some: "Kiarostami admits," Rupert Christiansen reported,

> that he knew virtually nothing about opera when he took on this project. He had never seen *Così*; he auditioned none of the cast. This absence of baggage and preconception means he doesn't feel impelled to strive for originality, and more experienced opera-goers might find his approach almost naïve in its trust in the text, its use of period costume, its eschewal of gags or gimmicks.

The production was also subject to its share of political controversy. When the opera was to be staged in London, the British embassy in Tehran had refused Kiarostami a visa, leading one British critic to object that English National Opera's "new *Così fan tutte* hit the headlines ... some time before it opened, owing to our Tehran Embassy's inability to provide director Abbas Kiarostami with a visa. After interminable wrangling,

---

12   See Rupert Christiansen, "*Così fan tutte*: When a Movie Maestro Focuses on the Opera Stage," *Telegraph*, July 10, 2008.

an exasperated Kiarostami eventually pulled out; he entrusted work in London, the production having been premiered last year at the Festival d'Aix-en-Provence, to his deputy, Elaine Tyler-Hall." The whole production thus became a textbook example of the globalized condition of the politics that at once enabled and compromised artistic production.

Kiarostami's production of Mozart's opera, however, had gone ahead and produced some enthusiastic responses. Bianca Bonomi tried to find a cinematic affinity between Kiarostami and the opera he was directing:

> He also recognized that the theatrical intimacy of the opera, which revolves around the dealings of six main characters, was not dissimilar to the intimacy promoted in much of his screen work. Such works include *The Wind Will Carry Us*, the story of a city engineer who journeys to rural Iran and discovers new social values; *Ten*, which details a female driver's conversations with passengers, and *A Taste of Cherry*, a contemplative tale of a middle-aged man who has resolved to commit suicide, for which Kiarostami won the Palme d'Or at Cannes in 1997.

The key historical significance of this moment, however, was that an Iranian filmmaker was trying his hand at an iconic operatic production in the heart of Europe, almost a century and a half after Mirza Aqa Tabrizi had first tried to introduce the European theatrical heritage onto the Iranian stage. The fact that Kiarostami was at home with Mozart in Europe speaks to a common creative ground shared beyond the ethnic territorialization of the nation-state. For Sergei Eisenstein to stage Richard Wagner's *Die Walküre*, or for any of the other non-Iranian directors named by Bonomi, to stage any number of other operas, had now been placed on the same field of play as Kiarostami's direction of Mozart on stage. What we were thus witnessing, from Mirza Aqa Tabrizi to Abbas Kiarostami, was the epistemic and aesthetic indeterminacy of worlds that had been intended to confine but had in fact liberated these artists.

Kiarostami is by no means the only example of such immediate and effervescent affinity between Iranian artists in and out of their homeland and their transnational aesthetics, politics, and audiences. When it comes to the theatricality of visual performances, the case of the globally celebrated Iranian artist Nicky Nodjoumi (b. 1942) exemplifies an equally significant staging of an Iranian artist far beyond his national confinements.[13] Born and raised in Iran, Nodjoumi became nationally prominent long before he immigrated to the United States, where he soon began to call New York home, bringing his earliest artistic sensibilities to a much more global audience. Both in and out of Iran, Nodjoumi's playful, flamboyant, decidedly theatrical, and deeply satirical art combines the political atrocities of Iran and its immediate and distant environs into a potent aesthetics now brought to bear on global politics. When we look at Nodjoumi's artwork today, we may not quite see the genealogy of his formal defiance of the politics of the day; but careful attention to his bitter satirical formalism cannot fail to show his ease and comfort in crossing aesthetic boundaries. His art is emblematic of a much larger artistic frame of reference, formed and brought to maturity inside Iran, and then expanded within a transnational public sphere where it was already at home.

Nation as Postcolonial Polity

As these varied cases of Iranian political and artistic adventures clearly testify, the formation of "the nation" as a postcolonial polity—in both its cultural and political registers—was

---

13 For more on Nicky Nodjoumi, see my essay, "Politics on Canvas: Nicky Nodjoumi and the New York Enclave," *Al Jazeera*, October 24, 2013, available at aljazeera.com.

Figure 2: Nicky Nodjoumi, *Caught on the Way* (2008–09).

a necessarily transnational product. Transnational European empires defeated and succeeded multinational Muslim empires, and from their historic clashes were born postcolonial nation-states like Iran. From that historic encounter we have inherited the overriding proposition of "the West and the Rest," as the iconic geopolitical imaginary of the last two hundred years—and it refuses to let go of the factual and lived realities of the world, as a result of the normative hegemony it has held over the public imagination, whether consenting or critical. Contemporary historians of European empires, like Niall Ferguson, continue to mark and mourn that binary in the very titles of the texts they continue to publish.[14] To

---

14   See Niall Ferguson, *Civilization: The West and the Rest* (London: Penguin, 2012).

liberate the mind from this distortion, we need to come to terms with the fact that what people make and inhabit is always through a double vision—looking simultaneously outwards from the inside and inwards from the outside. That we fail to see this double focus is partly because of the disciplinary boundaries that constrain our understanding of nation-states along their fictive frontiers.

The overwhelming majority of the knowledge—in both the social sciences and the humanities, in both manner and matter—produced over the last two hundred years is either in the form of grand narratives of the relationship of imperial domination between "the West and the Rest," or relates to the categorical formation of the postcolonial nation-states, or else is in the form of "area studies," which helped the United States and its European allies to retain political and epistemic control and domination over then-Soviet imperial expansionism. Lost among these departmental imperatives were the preceding (or emerging) geographies of affiliation, exchange, interaction, and solidarity across the old imperial borders and their emerging postcolonial counterparts. This was reinforced by the historical limitations that maintain a theoretical vacuity in the production of (self-centering) First World theories. From this inherently limited vantage point, the positing of the existence of other and alternative worlds always smacks of nativism, historicism, and ultimately theoretical irrelevance to the ears of a Europeanist who writes and reads the First World theories. But the anxiogenic notion of "Europe," precisely because it is so fundamentally suspicious of itself, falls into a crisis mode of identity the instant a country like Turkey wants to join it, or at the merest glimpse of a veiled woman walking the Champs-Élysées. But, since the geopolitics of fashions and frontiers are paramount, so are the efficacy and reality of the emerging worlds they entail.

Europe's anxiety over its identity conceals a dangerous

paranoia. Islamophobia now characterizes a defining moment for Europe as it struggles to remain "pure" and self-referential, in just the same way that anti-Semitism was (and remains) the defining feature of European Christianity. This makes the odd couple of Danish mass murderer Anders Breivik and Somali careerist Ayaan Hirsi Ali the real Europeanists. To turn to thinkers like José Martí, Américo Castro, Juan Goytisolo; or, more recently, Boaventura de Sousa Santos, Ramón Grosfoguel, Walter Mignolo, Enrique Dussel; or, reaching into the past, Ibn Khaldun or Al-Biruni, is precisely to retrieve and expand upon their particular moments of emancipatory anxiety and hope, when the epistemic indeterminacy of the world they inhabited and its emotive contingency had become politically evident and epistemically enabling. The objective of retrieving and expounding such worlds, of working out their hidden and repressed potentials, is the democratic dismantling of the tyranny of globalized Europeanism that is trying to colonize the world epistemically, now that it has lost it materially— in territorial terms, to the postcolonial nation-states, and in economic terms to China and India.

To achieve a comparative analysis that will overcome the epistemic limitations imposed by Europeanism's feigning of a moral and epistemic authority that it lacks in reality, we need to think outside the terms of the English and Comparative Literature or Continental Philosophy departments that have, over the last few decades, very much circumscribed theoretical approaches to this question in North America. We need to think of alternative worlds that have existed, that continue to exist, and that can easily emerge, in which alternative horizons of history are evident, potential, possible, or else repressed. Whether bygone or emerging, these worlds have a reality *sui generis*, and are irreducible to the limitations of colonial and postcolonial parameters. Vast geographies of effective histories have been glossed over by the postcolonial grid—perhaps most pertinently the expansive geographical crescent that stretches from Central Asia and the Caucasus, through the eastern domains of the Ottoman Empire, and down to its North African extensions. On that geography, the critical conjunctions in contemporary Arab, Turkish, and Iranian postcolonial nation-states (Iran and its environs) are self-evident but invisible and undertheorized.

CHAPTER 3

The Young and the Liberated

The Iranshahr Magazine *[published in Berlin] will do its best to prepare the groundwork upon which the young and liberated Iranian soul will be cultivated.*

Hossein Kazem-zadeh Iranshahr (1922)

The transnational disposition of politics and aesthetics I outlined in the previous chapter required a transnational public sphere within which Iran as a postcolonial polity was articulated. In the production of that public sphere, the earliest generations of newspapers and periodicals had a critical and enduring role to play. In the late nineteenth and early twentieth centuries, Calcutta, Tehran, Berlin, and London were the sites of the publication of some major periodicals that radically altered the language and diction of public discourse in Iran from a distinctively expatriate vantage point. These included *Qanun* (London), *Habl al-Matin* (Calcutta), *Sur-Israfil* (Tehran), *Kaveh* (Berlin), and *Iranshahr* (Berlin), which were all instrumental in facilitating the formation of a transnational public sphere, and thereby eventually directing the spirits of the French and Russian revolutions, as well as the anticolonial struggles of people in India, towards the making of the Constitutional Revolution of 1906–11 and the appearance of the earliest gestations of left, liberal, and Islamist political ideologies. Within this manufactured public sphere, Iranians within and outside their homeland began to reimagine their presence in the world. This was the worldly gift of expatriate Iranians to their homeland—one that did not come from "the West." It came from the world around

Iran, from India, Central Asia, the Arab and Ottoman worlds, and Europe. These periodicals were edited by leading Iranian literati and public intellectuals, who took advantage of their presence outside Iran to speak their mind free from the censorial and tyrannical repercussions of the ruling Qajar dynasty. There were of course many other periodicals edited and published inside Iran, at grave risk to their editors, but even these venues were deeply and decidedly influenced by those working from outside their homeland.[1] The expatriate journals were edited by the leading Iranian literati and public intellectuals who, residing outside of Iran, could speak more openly, free as they were from censorship and repercussions from the ruling Qajar dynasty.

When today we look back at a reformist of monumental stature, such as Mirza Malkam Khan (1833–1908), it is impossible to exaggerate his significance in pulling Iran out of its decadent degeneration under impotent Qajar rule by way of articulating a public reason to which he now had a claim as public intellectual. An Armenian by birth and breeding, though reportedly converting to Islam later, Malkam Khan, also known as Nazem al-Dowleh, attended a progressive Armenian school in Paris during 1843–51, and in 1852 began teaching at the pioneering polytechnic school Dar al-Fonun in Tehran. By 1857 Malkam Khan had entered diplomatic service at the Qajar court; but in 1862 he was exiled from his homeland because of his radical preoccupation with serious reform. He repeatedly fell in and out of favor at the Qajar court, and served in various capacities in European and Ottoman capitals. His final diplomatic position was that of Iranian ambassador to Italy, which he held until his death in 1908.[2]

---

1 A classical study of these periodicals is Yahya Aryanpour, *Az Saba ta Nima* ("From Saba to Nima") (Tehran: 1971–1995), vol. 1, pp. 233–52.

2 An account of Mirza Malkam Khan's life is given in Persian in Isma'il Ra'in, *Mirza Malkam Khan* (Tehran, 1974).

Malkam Khan facilitated the formation of a transnational public sphere within which ideas and ideals of the nation-state comparable to those thriving in Western Europe were to be articulated. A champion of the rule of law in his homeland, Malkam Khan published a widely popular and celebrated periodical in London, which, to make his point abundantly and immediately clear, he called *Qanun* ("Law"). The journal became critically influential in the course of the Constitutional Revolution, effectively introducing the key terms of the liberal democratic state with which the revolution articulated its aspirations. At the height of its popularity, even the ruling Qajar monarch and his courtiers read *Qanun*, while it was officially banned throughout the realm. Targeting reform-minded activists and students, and at times featuring such renowned essayists as Jamal al-Din al-Afghani, *Qanun* regularly criticized the Qajar monarchy for its dictatorial behavior. Published from London for some eight years (1889–1906), and widely circulated in Iran among the emerging literate public, Qajar officials, and members of the clergy, the prose of *Qanun* demonstrated a pioneering endeavor to simplify the Persian language for a wider and more politically engaged public.[3]

Even before the publication of *Qanun*, a number of expatriate Iranian intellectuals in Istanbul had started publishing a periodical in that city called *Akhtar* ("Star"). The paper became so influential, and its readers followed it so devotedly, that some people in Central Asia used the derogatory term of "Akhtarism" for those who read it.[4] Equally important in promoting the ideals and aspirations of an emerging bourgeoisie was the journal *Habl al-Matin* ("Solid Rope"—a Qur'anic reference), which was initially published in Calcutta but eventually also in Tehran. Edited by Seyyed

---

3 Aryanpour considers the prose of Qanun "simple and sweet." See Aryanpour, *Az Saba ta Nima*, p. 251.

4 Ibid.

Jalal al-Din Kashani (a.k.a. Adib), *Habl al-Matin* commenced publication in Calcutta in 1893, and in Tehran in 1907, and was vastly influential on the discourse of the Constitutional Revolution. The paper was repeatedly banned, at one point moving from Tehran to Rasht, but its pathbreaking ideas remained consistently influential among Iranian revolutionaries—both bourgeois and radical—now actively engaged in toppling the Qajar tyranny.[5] What is equally critical about these journals is the fact that they implicate an ever-widening reading public, within and outside Iran, concerned about Iranian and regional affairs. The publication of such periodicals from places like Calcutta reflects the local sensitivities of the editors to the colonial consequences of the British presence in the subcontinent, and thus plant Iranian political parlance in a much wider global context. Issues discussed in these periodicals included the rule of law, parliamentary democracy, women's rights, a reinterpretation of Iranian history from the bottom up rather than a mere dynastic chronicle, and descriptive accounts of progressive movements in Europe and the rest of the world.

Hekmat ("Wisdom") and *Sorayya* ("The Pleiades") were two highly influential periodicals published from Cairo, while *Sur-Israfil* ("The Horn of Israfil") was perhaps the most widely popular magazine published in Tehran at the height of the Constitutional Revolution. Edited by Jahangir Khan Shirazi, Qasem Khan Tabrizi, and Ali Akbar Dehkhoda, *Sur-Israfil* began publication in 1907. Featuring Ali Akbar Dehkhoda's pioneering satirical prose, the journal introduced a potently subversive comic element into the revolutionary momentum of the period. Provocatively titled *Charand-o-Parand* ("Gibberish"), these columns made Dehkhoda into the voice of the ordinary people engaged in a world-historic

---

5 Aryanpour considers this paper a major organ of political Islamism. See ibid., p. 252.

battle against tyranny. During the critical years of 1907–08, as the Constitutional Revolution succeeded in establishing the parliament and awaited its bombardment by the new king, Dehkhoda's "Gibberish" subverted Persian prose and radically altered the mood and manner of political writing. With such colloquial signatures as Dakhu ("Mr. Mayor"), Kharmagas ("Gadfly"), Sag-e Hassan Daleh ("Stray Dog"), Gholam Geda ("Gholam the Panhandler"), Khadem al-Foqara ("Servant of the Poor"), Nokhod Hameh Ash ("Mr. Know-it-all"), and so on, Dehkhoda fabricated so many social outcasts, using both proverbial and satirical registers, that Persian prose was suddenly flooded with powerful new possibilities. Literary, precise, eloquent, elegant, never collapsing into vulgarity or ad hominem attacks, he was always alert to the social and moral responsibility of his writings. Dehkhoda's prose echoed the Turkish (and occasionally Russian) prose of another major satirical publication, *Molla Nasreddin* (1906–17), edited by Jalil Mohammad Qoli Zadeh and published in the Caucasus. It is possible that the production of *Sur-e Israfil* was organically linked with that of *Molla Nasreddin*, the two publications dialectically expanding each other's domains of influence from the Caucasus to and from Iran.

From 1915 to 1921, the publication of *Kaveh* from Berlin inaugurated a major ideological movement conceptualizing Iranian history through the energetic resuscitation of its ancient heritage. Edited by a major public intellectual, Seyyed Hassan Taqizadeh (who I will discuss in greater detail below), and using the name of a mythical hero from Ferdowsi's *Shahnameh* as its title, *Kaveh* sought to revive a sense of pride in Persia's ancient history, literary heritage, and mythic foundations. The periodical was decidedly pro-German and anti-Russian, and even anti-British, in its politics. Though initially entirely political in its language and diction, *Kaveh* eventually assumed a more literary direction, though

Figure 3: A cartoon from the satirical magazine *Molla Nasreddin* (1906–17), published in Turkish and occasionally in Russian in the Caucasus. Muslim women wonder how Europeanized women can read and write and teach.

its pro-German politics were never compromised. Officially financed by the German government, leading Iranian literati such as Mohammad Qazvini and Mohammad Ali Jamalzadeh contributed to *Kaveh*. *Iranshahr* was yet another Berlin-based publication that reached an even wider readership, and covered an even more diversified domain of social and intellectual history. Edited by Hossein Kazem-zadeh Iranshahr and published between 1922 and 1928, *Iranshahr* regularly addressed a much wider range of social and intellectual issues than its counterparts. In 1876, a French-language newspaper was even published in Tehran. But when it was read in translation to the ruling monarch, he was angered by its democratic prose and ordered that it be shut down.[6]

These and similar periodicals were instrumental in facilitating the formation of a potent public sphere. The introduction

6   Ibid., pp. 241–2.

of the printing press, the publication of these periodicals, and the need for a simplified Persian prose contributed collectively to the formation of a new social persona we can now call a "public intellectual" in the strict sense of the term—no longer at the service of the royal court or financed by Shi'i endowments. They emerged from among the general public, who constituted their audience—*mardom* ("people"), *mellat* ("nation"), and so on. The polylocality of these periodicals—whose points of origin ranged from the Indian subcontinent to Central Asia, the Caucasus, the Arab and Ottoman worlds, and Europe—clearly points to the transnational disposition of the *public reason* they now helped constitute as Iran recast itself as a contemporary nation-state. The presence in this period of figures such as the Armenian, Mirza Malkam Khan, underlines the fact that these public intellectuals were not all Muslims. Thus, it cannot be said that Islam was the defining dimension of citizenship in this new nation-sate, of the nature and composition of its public sphere, or of the identity of its towering public intellectuals.

Epistemologies of the South

In his pioneering 2012 essay, "Public Sphere and Epistemologies of the South," Boaventura de Sousa Santos argues that the "theoretical and cultural presuppositions of [the public sphere] are entirely European. They are not necessarily universally valid, even when they purport to be general theories."[7] To the degree that the "idea" of civil society, most effectively theorized by Jürgen Habermas,[8] may in fact have any such global claim, Santos is of course right. But he has a more potent point to

---

7 See Boaventura de Sousa Santos, "Public Sphere and Epistemologies of the South," *Africa Development* 37: 1 (2012), available online at boaventuradesousasantos.pt.

8 See Jürgen Habermas, *The Structural Transformation of the Public Sphere* (Cambridge, MA: MIT Press, 1962)

make: "If the epistemological diversity of the world is to be accounted for, other theories must be developed and anchored in other epistemologies—the epistemologies of the South that adequately account for the realities of the global South." His project is therefore to emphasize "the need for intercultural translation, understood as a procedure that allows for mutual intelligibility among the diverse experiences of the world."[9]

This is a perfectly legitimate and perhaps even laudable project. But one critical factor that Santos fails to consider, in his otherwise pathbreaking project, is the fact that the capitalist machinery at the root of the structural transformation of the public sphere is always already global—precisely by virtue of its colonial tentacles. When we move from the self-centering ideologies of "the West" to its peripheralized colonial extensions (to the South and North or East and West of the globe), we can see that the transnational operation of capital has already manufactured a Europeanized bourgeoisie (in its material interests and ideological persuasions, its political manner and social demeanor), and thus a public sphere (in form but not content) whose central preoccupation is to service the local and regional operation of that globalized capital. What Santos calls "the epistemologies of the South," therefore, are required in order to achieve not an understanding of this public sphere, but its revolutionary transformation through opposition to the abusive activities of the globalized bourgeoisie. Towards that end, one could pursue any strategy of resistance, including "the epistemologies of the South," or epistemologies articulated from the vantage point of the disenfranchised by forces operative on such public spheres; for there are certainly, in a Europeanized bourgeoisie, segments of "the South" that are already the beneficiaries of the selfsame Northern epistemologies.

---

9   Santos, "Public Sphere."

A critical aspect of the globalized formation of the public sphere is the inner tension and dialectical opposition that it inevitably entails. These are primarily rooted in the agents and modalities of public discourse that enable and set in motion that public sphere, where the Northern public spheres will paradoxically enable the revolutionary disposition of the public sphere in the South. This paradoxical dialectic is innate to the conflicting interests that globalized capitalism generates and sustains, thus making it impossible to divide the world between its Northern beneficiaries and those enfranchised by it in the South. North and South share a common tension of globalized capital, between those who are privileged and those who are disenfranchised by it, and in which the Northern public spheres paradoxically enable the revolutionary disposition of the public spheres in the South. This makes it impossible to divide the world between its Northern beneficiaries and those enfranchised by it in the South.

Consider the fact that Karl Marx and Friedrich Engels published their *Communist Manifesto* in the year that Nasser al-Din Shah ascended to the Qajar throne (1848). For about a decade (1844–52), the Babi Movement—embracing the European revolutions of 1848—threatened the Qajar dynasty from within, though the combined efforts of the royal court and the clerical elite opposed and dismantled that robust revolutionary uprising. Throughout the long and languorous reign of Nasser al-Din Shah (1848–96), competition between the Russians and the British in using and abusing the arena of the Qajar court enabled both to advance their colonial and imperial interests (specifically, the acquisition of raw materials, cheap labor, expanded markets, and the military wherewithal to secure them). The Qajar court thus, in effect, facilitated the colonial domination of Iran by two superpowers. In the form of contractual concessions (*emtiyaz*), the Qajar court began a piecemeal auction of all of Iran's natural resources and the emerging national interests to the British and the Russians, in exchange for cash that the Qajar monarchs used to finance their extravagant trips to Europe. Both the British and the Russians established banks in Iran to facilitate this systematic theft of national wealth. This moment represented the absolute height of colonial thievery and imperial domination of Qajar Iran. The king was a fool, the clerical elite was a band of power-mongering fanatics, and the court was deeply and pervasively corrupt. A man named Mirza Reza Kermani, a follower of Seyyed Jamal al-Din-Afghani, finally assassinated Nasser al-Din Shah, bringing a dramatic end to this orgy of corruption.

However, the capitalist interests that had brought the British and the Russians to the Qajar court in search of their colonial and strategic interests—or, more specifically, raw materials, cheap labor, expanded markets, and the military wherewithal to secure them—had also generated a nascent bourgeois public sphere, including the introduction of the printing press, newspapers, and a simplified Persian prose, within which revolutionary ideas and aspirations were now articulated and spread in terms entirely hostile to colonial designs. Perhaps the most significant among these related factors was the simplification of Persian prose, as it began its historic exit from the royal court into the public sphere. The earliest signs of this formal simplification began to appear with such prominent figures as prose stylists Qa'em Maqam, Adib al-Mamalek Farahani, and Muhammad Hossein Foroughi Zoka al-Molk. Eventually, for purposes of their own, Christian missionaries introduced the printing press to Iran. But Mirza Saleh Shirazi, a pioneering Iranian student who was sent by Qajar Prince Abbas Mirza to England early in the nineteenth century, is credited with having first brought back a printing press to his homeland. The British interest in hosting Mirza Saleh Shirazi and his friends in the UK was entirely related to colonial competition with the

French, but the printing press and the simplified Persian prose that were the side effects of colonial interests began to pave the way for the Constitutional Revolution, which was, at least in part, a reaction against those interests.

It is only through this dialectic, organic to the operation of globalized capital, that we might approach the transnational prerequisite of resistance to European imperialism—in the formation of which emerging public intellectuals had an equally paradoxical role to play.

Consider the career of a leading example of such a figure, Seyyed Hassan Taqizadeh (1878–1970), editor of *Kaveh*, whose life and career—both literary and political—connects the waning of the Qajar dynasty to the waxing of the Pahlavis. Taqizadeh came from a learned clerical family, and was born and raised in the Azerbaijan province in the north during the tumultuous preparatory stages of the Constitutional Revolution. His early upbringing bridged the two divergent worlds of Shi'i scholasticism and the revolutionary ideas coming from both Russia and Europe. His mastery of Persian and Arabic languages and literatures was soon matched by his command of English and French. Taqizadeh was mesmerized by European achievements in science, industry, and the development of democratic institutions, and his support for the Constitutional Revolution was adopted from the perspective of an Enlightenment intellectual. The singular mission of *Kaveh* was to generate a new national consciousness, albeit from the safe distance afforded by publication in Berlin, where its contributors could think and write freely.

He was either entirely oblivious to the colonial designs on his homeland nursed by European powers, thought he could outmaneuver them, or else imagined them to be beneficial to Iran. Either way, he was instrumental in deepening the political entanglement of Iran in transnational politics. Taqizadeh soon moved to Berlin, where he joined force with a number of other leading public literary figures and published the highly influential periodical *Kaveh* (1916–22) widely distributed and read in both Iran and abroad. The singular mission of *Kaveh* was to generate a new national consciousness, though doing so from the safe distance of Berlin, where its contributors could freely think and write.

When the Pahlavi dynasty was established, in 1926, Taqizadeh returned to Iran, eventually assuming various high-ranking political positions, including that of governor-general of Khorasan province, minister of roads and transportation, minister of finance, and ambassador to the United Kingdom and France; he also spent some time as a leading parliamentarian. Driven by a conviction that Iran must find its place among the emerging group of nation-states, Taqizadeh was conversant and engaged with all of the major European and American powers in pursuit of this nationalist end. He thought he was outsmarting European powers in securing such interests, but the reverse may in fact have been true. He was exceptionally talented and learned, but the mighty political powers of Britain, Germany, and Russia were far too structurally rooted in the global geopolitics of the region for any man—politician or public intellectual—to dislodge them. The result, however, was the effective integration of Iranian politics into the geopolitics of the emerging superpowers. Taqizadeh was very much a man of his time: the embodiment of all the contradictions that defined an historical era.

The itinerary of Taqizadeh's life is perhaps the best indication of the transnational, cosmopolitan, and expatriate context of his career as a public intellectual. From his birth and upbringing in Tabriz in 1878 until 1903, he studied Shi'i scholasticism and Persian humanism with uncommon proficiency. He spent the two crucial years of 1904–05 traveling in the Caucasus, and went from there to Istanbul, Beirut, and

Cairo, where he published one of his earliest essays. From 1906 to 1908 he was an active parliamentarian in the newly founded Majlis, when he began publishing in the progressive journals of the time, until his forced exile to London, where he fled in fear of his life from the royal court. From 1908 to 1910 he was back in Tabriz, returning to Tehran as a parliamentarian again, relentlessly engaged in the course of the Constitutional Revolution. He then left Iran once more, initially for Istanbul but soon for Europe. From there he went to New York, staying until 1915. He then left the United States for Berlin, where he published *Kaveh* until 1922. From Europe he traveled to Moscow, shortly thereafter marrying a German wife, before his return to Iran in 1924. This pattern continued until his death in 1970, including prominent political positions in Iran, and travels to Europe and the United States in various official capacities. Without his periodic and systematic exits from Iran, he would never have achieved the prominence he eventually found. His was an itinerant, restless, and ultimately homeless mind.[10]

Perhaps the most significant aspect of Taqizadeh's political, literary, and scholarly career was the manner in which, at one point, he effectively became the embodiment of the public sphere that had been enabled and institutionalized during the course of the Constitutional Revolution. He was deeply and pervasively beholden to European Enlightenment modernity, showing not even the slightest suggestion of a critical grasp of its inner tensions and colonial contradictions. Taqizadeh thought it possible for Iran and Iranians to become completely, "from top to toe," as he once put it, European, just go through a metamorphosis and become something else. Taqizadeh was a serious scholar, teaching at Cambridge and

---

10 The best source of information about Taqizadeh's life is his biography, prepared based on Taqizadeh's own accounts, in Iraj Afshar, *Zendegani Toufani* ("Tumultuous Life") (Tehran: 1993).

Columbia universities for a short time, who produced some quite significant scholarly work about the Iranian calendar and Manichaeism. He was also a prominent literary figure in Iran, thoroughly familiar with Persian prose and poetry, and a close friend and ally of other leading Iranian literary scholars. Though later in his life he deeply regretted his unconditional enthusiasm for "Western Civilization," he was nevertheless among the modern advocates of replacing the Persian alphabet with its Roman counterpart. He went from this position to the opposite extreme of chauvinistic nationalism, arguing for the Iranian national interest at the expense of ethnicized subnational movements of regional revolt. These oscillations between radical extremes, and between enthusiastic endorsement of one cause and another, were a paradigmatic example of the ferment of the transnational public sphere of which he was now his homeland's best representative.

Generations after Taqizadeh, and halfway around the globe, Boaventura de Sousa Santos offered to think through "epistemologies of the South." This required a rectification of the slanted relation of power the self-centering project of ("Western") capitalist modernity had occasioned, by way of "creating new possibilities of progressive social transformation aimed at putting an end to the monumental Eurocentric theoretical justification of the unequal relations between the global North and the global South."[11] How was that exactly to be achieved? And what was it up against?

> The public sphere is the tribalism of the European bourgeoisie at the beginning of the eighteenth century. Both capitalism and colonialism converted such a localism into a global aspiration and a universal theoretical concept, at the same time that an abyssal divide between metropolitan and colonial societies

---

11 Santos, "Public Sphere."

made public sphere unthinkable in colonial societies and transformed such denial of universality into the vindication of the universal idea.[12]

The "public sphere" is not "the tribalism of the European bourgeoisie," by virtue of the fact that that tribalism was the modus operandi of a globalized capitalist modernity that had invented and designated "Europe" as its epicenter, and upon which the disenfranchised and the beneficiaries were no longer neatly divided between the North and the South. That "Europe," as Fanon suggested, is also "the invention of the Third World." The task at hand is to dismantle the false consciousness entailing the myth that North and South can be neatly divided, not to corroborate it by offering "epistemologies of the South" that are presumed to be quintessentially different from "the epistemologies of the North." Santos has set for himself the crucial task of "unthinking such historical construction [that] only becomes a credible theoretical task to the extent that theoretical work positions itself as the facilitating or supporting rearguard of the social movements and struggles that fight against capitalism and the many metamorphoses of colonialism."[13] This is of course a worthy and serious task, but manufacturing counter-myths of "Southern epistemologies" may turn out to be equally flawed, misleading, and in fact counter-productive. Capitalist modernity has unified the world in both misery and defiance—from the ruins and relics of that particular historical reality, as Walter Benjamin knew, we must begin to think of epistemologies of an entirely different liberatory geography than simply that of the Southern hemisphere of the same geography of domination and conquest within which "the West" has ruled from the North.

---

12 Ibid.
13 Ibid.

Ending States

In the heat of George W. Bush's neocon imperialism, commenced soon after 9/11, one of his chief lieutenants, Paul Wolfowitz, at the time US deputy secretary of defense, once said in clear and forceful language that the United States was now bent on "ending states who sponsor terrorism."[14] By now the term "terrorism" was squarely codified as the catchword for the US intention to dominate a "monopolar world," and the declaration was of course immediately meant to inaugurate the US-led war against Afghanistan, and soon Iraq—two catastrophic invasions from which the world continues to suffer. But the statement had a far more cataclysmic ring to it, which still continues to resonate. What did it mean exactly to "end states?"

The nation-state is a postcolonial proposition predicated on the accumulated, shared memories of the nation gathered within a *public sphere* called a "homeland," freed from monarchical and clerical elites. It is precisely this idea of "the nation" as shared memories of a homeland that Israel and ISIS identically negate. To oppose and resist that continued colonial project, we need to go back to the transnational, and thus postnational, origin of the nation as public sphere and rearticulate its origin and logic. We perform a negative dialectic on the design of "ending states" by going behind and before it, and re-positing the public sphere as precarious, vicarious, and a proxy space, and thus dodging the vacated state (from Iraq to Syria) to oppose it. We in effect reverse-engineer the "soft power" designed to "end states" in order to oppose it. From both the royal court and the defiant mosque that predate European colonial incursions, public spheres, public intellectuals, and public reason eventually emerged on the site of people's shared memories, replacing the courtiers and the

---

14 See David Plotz, "Paul Wolfowitz: Bush's Testosterone Man at Defense," *Slate*, October 12, 2001, slate.com.

clerics. This public sphere, *ipso facto*, was cosmopolitan and worldly, as the nation or *mellat* that it designed was articulated by and large by expatriates looking at its fictive frontiers from the outside. Postcolonial nation-states like Iran, Afghanistan, Iraq, and Egypt had imperial pedigrees, evident in the form and formation of their public spheres, as the locus classicus of their nationhood. Worldly national self-consciousness thus informed and animated their postcolonial self-consciousness.

To think critically beyond the frontier fiction of the nation-state is not to abandon the nation-state as the unit of critical thinking. On the contrary, precisely because of their condition of coloniality, including their colonially conditioned frontiers, postcolonial nations have generated, sustained, and enriched shared memories that are definitive of their sense of revolutionary justice. But it is the free, democratic, and federative disposition of their de-centered power-sharing that can further those shared memories, preventing a bourgeois ethnic nationalism from claiming and controlling them. Those shared memories are multifaceted and cosmopolitan from the ground up, and by virtue of common experiences, and are the exact opposite of an ethnicized bourgeois nationalism—whether Persian, Turkish, Arab, or other—that is built against the very grain of the cosmopolitanism represented by successive labor migrations. A loosening of the fictive frontiers of nations in order to retrieve their transnational origin is meant to discover the hidden cosmopolitan worldliness concealed by colonialism beneath the self-centering imperial myth of "the West."

What I propose here is a radical reconceptualization not of the nation-state, or even of state sovereignty, but rather of the transnational genealogy of the nation beyond its aggressive ethnic nationalization and its emergence as a fragment of three Muslim empires—the Mughals, the Safavids, and the Ottomans—in the course of their respective clashes with the

European imperial incursion into the Muslim world. The historical moment I am trying to capture here occurred some time before what we have now coded as "globalization" and the purported collapse of the nation-state and national sovereignty. This moment did not fall after Fukuyama's "end of history,"[15] or Niall Ferguson's "Westernization of the world."[16] It occurred decidedly before any such delusions of ideology. Indeed, we may now have entered the moment that Giacomo Marramao considers "Post Nation-State."[17]

But, for that eventuality even to be recognized as such, we need to de-fetishize the frontier fiction of the postcolonial nations at the point of their origin, and observe how, from the fragments and upon the ruins of Muslim empires, modern polities and their corresponding political cultures have emerged.[18] The moment at which postcolonial national identities were mythologized needs to be reverse-engineered, as it were, so that we can retrieve the *transnational public sphere* that had constitutionally informed the formation of national polities and cultures, and above all conditioned national economies. The nature and function of labor migrations, of expansive markets, and of rootless capital are far truer to this idea of transnational public spheres within which postcolonial nation-states were formed.

The ultimate goal of such a work of genealogy is to retrieve the hidden and repressed worlds that the fiction of "the West" and the artificial binary of "the West and the rest" have hitherto

---

15   See Francis Fukuyama, *The End of History and the Last Man* (New York: Free Press, 1992 [1989]).

16   See Niall Ferguson, *Civilization: The West and the Rest* (London: Penguin, 2011).

17   See Giacomo Marramao, *The Passage West: Philosophy After the Age of the Nation State* (London: Verso, 2012).

18   As admirably suggested by Pankaj Mishra in *From the Ruins of Empire: The Revolt Against the West and the Remaking of Asia* (London: Penguin, 2013).

successfully concealed. The point here is not just to mark the pluralism and hybridity on both sides of the binary myths of orient and occident,[19] which seems still to retain some significance for poststructuralist European thinkers. Of course there are "several Orients and several Occidents" characterized by both "synchronic plurality [and] diachronic mutation."[20] The point is the enduring and plural historical genealogies of such pluralities and mutations. Such genealogies, which are still in need of serious and systematic retrieval and reconstruction, overcome the intermediary state of postcoloniality, and link the ruins of Muslim empires to this newer, amorphous empire with which caring philosophers like Marramao wish to associate "a universal politics of difference." For that "difference" not to degenerate into yet another mutation of "the West and the rest," we first need to know what exactly constitutes the differential axis of the emerging universalism. My contention, here as in previous work, is that, without deliberately and consciously retrieving the repressed worldliness of the violently othered (and thus denied and neutered) worlds, it is impossible to recognize and cultivate the differential organicity of any claim to universalism we may wish to articulate and achieve. In loosening the fictive frontiers of the postcolonial nation-state, and relocating it back to its transnational public sphere, I have found one particularly potent strategy.

The interwar German social and intellectual history that gave birth to texts such as Carl Schmitt's *The Concept of the Political* (1932) is critically important in our understanding of the colonial condition of what we now call "the global South." Schmitt's purposeful hostility to liberalism was definitive of his conception of the political not in terms of state authority and power but in terms of a politically self-conscious and socially significant exercise of hostility towards an enemy. It

---

19 Marramao, *Passage West*, pp. 230–1.
20 Ibid., p. 231.

is instructive to compare this notion of the political held by Schmitt in 1932 with Max Weber's in 1919, in his "Politics as a Vocation" (1919), where he defines politics in terms of its means (not its ends), referring to the physical force (the violence) with which politics defines itself. Schmitt takes the Weberian "ends" and transforms it into an object of hostility (the enemy), as the defining locus of *the political*.

In the case of *the colonial*, to posit it in juxtaposition to the *political*, the notion of "the enemy" is, for Schmitt, transfigured into an externalized collective, and a significant other. The colonial relation to this significant other is much more complicated than that of the political towards the enemy. Unlike the enemy for the political, the other ("the West") for the colonial is an object of collective *ressentiment* (as theorized from Friedrich Nietzsche to Max Scheler), of the transvaluation of values, of desire becoming denunciation. *Ressentiment*, and not animosity, thus becomes the defining moment of the colonial—of not just the transvaluation of values but of the generation of values. The transnational public sphere that European imperialism paradoxically generates and facilitates becomes the site of the production of knowledge and sentiment within this historical framing. Schmitt thought that the identity, character, and culture of the state is formed through the operation of the political in terms of hostility and animosity towards the enemy. But, in the colonial context, the enemy upon which Schmitt was fixated is far more amorphous and scattered within the active counter-formation of "the West" as an *absolute metaphor* that, through a negative dialectic of alienation and identification, generates a systematic constellation of political virtues and vices whose emotive matrix has defined the spectrum of postcolonial politics.

Public Spheres: Classed and Gendered

The effervescent rise of new periodicals widely circulated outside Iran did not, of course, leave Iran unaffected, but soon generated a similar phenomenon in major Iranian cities. The formation of the public sphere as the simulacrum of the nation by the emerging generation of public intellectuals, from both inside and outside their homeland, was instrumental in the making of the politics and purpose of organic solidarities in multiple forms. Revolutionary leaders (later parliamentarians) and artists; nascent labor unions and reformist religious leaders; women's rights organizations and student assemblies—these were the primary audience of such periodicals, and became the formative forces of the nascent public space. They read, discussed, and debated the merits of what they were reading in these periodicals. This new public sphere soon came to be gendered, and numerous women's rights organizations emerged advancing the cause of liberty for the nation at large and for women in particular. Such organizations as Anjoman-e Azadi Zanan (Society for Women's Liberation), Anjoman Gheybi-ye Nesvan (Secret Society of Women), Anjoman Nesvan-e Vatan (Society of the Nation's Women), and Etehadiyeh Nesvan (Union of Women) claimed sizable memberships throughout the emerging nation-state.[21]

A number of leading women's rights activists emerged at this critical juncture. Sediqeh Dowlatabadi (1882–1961) was a leading women's rights advocate and journalist with a wide-ranging body of work on institution-building. Born to a progressive clerical family in Isfahan, she received her early education in her hometown, and later in Tehran, soon becoming a founding member of Anjoman-e Mokhadrat Vatan (Society of Patriotic Women), and publishing the

---

21 For a detailed discussion of these women's rights organizations, see Chapter 7 (pp. 177f) of Janet Afary, *The Iranian Constitutional Revolution, 1906–1911* (New York: Columbia University Press, 1996).

pioneering journal *Zaban-e Zanan* ("Women's Discourse").[22] From this same milieu emerged the most prominent woman poet of the Constitutional period, Parvin E'tesami (1907–41). She, too, was born to a prominent, learned family, and her exquisite poetry soon became a staple of progressive circles in her homeland, with the particular attention it paid to the fate of the poor and women's rights.[23] From leading revolutionary activists and poets emerged a body of writing linking the sites of progressive politics inside and outside the fictive frontiers of Iran. The emerging public sphere was rooted in the gendered politics of a nation recasting itself on the track of colonial modernity, with widening horizons of an emancipatory liberation geography written into the very fabric of the nation it thus enabled.

22   For a pioneering study of the women's rights movement in Iran, see Eliz Sanasarian, *The Women's Movement in Iran: Mutiny, Appeasement, and Repression from 1900 to Khomeini* (New York: Praeger, 1982).

23   For more on Parvin E'tesami's life and poetry, see Heshmat Moayyad, ed., *Once a Dewdrop: Essays on the Poetry of Parvin E'tesami* (Costa Mesa, CA: Mazda, 1994).

CHAPTER 4

The Sphere of the Earth

I wish I could
For a moment I wish I could
Have sat upon my shoulder
This countless mass
And taken them around
The sphere of the earth
So they could see with their own eyes
Where their sun rises—
And they would believe me.
I wish I could

Ahmad Shamlou (1967)

The paradox of the *colonial* I proposed in Chapter 3 came to full fruition in the course of the revolutionary atmosphere of the late nineteenth and early twentieth centuries. In this chapter I intend to shift focus towards the 1950s and map out the formation of a liberation geography that still informs the geopolitics of the region. An immediate manifestation of these political border-crossings is in the realm of poetry, with the coming together of several leading poets from four corners of the world to imagine an alternative universe to the one determined by domestic tyranny and amorphous imperialism. But first let us establish some historical context.

What is affectionately referred to as the Tobacco Revolt (Jonbesh-e Tanbaku) (1890–91)—a widespread uprising against a tobacco concession granted by the Qajar monarch to Great Britain—in many ways marks the rise of an enduring revolutionary consciousness late in the Qajar period. It was arguably something of a dress rehearsal for the world-historic Constitutional Revolution of 1906–11. But between the Tobacco Revolt and the Constitutional Revolution something equally significant took place: the first ever expression of colonial interest in Iran's oil reserves. In 1901 a British millionaire entrepreneur named William Knox D'Arcy (1849–1917) managed to strike a deal with Mozaffar al-Din Shah, the Qajar monarch, giving him an exclusive right to excavate for oil in a vast territory in His Majesty's realm. In exchange, the shah received a generous sum to finance his insatiable lust for traveling to Europe. British and Russian, and thus by extension European, interests in Iran, which dated back at least to the early nineteenth century—and had almost entirely concerned strategic considerations relating to the Indian subcontinent—now also found a major economic impetus. The combined forces of strategic, geopolitical, and economic factors now converged to define the emerging globalized economy of oil, in which Iran was to play a central role in world politics.

As fate would have it, D'Arcy did not in fact succeed in his deal, finding no oil to extract, and so sold his rights to a Scottish entity called Burmah Oil Company. In 1908, just as they were about to abandon hope, Burmah struck oil. By the following year, Burmah Oil had created the Anglo-Persian Oil Company (APOC)—later to be renamed British Petroleum (BP)—and soon Iranian crude became a hot commodity on the global market. By 1913 Abadan refinery had been built, and Iranian oil began to circulate around the globe. What soon followed the development of this new source of energy was a critical adjustment in the direction of British imperialism. Just before the commencement of World War II, when Winston Churchill, as the first lord of the admiralty, was determined to modernize the British navy, and thus the British crown became a major stakeholder in the operation of APOC in Iran. It was through the force and urgency of two successive world wars that Iranian oil became the boiling blood running through the veins of British imperialism.[1]

Oil was the pressure point that pushed Iran into the global limelight during the tumultuous onset of the twentieth century. Increasing colonial interest in Iranian crude mirrored, and ultimately exceeded, the strategic significance held by the Persian Gulf for the British navy, in its movements in and out of its vast imperial domains, which spread from the Indian subcontinent deep into the heart of the Arab world. It might be thought that the anticolonial revolt that resulted in Indian independence in 1947 put an end to the British interest in that domain; in 1953, however, the British joined forces with the United States to stage a coup in Iran, ensuring the protection of that interest for yet another historic epoch. The flow of oil overrode the fictive frontiers of Iran, running deeply into the wider global markets of colonial interests and anticolonial ideas. People in four corners of the world who might never have heard of a Tobacco Revolt or a Constitutional Revolution were never further from the dark blood of the Iranian soil than their nearest gas station. Oil gave the transnational public sphere a decidedly Persian pigmentation.

The Transnational Public Sphere and the Rebirth of a Nation

The preparatory stages of the revolutionary turn of the century were laid down within the transnational public sphere encompassing India, the Arab World, and Europe, cultivated by Iranian public intellectuals within and beyond their homeland. The printing press that Mirza Saleh Shirazi had brought back from England; the simplified prose of journalists from

---

1 Stephen Kinzer revisits this history in his *All the Shah's Men: An American Coup and the Roots of Middle East Terror* (Hoboken, NJ: Wiley, 2003), Chapter 4.

Calcutta to Cairo, Istanbul, and London; the revolutionary agitation of Seyyed Jamal al-Din al-Afghani and his comrades throughout the Arab and Muslim world; the emergence of a lively tradition of Persian fiction and drama, accompanied by an energetic movement of translation from European sources; familiarity with the French Revolution of 1789, the European revolutions of 1848, the Japanese victory over Russia after the Russo-Japanese War (1904–05), and the Russian Revolution of 1905—all were instrumental in cultivating and enriching this public sphere. Napoleon was defeated by the British at Waterloo on June 18, 1815, when Mirza Saleh Shirazi and his fellow students were en route from Iran to England. This was among the earliest recorded instances of an awareness of global events entering the political consciousness of Iranian public intellectuals—now far removed from their own imperial history, conditioned by Safavid rivalry with the Ottomans and the Mughals. The public sphere on which all these world-historic events were being recorded was decidedly transnational—its written language a simplified Persian prose, its audience increasingly conscious of its civil liberties and inalienable rights.

The Constitutional Revolution was the final and most dramatic fruition of two successive phases of revolutionary posturing—the Babi Movement of 1844–52 and the Tobacco Revolt of 1890–91. The Babi Movement had its origin inside Iran, but soon expanded into Ottoman territories. The ideas of the Iraqi, Shaykh Ahmad Ahsa'i, were at its ideological epicenter. Though it was a homegrown Shi'i revolution, the Babi Movement spread widely into other territories, reaching as far as Cyprus and Palestine.[2] The Tobacco Revolt, meanwhile, was deeply rooted in the colonial concessions that the Qajar monarchs had continued to bestow upon European interests, as the emerging Iranian merchant class and bourgeoisie finally

---

2 See Amanat, *Resurrection and Renewal*.

asserted themselves against a monarchic court with no structural link to their commercial interests. The Constitutional Revolution brought all of these elements onto the much-expanded transnational public sphere, giving birth to whole new notions of nationhood, citizenry, and national interest against colonial domination.[3]

The Constitutional Revolution succeeded in dismantling an absolutist monarchy, drafting a constitution that established a range of protected civil liberties and a classic division of power between the executive, the legislature, and the judiciary. But, just as the constitution had been drafted, World War I erupted, dividing Iran into two spheres of influence—Russian in the north and British in the south. The chaos and confusion that ensued were ultimately resolved in a military coup by Reza Khan, endorsed by the British.[4] Reza Shah founded the Pahlavi dynasty, which ruled ruthlessly from 1925 to the commencement of the Allied occupation of Iran in 1941, when he was forced to abdicate in favor of his son. Mohammed Reza Shah reigned with an unsteady hold over his tumultuous homeland, until, in 1953, he was forced to flee. But he was soon returned to power by a military coup organized and overseen by the CIA and MI6.[5]

Border-Crossings: From Politics to Poetics

Although the link between the interconnected histories, politics, and cultures of the Iranian plateau and the Indian

---

3 One of the best accounts of the Constitutional Revolution is given in Janet Afary, *The Iranian Constitutional Revolution, 1906–1911* (New York: Columbia University Press, 1996).

4 For an account of Reza Shah's reign, see Cyrus Ghani, *Iran and the Rise of Reza Shah: From Qajar Collapse to Pahlavi Power* (London: I. B. Tauris, 1998).

5 The most recent account of the CIA-sponsored coup is Ervand Abrahamian, *The Coup: 1953, the CIA, and the Roots of Modern U.S.-Iranian Relations* (New York: New Press, 2013).

subcontinent stretches back before the written record, the inauguration of the colonial interests of the East India Company in India (1612–1757) coincided with the presence of the British and the Portuguese in the Persian Gulf during the Safavid period. The same colonial interests had brought them all to the Indian Ocean, the Arabian Sea, and the Persian Gulf. The Company's rule in India (1757–1858) was likewise coterminous with the height of Qajar power, and with increasing Russian, British, and French colonial interests in the same region. Napoleon's determination to upset British rule over India early in the nineteenth century had occasioned his interest in the Qajar court, which in turn resulted in the British offering even greater incentives for the Qajar to remain in its camp, including an agreement to dispatch a first group of Iranian students to England. During the British Raj (1858–1947), contacts between Iran and India sharply increased. The final victory of the Indian anticolonial movement in the mid-to-late 1940s dovetailed with the rise of anticolonial nationalism in the early 1950s in Iran. The almost identical aspirations of Jawaharlal Nehru, Mohammad Mosaddegh, and Gamal Abdel Nasser came together in the making of a liberation geography that deeply informed the geopolitics of the region. The anticolonial nationalism that motivated Mohammad Mosaddegh's nationalization of the Iranian oil industry was very much informed by this transnational environment, extending from the Indian subcontinent to North Africa. The CIA-sponsored coup of 1953 put a damper on this mood, but failed to curtail it.

To underline this, and even indicate a wider liberation geography, we might also note the presence of a number of seminal poets who were celebrated together in a transnational pantheon, including Faiz Ahmad Faiz (1911–84) from Pakistan; Vladimir Mayakovsky (1893–1930) from Russia; Aimé Césaire (1913–2008), echoing the voices of anticolonial resilience from the Caribbean to Africa; Federico García Lorca (1898–1936) and Pablo Neruda (1904–73), representing the larger Hispanic and Latin American world; Nâzim Hikmet (1902–63) from Turkey; Mahmoud Darwish (1941–2008) from Palestine, also representing the larger Arab world; Langston Hughes (1902–67) from the United States; and Ahmad Shamlou (1925–2000) from Iran. The poetic representatives of a widespread solidarity in the global South, these poets were simultaneously known and celebrated, after 1953, by a post-coup generation that had a greatly expanded conception of its political consciousness. These poets were translated into Persian, read and memorized by an expanded readership among young Iranian students, teachers, literati, and public intellectuals, just as if they were all born-and-bred Persian poets. A transnational revolutionary public sphere was implicated in the poetry of these towering figures that located Iran and Iranians squarely within a much more global conception of themselves. When, in one poem, the Palestinian national poet Mahmoud Darwish says, "Write down I am an Arab," in defiance of Israeli occupation of his homeland and denial of his identity, that line very easily could have been read as, "Write down I am an Iranian" (or Turk, or Kurd, or Indian), retaining its original resonance intact.

As is perhaps best exemplified by Lorca (but widely echoed by all the other poets mentioned above), a defiant combination of lyricism and politics informed the poetics of this global pantheon of iconoclastic poets. In his own Persian poetry, Ahmad Shamlou, the most widely celebrated poet of his time, evocatively represented that universal pantheon, achieving a poetic diction with a cosmic certainty. "Dar enteha-ye zaminam kumeh-'i has" ("At the End of the World I Have a Little Cottage"), he says in one of his signature poems,

Where the steadfastness of the earth—
Just like a mirage dancing—
Relies on the delusion of thirst—
Where Man and God are joined,
Yes where the earth and nullity meet
Do I reside in an unstable little cottage.[6]

That Olympian certainty, rooted in a combustible combination of truth and terror, became definitive for a politically engaged generation beyond the banal borders of party politics or ideological fanaticism. Shamlou, the Iranian national poet laureate, was entirely beholden to Lorca, whose work he translated into Persian, and whose strong influence can be detected upon his own. Through Shamlou, Lorca was brought home to Iranians, who were thereby transported into a Spanish and Latin American emotive universe that categorically changed what it meant to be an Iranian (and Iranian poet). Lorca's erotic politics and lyrical materialism were so thoroughly at home in Iran that, at times, the border between Shamlou's and Lorca's work entirely disappeared. The combined influence of Lorca and Neruda on Shamlou meant the effusive presence of a Spanish/Latin American poetic twist on the world deeply interwoven into the emotive taxonomy of the nation. The presence of a Lorca/Neruda register in the Persian poetic universe was radically transformative of an entire poetic lexicon far beyond Iran's immediate borders, and deep into the moral and normative imagination of anything integral to its climate and character. By this time, the world of Persian literary humanism had given right of passage to a worldly domain in which the Persian poetic lexicon was squarely at home. The classical figure of the Persian poet had by now thoroughly exited the

---

6 Ahmad Shamlou, "Oqubat" ("Penance"), in *Shekoftan dar Meh* ("Blooming in Fog") (Tehran: 1970). My translation.

royal court, and entered a public domain that she and he had helped to craft.

What made the reception of Lorca and Neruda possible was a pantheon of other poets much closer to Iran. Vladimir Mayakovsky had a towering presence in Iran because of his significance in the course of the Russian Revolution of 1917. This was matched by the prominence of the Turkish poet Nâzim Hikmet, whose poetry resonated with the socialist aspirations of his admirers. Two other poets from neighboring regions soon joined in: Mahmoud Darwish made the Palestinian cause palpable in the Persian poetic repertoire, while Faiz Ahmad Faiz echoed the trauma of post-partition anxieties in the India subcontinent. Meanwhile, leading African-American poet Langston Hughes (1902–67) entered the Persian poetic pantheon via references in Ahmad Shamlou's poetry, delivering a clear awareness of the pains and promises of African-Americans into Persian poetic consciousness. These poets and many others redefined the very meaning of time and timeliness in a renewed conception of a widely liberating geography. When Shamlou translated Hughes's "Florida Road Workers" into Persian, he opted for a colloquial and conversational tone, bringing the poem much closer to the working-class sentiments of the original, thereby reaching out to a working-class readership in Iran.

The synergy that was created among poets within and outside their homeland, composing poetry in Persian or another language, lent legitimacy to and fostered critical thinking in the transnational public sphere within which they were all gathered. At the height of the Constitutional Revolution, the rise of a whole constellation of Persian poets gave a lyrical momentum to their political causes that extended beyond all borders. Aref Qazvini (1882–1934), a hugely popular poet, lyricist, musician, singer, and songwriter, grew to prominence in Iran, but was given wider currency by being published by his admirers in Europe, and honored by his readers among the Parsees in India. Mirzadeh Eshghi (1893–1924), a leading political writer and poet, learned French in a French school in Iran, achieving the height of his popularity after moving to Istanbul. Mohammad-Taqi Bahar (1884–1951), a gifted poet, scholar, journalist, and literary historian, mastered both Arabic and French, and his scholarship was deeply influenced by his familiarity with French literature. Prince Iraj Mirza (1874–1926), a satirist of unparalleled poetic gifts placed squarely at the service of social causes, received an elite early education in Persian, French, Arabic, Turkish, and some Russian, too, before traveling to Europe, and then returning to advance the cause of liberty in his homeland. Mirza Mohammad Farrokhi Yazdi (1889–1939), a leading Marxist and popular poet, had a particular following in Afghanistan. When his political activism in Iran made life impossible for him, he moved to Germany via the Soviet Union. Abolqasem Lahouti (1887–1957), a gifted poet and political activist, was as important in Iran as he was in Tajikistan in the early Soviet era. Like many of his contemporaries, he had started his education at a clerical school in Iran, but spent close to four decades of his life outside Iran. A committed communist, for a time he published a bilingual periodical called *Pars* (in both Persian and French) in Istanbul. He spent most of his life in the former Soviet Union, deeply involved in the Tajik literary scene.[7] For all these poets, "freedom" was the talisman of all other ideals and aspirations of a people. In the words of Farrokhi Yazdi,

> I swear by the dignity, sublimity, and gravity of Freedom
> That the very name of Freedom lends this world its soul—
> People around the world respect only those
> Who wholeheartedly honor Freedom …

---

7 For more on these poets, see Mohammad Ali Sepanlu, *Chahar Sha'er-e Azadi* ("Four Poets of Liberty") (Tehran: Negah, 1369/1990).

Without having access to surrounding countries, from India to the Ottoman territories and Europe, none of these poets could have been nearly as effective in their homeland as they were, in effect constituting and coining the term *vatan* ("homeland"). Among these poets, a critical synergy was created so that, even if one of them—say, Aref—had not personally traveled abroad, his poetic prowess was infused by the experience of those who had, with whom he both affiliated and competed. Aref, in turn, remained popular in his homeland for generations to come, his name and his poetry in effect inseparable from the Constitutional Revolution. Whenever there was a critical event happening in his homeland, he was there with his poetry to preserve it for posterity. When the nationalist leader Colonel Mohammad Taqi-Khan Pesyan (1892–1921) was killed, he was there to honor his patriotism, as he had been throughout the crucial turning points of the Constitutional Revolution and its tumultuous aftermath. To this day, his songs and lyrics have remained popular:

> *Az khun-e Javanan-e vatan laleh damideh,*
> *Nemidanam cheh dar peymaneh kardi,*
> *Bolbol-e shurideh faqan mikonad,*
> *Cheh azar-ha beh jan az eshq Azerbaijan daram …*

> Tulips have grown from the blood of the patriotic youth,
> Have no idea what you put in my wine cup,
> The ecstatic sparrow is crying,
> What fires have afflicted my soul for my love of Azerbaijan …

Because of the lyrical ecstasy, political audacity, musical simplicity, and moral generosity of his songs, his popular ballads were sung not just by leading pop singers from his own time up to our own, but in fact by ordinary people, since they did not require a very sophisticated command of Persian poetry or music.

How are we to understand that time and timeliness, that spirit of the age, when these poets were complementing one another, competing for our attention from the four corners of our liberated geographical imagination? If we were to consider one other towering contemporary poet, Forough Farrokhzad (1935–67), and her articulation of the nature of poetry, we would come closer to that spirit. Paramount in Farrokhzad's conception of poetry were *time* and *timeliness*—present, contemporary time, the time of the poet; and the time she had made into the time of her audience, or the time of her world. "In my opinion," she once said, "this is no longer the time to talk about old and new in poetry"[8]—by which she meant that the battle between the old and the new had dissolved into the crucible of the urgency of the present. The real meaning of poetry, she insisted, could not be further from such discussions. True poetry was rooted in people's pains, and it was capable of "making its birth accepted and thereafter continuing with its magical maturity."[9] She insisted: "[R]ight now the time has come to examine and be particular about the poetry that today we call 'New Poetry.'" What was the time that had arrived? Not a time to be measured by any watch. A time that was in the air, that was the time of the world we inhabited—and she had her finger on the pulse of that time. Her criticism was that this poetry was not yet sincere enough, not sufficiently in touch with its own time, and thus she purposefully declared: "The poetry of today lacks the insight and understanding of its own specific time."[10] She was

---

8   Forough Farrokhzad, *Chand Neveshteh v Goft-o-Shonud Parakandeh dar She'r va Sha'eri* ("A Few Scattered Writings and Conversations on Poets and Poetry") (Arash: Esfand, 1345/1966), p. 11.

9   Ibid., p. 12.

10   Ibid.

referring here to the vacuous poetry of the neo-classicists, who were simply regurgitating received and clichéd metaphors of love and passion without any worldly specificity. Against this stagnation, she spoke specifically of her own erotic encounters and existential angst. She began one of her signature poems, "Sin," with a stanza oozing with sensuality and passion:

> I sinned
> A sin full of pleasure!
> Next to a body
> Shivering and unconscious—
> God Almighty what do I know what I did
> In that dark, silent, and secluded room!

She challenged contemporary poets to make a hard choice: "[T]he poetry of today is scared of naming the objects and locations with which it deals all day and night, and to express itself it still resorts to words that have hundreds of years of poetic tradition about them."[11] She was determined, and she succeeded in bringing her poetry more into tune with the pulse of her world. More specifically, she declared:

> The poetry of today looks at the world through the narrow and pathetic window upon which the spiders of selfish laziness, and most of the time illiteracy and short-sightedness, prevail, and it wastes its time soliciting the acceptance of different people, as if it does not believe in its own existence, as if it can only stand on its feet through the acceptance and acknowledgment of others, and thus lacks its own sparkle.[12]

---

11   Ibid.
12   Ibid.

The gauntlet was thus thrown to bring the poets closer to the spirit of their own age, the time of their history, the poetic awareness of the world. The entire spectrum of Forough Farrokhzad's poetry was a testimony to that timely worldliness.

Iran and Its Environs

In the vast spectrum of Iranian history ever since the collapse of the Safavid Empire in the eighteenth century, and the eventual replacement of Iran as a postcolonial nation-state during and in the aftermath of the Qajar dynasty there is one abiding fact: there is a dialectic of reciprocity between Iran and its environs, as between any postcolonial nation-state and the geopolitics of its regional and global self-transcendence. That fact is decided by the successive collapse of Muslim empires, the onslaught of European empires, and the eventful formation of fictive frontiers that now claimed a national history for themselves. The Muslim empires that preceded the rise of nation-states, and the European imperial forces that descended from nowhere to colonize them, were by nature transnational, and thus so was the public sphere their clash gave rise to, and upon which these nations were imaginatively formed. Under the normative and imaginative domination of "the West"—the most potent ideological talisman of capitalist modernity—Iran has been forced, like all other postcolonial nation-states, to define and posit itself against and in response to a compelling figment of dialogical imagination. Jalal Al-e-Ahmad's iconic text, *Gharbzadegi* ("Westoxification") (1962), was a potent critique of that self-fashioning by "the West," while the text itself paradoxically became a central referent in corroborating the very "West" at which Al-e-Ahmad had aimed his critique.

Perhaps the most significant public intellectual of his time, Al-e-Ahmad (1923–69) emerged from a clerical family. He soon rejected family pressure to become a seminarian, and joined the Iranian Socialist Tudeh Party. Both before and after leaving the Tudeh Party because of its too cozy relationship with the Soviet Union, Al-e-Ahmad wrote a number of seminal literary and political essays that became definitive of the political culture of his time. Among all his work, Al-e-Ahmad's "Westoxification" remains the most influential text, having something of the resonance of Edward Said's *Orientalism* (1978) in the West. Partly under his enduring influence, the trope of "Iran versus the West" became a compelling register of "Islam versus the West." This powerful colonial construct became the ontic, epistemic, and existential paradigm—the syntax and morphology, the absolute metaphor of reality and how to understand it, producing and describing the diagnoses and prognoses of Iran as a polity, a culture, a commodified product, in the geopolitics of its region and beyond. The talismanic force of this binary of "Iran versus the West" limited the moral imagination of the nation by going directly against the grain of the cosmopolitan worldliness that had in fact formed the transnational public sphere of which this binary notion was a product.

Whether by its monarchic or clerical custodians, Iran was read and written back into its imperial history from one direction, and placed next to the absolute metaphors of "the West" from another, and thus trapped inside a matrix from which it is yet to be liberated. To be sure, that entrapment has entailed its blindness and insights. It has produced useful knowledge while, at the same time, blocking liberating possibilities. It is safe to say that, over the last two hundred years or more, since the fateful encounter of the Qajars with the European and Russian empires, and their colonial acquisitions and ambitions, Iran has been trapped inside this matrix of "Iran versus the West," both enabling and disabling—its liberating possibilities confined entirely within this scripted metaphor. The Islamic liberation theology that was integral to (but not definitive of) the Iranian Revolution of 1979 was itself the most potent colonial product of contemporary history—entirely the doppelganger of "the West." But so, too, were other liberatory ideologies of anticolonial nationalism and Third World socialism the byproduct of this same ideological matrix. All of these modes of ideology production remained in contestation and defiant dialogue with "the West." A figment of their own arrested imaginations, "the West" defined the terms of their political liberation and normative idiomaticity. The binary opposition and epistemic matrix manufactured and sustained by "Islam versus the West" and "Iran versus the West" were long ago categorically exhausted. The monarchical and clerical orders that took turns ruling over Iranians are indigenous to this political culture, but were enabled by and codified against the colonial conditions and hegemonic entrapments that had activated their interests. Underlying both of these orders were the defiant potentialities of the public and parapublic spheres, which both the Pahlavis and the Islamic Republic have tyrannically sought (but failed) to dominate and delimit. Active recognition of the transnational public sphere that has historically defied them both is now instrumental in a far more potent defiance of both domestic tyranny and imperial domination.

The clearest expression of this transnational public sphere is the fact that the formation of Iranian national identity has always been historically dialogical—a contrapuntal entity produced in interaction with the consistently expanding horizons of what it means to be a worldly, conscious Iranian. The cosmopolitan worldliness that defines this dialogical self is entirely a result of historical development, and not subject to any ideological claim or counter-claim. The only properly political project deeply rooted in the transnational fact of the postcolonial national frontiers is of course socialism, since it is materially rooted in the lived experiences of the nation, and thus transcends both militant Islamism and bourgeois nationalism as the key ideological products of the colonial encounter. By injecting *class* into the formation of national identity, this rooted socialism effectively dismantles it. Equally critical in this dismantling have been successive waves of increasingly class-conscious feminism, which do the same by adding gender to the range of inequities within patriarchal culture. The combined effects of transnational socialism and class-conscious feminism then confront the formation of racialized minorities (Kurds, Arabs, Turks, and so on), and thus the animating energies of race, gender, and class demystify the violent formation of the frontier fiction of both bourgeois nationalism and militant Islamism.

The central paradox of colonial modernity for much of the colonial world (which in turn extends into and exacerbates its postcolonial political disposition) is the fact that, while postcolonial nation-states are ruled by colonially mitigated ideologies of militant Islamism and/or bourgeois nationalism (both absolutist), their societies are culturally cosmopolitan by virtue of their emotive and normative location within the transnational public sphere. What exactly does the term "cosmopolitanism" mean as I am using it here? I have used two complementary concepts to identify this type of cosmopolitanism—in Persian, *jahanshahri* ("cosmopolitanism") and *Iranshahri* ("Persopolitanism").[13] The emplotment of

---

13 I originally developed these two related concepts in Persian at the height of the Green Movement in Iran in 2009. See my "Jonbesh-e Sabz Bazgasht-e Farhang-e Jahanshahri-ye Mast" ("The Green Movement Is the Return of Our Cosmopolitan Culture"), *Jaras*, Ordibehesht 8, 1389 (April 28, 2010); and "Tamamiyat Arzi-ye Iran dar Geruv-e Farhang-e Iranshahri-ye Mast" ("Iranian Territorial Integrity is Contingent on our Iranshahri Culture"), *Jaras*, Tir 13, 1389 (July 4, 2010), both available at rahesabz.net. I expanded the ideas in these two essays in English in my book on the Green Movement: *Iran, the US, and the Green Movement: The Fox and the Paradox* (London: Zed, 2010).

Iran within the transnational public sphere I have termed the occasion of its *jahanshahri*, whereas I term its local reflection *Iranshahri*. *Jahanshahri* is the regional, transnational, global disposition of this cosmopolitanism, while *Iranshahri* is its internal dynamism, generating common memories from divergent elements of a people's history far beyond their ethnicized proclivities. This dual dynamics articulates a structural dissonance with the conditions of tyranny domestically, reflecting the colonial and imperial domination of the last two centuries and more. So, while the Islamic Republic insists on opposing US imperialism and/or British colonialism, in strategic and geopolitical terms that are quite plausible, it is in fact politically the most perfect and complete manifestation of their complementary logics of domination. This self-negating paradox will continue until the postcolonial state is either completely dismantled or else reflects the cosmopolitan realities that it has violently suppressed, and the nation is allowed to come to terms with its transnational birth and heritage.

What I am in effect proposing is a paradoxical political culture, deeply rooted in Shi'ism but not entirely reducible to it, in which the colliding elements of the culture, its *Iranshahri* and *jahanshahri*, posit an *armanshahri* ("utopianism") that is never completely contained in any political ideology, or captured by any political regime. This does give the political culture a characteristically anarchic disposition, though in the strict sense of the term, denoting a constitutional mistrust of the state apparatus, and thus of the nation-state as a polity. As the Islamic Republic tries to manipulate the public and parapublic spheres to sustain itself in power and fabricate its own legitimacy, it in fact inadvertently further expands the distance between its beleaguered state apparatus and the increasingly cosmopolitan culture of citizenship it has never been able completely to claim or represent. The Principalist–Reformist binary, though real in certain limited terms, categorically fails to represent the factual disposition and runaway political sentiments of the society at large. In cultural, societal, and political terms, this binary is seriously limited in its representation of the much wider and more multifaceted culture over which it wishes to preside. The whole production that calls itself *Roshanfekr-e Dini* ("religious intellectual") is a byproduct of this ailing environment. They emerged under circumstances of political triumphalism, and thus mistook the benefits of their ideological alliance with the ruling regime for theoretical potency. Nothing of any enduring significance emerged from this group of "religious intellectuals"—not even anything comparable with ideas produced in the heyday of Jalal Al-e-Ahmad and the leading Muslim revolutionary who emerged after him, Ali Shari'ati. Nevertheless, this faction disseminated its short-lived intellectual parlance with mystical panache and extreme verbosity. From a position of ideological power they had made Islamism the hegemonic term of engagement, cannibalizing ideas not generated by them just to pretend to articulate sentiments whose universality their thinking categorically lacked.

From Oil to Cinema

Nothing exposes the vacuity of the Iranian "religious intellectuals," their myopic conception of the cultural continuum of their homeland—and thus the nativist disposition of the state apparatus that enabled them in the first place—more emphatically than Iranian cinema. When the ruling monarch Mozaffar al-Din Shah Qajar (1853–1907) was in Paris, in July 1900—during one of the European visits that so obsessed him, paid for by the auctioning of his kingdom—he attended the Paris Expo, where, in the Lumière film exhibit, he saw the "cinematograph." He had one of the earliest models of camera purchased for his official photographer, Ebrahim Khan Akkasbashi, who used it to capture his European visit in motion pictures. Usually taken as the first page of the long and illustrious history of Iranian cinema, this auspicious episode might very well also be understood as one of the unintended consequences of Iranian oil—however indirectly—paying for the introduction of cinema in Iran. The flow of oil from Iranian soil brought back a camera, and with it inaugurated the preparatory stages of a cinema industry that would eventually grow to dazzle the whole world. That industry would grow from the Qajar period to that of the Pahlavis, and, under the Islamic Republic, it would become perhaps the most globally familiar and celebrated visual medium representing Iran to the outside world. Throughout the world, Iranian cinema was loved and admired as a distillation of the world in its own specific cinematic vocabulary. As the Iranian oil industry drew the productive juice from the soil and transported it around the world, cinema brought the visual *jouissance* of the world back to Iran. This circulation became reproductive, and soon Iranian cinema began to reproduce the visual languages whose idioms it had borrowed from around the world, which it nurtured and finally made its own.

Musicals from India, the Arab world, and Hollywood became the first staples of the Iranian cinema scene, to which were now added Iranian melodramas and musicals. A rich and diversified cinematic culture emerged in the post-war era, bringing vistas of the wider world to local movie theaters throughout Iran. Popular cinema soon cultivated a much more serious interest in art films. Introduction to the Bengali master Satyajit Ray, Japan's Yasujirō Ozu and Akira Kurosawa, and America's John Ford was soon followed by an enthusiastic and cultivated exposure to Russian formalism, the French New Wave, Italian neorealism, and New German Cinema. The establishment of the Tehran Film Festival soon brought world masters to Iran, and strengthened the courage and imagination of Iranian filmmakers. Iranian filmmakers likewise began to visit European and other major film festivals around the world. What Mozaffar al-Din Shah had initiated by serendipity and a wide-eyed wonder, squandering Iranian natural resources on a personal enthusiasm, went on to have planetary consequences for the emplotment of the nation within the transnational public sphere. From oil to cinema, a borderless Iran extended from the subterranean layers of its land to the sublimest spectrums of its transnational consciousness.

CHAPTER 5

Sailing Upon the Waters Round the Globe

> I still am traveling.
> I imagine a boat
> Sailing upon the waters round the globe and in it I—
> The traveler on this boat—
> Have been singing for thousands of years
> The living hymn of ancient mariners
> Into the orifices of the seasons' ears—
> And I sail—where
> Will the journey take me?
>
> Sohrab Sepehri (1966)

In the 1960s a fully blown cosmopolitan culture formed in Iran—a world and a worldliness in which Iranians actually lived and recognized themselves. This was the time when Forough Farrokhzad went to Italy, Ali Shari'ati to Paris, while Jalal Al-e-Ahmad traveled in and out of Iran and then around the world, and Frantz Fanon and Aimé Césaire entered the Iranian political consciousness in earnest, as well as that of Algeria, Cuba, and the rest of Africa and Latin America. As Bertolt Brecht, Anton Chekhov, Henrik Ibsen, and Arthur Miller were translated into Persian, Bahram Beiza'i, Akbar Radi, and Gholam Hossein Saedi emerged as the leading dramatists of their generation, and all came together to erase the political boundaries of the nation, of Iran and its environs. The Nimaic revolution in poetry was now in full swing, captivating the moral and revolutionary imagination of an entire generation. Iranian cinema was blooming, connecting its domestic audience to its global admirers. The post-1953 coup blues were actively and creatively transforming themselves in creative and defiant ways. Ayatollah Khomeini's 1963 uprising during this period was as much against the Pahlavi monarchy as it was against the cosmopolitan worldliness of this era, which he considered "secular," "Western," "ungodly," and thus inimical to his Islamist ideology. Before long, he, too, left Iran for Iraq and then for France, from where he would launch his final putsch against the Pahlavi regime. Lands were not nailed onto any colonial geography, seas connected rivers to oceans, and the fate of nations was spelled out within a transnational public sphere that respected no fictive frontier.

"I wish I was born somewhere else"

One can persuasively argue that, when the singularly iconoclastic poet Forough Farrokhzad (1935–67), an extraordinarily significant woman whose poetry single-handedly created the very fabric of feminine sensuality in Persian, took her groundbreaking film about a leprosy colony, "The House Is Black" (1962), to the Oberhausen Short Film Festival, Iranian cinema was officially issued with its ticket of entry onto the global scene. Farrokhzad was already a renowned and groundbreaking poet of uncommon courage and imagination, widely known and loved in her homeland. Her visual language film inaugurating the Iranian New Wave also gave birth to a documentary style of realism that has remained definitive of Iranian cinema to this day. It firmly established her reputation as a poet with an equally compelling cinematic imagination. One can argue that Farrokhzad's combination of poetry and realism very much anticipated the principal characteristic of Iranian cinema for decades to come. Born and raised in Tehran, soon after a short-lived marriage she began a career as a public intellectual and an increasingly daring poet. Both her life and her poetry became matters of uninterrupted attention by her contemporaries. In the midst of her successful career, Farrokhzad made a number of crucial trips to Europe, and through the travelogues and letters she wrote to her lover Ebrahim Golestan she made detailed records of these trips and their impact on her. "There is a painting of Leonardo in the National Gallery that I had not seen during my previous trips to London," she once wrote to Golestan. "It is extraordinary. Everything is dissolved in a light blue—like a human being and the dawn. I wanted to bow down and pray. This is the meaning of religion. I only feel religious at times of love and prayer."[1] This whole language was provocatively iconoclastic in the normative diction of Farrokhzad's time, and she thereby began to develop an ambivalent relationship with her homeland. After attending a festival at which her film was widely praised, she wrote to Golestan: "I wish I was born somewhere else, somewhere closer to the center of living excitements and movements. Alas I have to waste all my life and all my abilities—just because of my love for my homeland and my attachments to my memories—waste my life in a dilapidated domicile that is replete with death, inferiority, and uselessness."[2] But this sentiment was not lasting, for she immediately wrote: "I love our own Tehran, for whatever it is. I love it. It is only there that my life finds meaning and purpose. I love that sun that makes me lazy, those heavy sunsets, those dirt roads, those godforsaken, vicious, and corrupt people."[3] She wrote these lines, missing Tehran, while in Europe. When she returned to Tehran, she would carry the lasting memories of Europe with her back to her homeland. The effect was not one of ambivalence or confusion, identity crisis or misplaced emotions. Quite to the contrary: the effect was an emotive

---

1 As cited in Amir Isma'ili and Abolqasem Sedarat, eds., *Javdaneh Forough Farrokhzad* ("The Eternal Forough Farrokhzad") (Tehran: 1972), p. 17.

2 Ibid., p. 16.

3 Ibid., p. 17.

universe that was rooted in Iran but global in its sentiments, rooted in the world but effervescent in its worldly conception of her homeland.

While Farrokhzad visited Europe only for short trips, Ali Shari'ati (1933–77) had a much longer European sojourn with even more lasting impacts. The leading Islamist ideologue of the Iranian revolution of 1977–79 (though he was not alive to see it), Shari'ati's spell as a student in Paris had a radically transformative impact on his ideals and revolutionary aspirations.[4] As Ali Rahnema, who wrote a definitive biography of Shari'ati, notes, Shari'ati had a paradoxical attitude towards Paris—a combination of "attraction and repulsion."[5] He had come to the city after a rather ordinary upbringing in a devout Muslim family, in the provincial environment of his birthplace in Khorasan, in Northern Iran. While in Paris in 1960–64, Shari'ati was radicalized in an entirely different political milieu, with a vibrantly cosmopolitan frame of reference. A number of prominent French thinkers and scholars had a lasting impact on Shari'ati, among them the eminent scholar of Islamic mysticism Louis Massignon, leading sociologist George Gurvitch, and French Islamologist Jacques Baroque. But his most significant influence was perhaps that of Frantz Fanon, whose *Wretched of the Earth* (1961) had just been published. Of course, the existentialist thought of the leading French philosopher and public intellectual of the time, Jean-Paul Sartre, would have an enduring impact on him. It is thus crucial for us to see Shari'ati's presence in Paris as the intellectual and political hub of his exposure of transregional politics from Europe to Africa (through Algeria) and Latin

---

4 For more on Ali Shari'ati, see Hamid Dabashi, *Theology of Discontent: The Foundations of the Islamic Revolution in Iran* (New York: New York University Press, 1993), Chapter 2.

5 See Ali Rahnema, *An Islamic Utopian: A Political Biography of Ali Shari'ati* (London: I. B. Tauris, 2014 [1998]), p. 88.

America (through Cuba). The Cuban Revolution of 1959 and the Algerian Revolution of 1962, as well as the anti-war and Civil Rights movements of the same period in the United States, were seismic events of the period, and thus paramount in Shari'ati's mind. In political terms, he wedded Sartre's existentialism to Fanon's critique of colonialism, invoking a personal responsibility to rethink the history and dogmas of Islam in pursuit of a purposeful revolutionary commitment.

Ali Shari'ati ascended to prominence soon after the untimely death of another towering public intellectual, Jalal Al-e-Ahmad (1923–69).[6] Although Al-e-Ahmad became most famous for his critical essay, *Gharbzadegi* ("Westoxification") (1962), plus a number of other less significant short stories and novellas, it was really his travelogues that left an indelible mark on his generation. His travels were basically in two opposite directions—deep inside Iranian villages, and far into the wider world. His *Khasi dar Miqat* ("A Straw upon the Sacred Site"), an account of his Hajj pilgrimage, is a typical example of how amply his travels afforded him the opportunity to expand the horizons of his thinking—effectively, in this case, overcoming the false binary between "the religious" and "the secular." His travelogue on Israel—to which he traveled with his wife Simin Daneshvar in February 1963—consists of two contradictory parts, written at two different times (1964 and 1967), the first praising and the second denouncing Israel.[7] He had intended

6 For more on Ali Shari'ati, see Dabashi, *Theology of Discontent*, Chapter 1.

7 See Jalal Al-e-Ahmad, *Safar beh Velayat-e Ezra'il* ("Journey to the Land of Israel") (Tehran: 1984). This volume was first published in 1984, some five years after the establishment of the Islamic Republic. We know from the introduction to this volume that the current leader of the Islamic Republic, Ayatollah Ali Khamenei, was not much impressed with the first part of this travelogue, in which Al-e-Ahmad praises Israel—and that he made a trip from Qom to Tehran in 1963, when the first part was published, to register his complaint with Al-e-Ahmad by telephone. The editor of this volume, Al-e-Ahmad's brother Shahs Al-e-Ahmad, claims that the

to collect writings on his travels abroad into four categories, and call them "Chahar Ka'bah" ("Four Ka'bah"), covering Mecca, Jerusalem, Russia, and the United States. His ethnographic studies of Urazan (a temperate village in Northern Iran, from which Al-e-Ahmad's paternal family had emerged) are the best example of what these travels meant for him. Al-e-Ahmad had emerged from a clerical family to become perhaps the most widely celebrated public intellectual of his generation—while his ideas and convictions transcended the religious–secular binary, reflecting a much wider transnational exposure to the predicament of his generation, caught between an invented "tradition" beyond their reach and a "modernity" mitigated by colonialism.

Through such seminal figures as Farrokhzad, Al-e-Ahmad, and Shari'ati, the poetics and politics of the anticolonial struggles around the globe were brought home to Iran— domesticated, normalized, and made into the fabric of the worldly consciousness of the nation. The rise of these and similarly important public intellectuals was predicated on an already transregional solidarity with liberatory causes emanating from Latin America, Africa, and Asia. Through the writings of Fanon and Césaire, the awakening postcolonial consciousness of Algeria, Cuba, and the rest of the world entered the Iranian political vernacular, placing the prose and politics of the nation in the wider fold of a worldly awareness. When, at the age of eighteen, I took an overnight bus from my hometown of Ahvaz in the south and arrived early

---

second part was first published in two different venues, in Tehran and Qom, in 1967. In the second part we read a note presumably by Al-e-Ahmad in which he says this text is actually by a friend of his from Paris, to which he has added: "its gibberish is all mine, the good parts are his" (p. 86). But this whole second part and its radical change of tone, perhaps in part understandable in the aftermath of the 1967 war, has to be read very carefully, for in its book format it was published under the strict censorship of the Islamic Republic.

in the morning in Tehran one fine August morning in 1970, the Iranian capital was more abuzz with a cosmopolitan energy than Paris, London, or New York would be decades later in my own lifetime. From the highest echelons of the ruling regime down to the police officers patrolling the busy streets, no one had much authority over the politics of our convictions. A cheap copy of a leading progressive magazine like *Ferdowsi*, which included the essays, article, translations, and poems by these intellectuals, carried tremendous power and cultural charge. Such publications meant the world to us.

This was a time of creative effervescence in Iranian urban culture. The Tehran Film Festival would soon bring the best film directors from around the world to the Iranian capital. As a wide-eyed cineaste, I sat mesmerized just a few steps away from Michelangelo Antonioni when he brought his *The Passenger* (1975) to Tehran. The recently built Teatr-e Shahr (City Theater) was staging the widest spectrum of drama from around the world. As Bertolt Brecht, Anton Chekhov, Henrik Ibsen, and Arthur Miller were being staged in Persian translations, while Iranian dramatists like Bahram Beiza'i (b. 1938), Akbar Radi (1939–2007), and Gholam Hossein Sa'edi (1936–85) were emerging as the leading dramatists of their generation. Students of my political persuasion had serious issues with the Shiraz Art Festival, because of its affiliations with the royal court; but the fact is that it set off a seismic change in the Iranian artistic scene. Directors like Arby Ovanessian were in the vanguard of a movement involved in staging the best plays from around the world. Farhad Mechkat had just come back to Tehran after years of education and training in Europe and the United States to become the principal conductor of the Tehran Philharmonic Orchestra. As a young undergraduate student in Tehran, I slept all night (with a group of other enthusiasts) in front of Rudakai Hall, to get up early in the morning and purchase tickets to see the legendary Austrian conductor Herbert von Karajan conduct Beethoven's Fifth Symphony. A great number of other European composers were introduced to the young generation by carefully produced LPs issued by Kanun-e Parvaresh-e Fekri-ye Kudakan va No-javanan (Center for the Intellectual Development of Children and Young Adults). I recall that there was a record store named "Beethoven" in Pahlavi Avenue, where we could listen to and purchase from the widest collection of classical and pop music anywhere in the world—from Mozart to Ravi Shankar, from Edith Piaf to Ella Fitzgerald. Soon a worldly musical and artistic repertoire had emerged, within which Iranian and non-Iranian artists, filmmakers, composers, and dramatists took equally integral positions. Meanwhile, the Nimaic revolution in poetry was in full swing, dismantling classical Persian prosody and wedding the poetics of the time to an entirely different set of sensibilities. When, in an iconic poem, Nima declared: "Oh People / Sitting comfortably / Upon the Shore / Someone is drowning in the water," suddenly an entire generation realized that this was the harbinger of a new age. The dejection following the 1953 coup was transforming itself in creative and defiant ways.

The vascular channels that brought world literature from the four corners of the globe—from Japanese Haiku to Russian novels, Latin American magic realism, and, with Aimé Césaire, the poetry of Africa—into the Persian literary public sphere multiplied and expanded the channels through which Iranian oil and cinema had crossed beyond the borders of the homeland to travel far and wide. As oil oozed from the land to lubricate globalized capitalism, in came world film, fiction, drama, and poetry to nourish the expectant soul of the inhabitants of the postcolonial nation-state. On this site, "world literature" was defined and articulated not by a German humanist or an American comparatist trying to expand their literary horizons by cannibalizing the world literatures of peoples and histories about which they knew very little, but through the imaginative wherewithal of an urbanity with an urgent need to breathe life normally. With every breath Iranians collectively took, the lungs of their natural habitat expanded and contracted in and out of a frontier fiction that was only there for trespassing. Today, as we watch Iranian soft power stretching its limbs like an octopus from Afghanistan to Iraq, Syria, Lebanon, Palestine, Bahrain, Yemen, and beyond, we are witness to a ruling regime that uses and abuses the navigational routes of an existing cosmopolitanism for the narrow purpose of its own survival. The Islamist regime has sought ideologically to claim those breathing grounds for itself; but they are embedded in far more fertile and diversified soils, which contain forces that dismantle the ruling metaphors of that regime itself.

But the ruling Islamists are not the only culprit in this process of categorical distortion. The opposites of "Islam and the West," "Iran and the West," and "tradition versus modernity" are chief among the false binaries that have consistently falsified generations of understanding and interpretation of Iranian history throughout its colonial encounters and postcolonial history—and the Iranian Islamists are only one group among those that have contributed to the making of this foggy hall of mirrors. The so-called "secularists" are even worse. A far richer, more regionally diversified and globally informed political culture has foregrounded the Iranian political culture of the last two hundred years or more that this binary violently conceals. More than anything else, that falsifying history has severed Iran from its natural habitat in Asian history, and beyond that from its affinity with historic events in Africa and Latin America. As a result, a whitewashed generation of Iranians have seen themselves as "really Europeans" unfortunately thrown among a band of "Arabs and Turks and Indians." A whitewashed, Eurocentric generation of Iranian intellectuals has been mesmerized by what they have understood of European modernity, surrendering all critical sensibilities in the process. They have been, and remain, instrumental in the conceptual calamity of this severance of Iran from its regional and global context through its submission to the deceptive and deceitful lexicon of "Iran and the West." In this respect, the self-designated "secularists" were in fact worse than the so-called Islamists, paving the way for the Islamist takeover of Iranian cosmopolitan culture (cosmopolitan in the sense of having emotive, experiential, and conceptual roots in Asia, Africa, and Latin America, as well as relying on Western European and North American traditions of critical thinking). A banal, bourgeois fanaticism characterized by an artificial and skin-deep encounter with the Champs-Élysées and Fifth Avenues of their imaginations drafted the contours of what it meant to be "modern" for this afflicted generation, entirely ignorant of the critical responses such a version of "modernity" had generated not just in Asia, Africa, and Latin America, but also in Western Europe and North America. It was this lingering generation of fanatical secularists who distorted the world picture by designating it the "modern West" against which the Islamists (and their "religious intellectuals"), led by Khomeini and his followers, mobilized their forces. Khomeini's takeover of the Iranian Revolution of 1977–79 can very well be read as that of a decidedly nativist (though clerically Islamized) backlash not just against the self-designated secularists but against the very grain of a transnational, cosmopolitan culture they had both collaborated to conceal and deny.

A crowning achievement of that cosmopolitan setting was the work of the wildly creative cartoonist Ardeshir Mohassess (1938–2008). Rambunctious and rowdy in his satirical defiance of the seriously flawed order of things, Mohassess turned his pen to the boisterous depiction of his homeland and its follies. Riotous in his satire, he thrived on pictorial abstractions. His linear, lean depictions exposed the mad reasoning of the life he lived and witnessed. Mohassess achieved an allegorical transcendence that thrived on his visual parables—all worldly, tangible, funny, and furious. He poked fun at everything, stripping politics of all its paraphernalia of legitimacy and exposing its naked violence. Using his keen nose for absurdity, he placed national and global politics under a magnifying glass that revealed its innate brutality. He sketched social castes, kings, clerics, merchants, men, and women in a way that stripped them back to their bare bones, summarizing their twisted realities in just a few lines. He laughed both at and with the world around him, leaving no space safe from his ridicule. He was decidedly not on your side: he was on no one's side. As soon as you felt comfortable with him, he forced you to see yourself in his brutally honest mirror. Turning everything and everyone upside down, his work nonetheless seemed to reveal the reality of many situations for the first time.

Mohassess's visual lexicon was global from the beginning. He left Iran for New York in the aftermath of the totalitarian brutalities of the Islamic Republic, and lived in New York until his death. Once in New York, he made only minimal adjustments to his iconography. His villains now looked American and European, while monarchs and mollas found themselves in the company of Nazi generals and Latin American dictators. When he was in Iran, a globality of vision informed his style; once he was in New York, a cosmopolitan politics began to energize his particular penchant for the absurd. "I was three years old when my brother and I went to see the movie *Bala-ye Jan Nazi-ha*," he once recalled. "When we returned home they asked me what was the movie about. Instead of talking about the film I began drawing it. From then on whenever I saw a film I would draw its scenes and story.

I was madly in love with Western films, with thrillers, and with Tarzan."[8] What was this *Bala-ye Jan Nazi-ha* ("A Pain in the Neck of the Nazis") that he had seen? What Mohassess means is William Whitney's *Spy Smasher* (1942), a twelve-episode serial based on the comic character "Spy Smasher," with Kane Richmond and Marguerite Chapman, which in Iran was shown under the title he reported. Many prominent painters—from Brueghel to Bosch, Goya, and Picasso—have rightly been identified as having influenced Mohassess. But it was these American comics created by Bill Parker and C. C. Beck that left the most lasting impact on his creative and critical imagination. Mohassess travelled far and wide beyond those childhood impressions—the geographical distance magnified by a superior critical intelligence, and a special eye for a world gone mad with brutish absurdities.

When, in June 1963, Ayatollah Khomeini launched his first, unsuccessful uprising against the Pahlavi regime, it was as much against the ruling monarchy as it was against the cosmopolitan worldliness of the era, which he considered "secular" and "Western," and thus inimical to his brand of militant and absolutist Islamist ideology. As for Khomeini himself—where did he live between 1963, when he had failed to topple the Pahlavi regime, and 1979, when he triumphantly emerged to do precisely that? He did not live in Qom or Tehran, or any other Iranian city. Forced to leave Iran by the late shah, he lived in Najaf in Iraq, and then in Neauphle-le-Château in France—the two crucial locations from which he could continue to read, write, and gather followers and momentum, until his triumphant return to Iran. The term "exile" singularly fails to do justice to the fact that Khomeini was far freer and more politically agile in Iraq and France than he would have been in Iran. His physical absence from Iran enabled him

---

8 See Ismail Kho'i, *Shenakhnameh Ardeshir Mohassess* ("An Introduction to Ardeshir Mohassess") (Tehran: 1978), pp. 55–6.

Figure 4: Ardeshir Mohassess, *Untitled* (1996). Bill Parker and C. C. Beck's *Spy Smasher* (1940).

to be far more effectively present in Iran. Through the use of correspondence and cassette tapes, he managed to cultivate and sustain an ever-expanding body of revolutionary followers who, when the moment was ripe, rose up to support his aspiration of toppling the ruling regime. The fictive frontiers of "Iran" meant nothing to the mobilizing force of the most significant revolutionary event of the latter part of the twentieth century. It is known that, when Khomeini was on his flight back from Paris to Tehran, someone asked him what he felt upon returning to his homeland after so many years. "Nothing," he is reported to have responded—for he had never left it, in its larger emotive meaning, formed beyond its postcolonial borders.[9]

A significant proportion of Khomeini's followers during the crucial years between his departure from Iran in 1963 and his triumphant return in 1979 were in fact Iranian students living in Europe and the United States. He maintained regular correspondence with these students, encouraging and mobilizing them, and guiding their revolutionary sentiments. Active

---

9 For more on Ayatollah Khomeini, see Dabashi, *Theology of Discontent*, the eighth chapter.

Muslim students who were attracted to Khomeini's ideas were not, of course, the only Iranian students abroad. An equally significant segment of these students were Marxists, Maoists, Leninists, or else staunch nationalists. The "Confederation of Iranian Students (National Union)" was the umbrella organization of Iranian students abroad, mostly in Western Europe and North America, who were active in particular during the 1960s and 1970s. Their oppositional politics were informed mostly by Marxist and nationalist ideologies. Deeply involved in Iranian and other national liberation movements—from Palestine to Vietnam—these students were instrumental in wedding Iranian political causes to their transnational and global contexts. As a leading historian of the Confederation puts it,

> in the next fifteen years [after the June 1963 uprising] the only openly active and organized opposition group that survived was the student movement abroad, led by the Confederation. The expanding influence of this movement was generally recognized in the Western news media, and the shah himself considered it an effective element in the coalition of forces that eventually brought about the overthrow of the monarchy.[10]

Though rooted in Iran by political sentiment and family connections, these students were effective entirely outside their homeland:

> Through militant demonstrations and close cooperation with human rights, legal, and student organizations, the Confederation spearheaded an international campaign exposing the shah's regime as a repressive dictatorship. After the failure of 1963, the Confederation began to shift to a more

---

10 See Afshin Matin-Asgari, "Confederation of Iranian Students, National Union," *Encyclopædia Iranica*, at iranicaonline.org.

radical line, following a similar shift within the opposition at home. While a new generation of Marxist and Islamic activists were working underground to mount a guerilla campaign in Persia, some members of the opposition abroad, including Confederation activists, also decided to prepare for armed opposition. They approached Cuba, Algeria, China, and Palestinian guerrilla organizations for support.[11]

No such facilities were available to any student inside Iran. Had Khomeini been back in Qom under the surveillance of the shah's secret police, and the students back within the forced frontiers of their country rather than in major cities in Europe and the United States, there would have been no revolution in 1979. But placing Qom and Tehran next to Najaf, Neauphle-le-Château, Paris, London, New York, San Francisco, Tokyo, New Delhi, and Mumbai yields a far more realistic geography of the political struggle that enables revolutions such as the one that broke out in Iran in 1977–79, predicated on a transnational public sphere exceeding the constraints of national frontiers—and thus making use of a cosmopolitan space that Khomeini and his lieutenants sought immediately to dismantle as soon as they ascended to power in Tehran. In this, of course, they failed—for the selfsame transnational public sphere that had borne them to power was now discrediting their claim to exclusive legitimacy.

Reimagining the Imagined Community

Every aspect and every period of Iranian history during its last two hundred years or more that are under consideration here point to one irreducible fact: the formation of this nation-state was predicated on a transnational public sphere that linked its imperial past to its postcolonial present. Scarcely

---

11   Ibid.

a single public intellectual instrumental in the imagining and making of Iran as a postcolonial nation-state did not live a crucial period of their lives abroad—or at least have contact with those doing so—from India to the Ottoman territories to Europe. All of the most recent discussions of the nation as an "imagined community," or of the link between "nation and narration," mystify the nation-state far more than they theorize it within site-specific locations, paying detailed attention to the particular conditions of nation-states in non-European contexts. Of course, nations are indeed imagined communities, as are empires, tribes, and clans—and even extended families. We have not said anything particular about nationalism when we have catalogued the details of its active imagination by the institutions of nation-building—from state to society to culture. As for the link between the nation and narration, the same applies. Cancer and all other diseases are also narratives, as is our understanding of the solar system, and of course heliocentric astrophysics, when compared to its geocentric antecedent. Both Benedict Anderson and Homi Bhabha disregard two fundamental facts about postcolonial nations: (1) their own imperial pedigree, and (2) their subsequent, historically accumulated, shared memories of struggle against European colonial domination—which is neither imaginative nor merely narrative, but bone-deep and bloodily real.

Beyond the inherent limitations of thinking the nation as an imagined community or literary trope, we can think of national history outside the colonial bordering of nation-states and the postcolonial politics of national liberation—both rather self-evident historical facts that are mystified by an excessive postmodern preoccupation with cliché alliterations such as "nation and narration." The example of contemporary Iranian history allows us to chart a radically alternative way of reading the fictive frontiers of nation-states. Here we can base our reading of the nation not on the imaginatively manufactured nations and nationalism that it occasions, but on the factual evidence of a transnational public sphere that fosters and embraces that political project. A nation might indeed be a socially constructed community, as Benedict Anderson rightly proposes, imagined by its members; but that imagination is perceived and performed within a transnational public space that is formed on the borderlines of any geopolitics of regional border-crossing, incorporating public intellectuals beyond the borders of that nation, well before they are fully drawn, or as they are being drawn—then only to be creatively and effectively crossed.

The nation is thus "imagined" (if we are compelled to use that word) long before the paraphernalia of nationhood—a common currency, a flag, a national newspaper, a national soccer team, a national airline, national television and radio—is set in motion, and by virtue of a discursive articulation that narrates the nation mostly from outside its cartographic boundaries. Today there is still no Palestine as a nation-state, but Palestinians are more convinced of their sense of belonging precisely by virtue of that dispossession. Palestine is not a narration, nor is it imagined. It is the product of generations of bloody and painful struggle, and it gets stronger by the day, articulated by Palestinians from refugee camps in Lebanon to Ivy League universities in North America. The example of Iran clearly indicates that expatriate intellectuals in areas ranging from India to the Ottoman territories to Europe were instrumental in the articulation of Iran as an imagined community. This transnational site of the nation and nationalism softens and dissolves the postcolonial frontier fictions it implicates into the larger domain of the geopolitics of liberation that is located decidedly outside the colonial boundaries of the nation.

Anderson defined the nation as "an imagined political community—and imagined as both inherently limited and sovereign."[12] That imagination, I propose, is a feat performed for the nation from outside the colonially constituted borders of that nation; and thus, as politically limited as it might be, imaginatively it is in fact entirely unlimited and open-ended in its articulation of sovereignty. "Iran" was imagined in Calcutta, Berlin, Paris, and Cairo far more vividly and passionately than it was in Tehran, Isfahan, or Qom. Anderson's definition has a proclivity to become structural-functional and ex post facto, while the transnational origins of nations have given them an inherently defiant disposition against the stabilizing requirements of sovereignty. He privileges the power of the state to define the nation, whereas it is far more defiantly imagined and performed in opposition to the power of states. Given the transnational and multicultural disposition of the public sphere upon which the nation is imagined, if its sovereignty is defined in, say, nationalistic terms, it might be challenged in socialist or Islamist terms—both transnational by their ideological nature. Neglecting this transnational proclivity of the nation leads Anderson to another serious folly. He states:

> The nation is imagined as limited because even the largest of them, encompassing perhaps a billion living human beings, has finite, if elastic, boundaries, beyond which lie other nations. No nation imagines itself coterminous with mankind. The most messianic nationalists do not dream of a day when all the members of the human race will join their nation in the way that it was possible, in certain epochs, for, say, Christians to dream of a wholly Christian planet.[13]

---

12 Benedict Anderson, *Imagined Communities: Reflections on the Origin and Spread of Nationalism* (London: Verso, 1983), p. 6.
13 Ibid.

Here Anderson has strayed onto a flawed path. Indeed, "no nation imagines itself coterminous with mankind." But between the *nation* and the *mankind* stands the historical fact of *empires*, from which nations within the vast territories of the three simultaneous Muslim empires of the Mughals, the Safavids, and the Ottomans eventually emerged. Postcolonial nation-states ranging from India to Iran, Turkey, Egypt, and so on, have emerged not only on the model of the European experience that is so paramount in Anderson's theorization, but wholly conscious of the non-European, Muslim empires to which they once belonged. The Eurocentricity of Anderson's conception of the nation is quite specific. The nation, he writes,

> is imagined as sovereign because the concept was born in an age in which Enlightenment and Revolution were destroying the legitimacy of the divinely-ordained, hierarchical dynastic realm. Coming to maturity at a stage of human history when even the most devout adherents of any universal religion were inescapably confronted with the living pluralism of such religions, and the allomorphism between each faith's ontological claims and territorial stretch, nations dream of being free, and, if under God, directly so. The gage and emblem of this freedom is the sovereign state.[14]

Here again, Anderson bypasses the historical fact of empires and goes directly from the post-Enlightenment formation of the nation back to the "divinely-ordained, hierarchical dynastic" terms facilitated by way of "Enlightenment and Revolution." This succession of Enlightenment and Revolution is an entirely European experience, though it had global repercussions in the formation of postcolonial nations around the world. But categorically absent from Anderson's theory is the factual evidence that vast Muslim empires, from the Mughals

---

14   Ibid., p. 7.

to the Safavids to the Ottomans, were not "divinely-ordained, hierarchical dynastic realms," but in fact vastly cosmopolitan political cultures embedded in a "living pluralism" of their own, long before European notions of the post-Enlightenment nations reached their shores. The structural transformation of institutions of power and authority into a transnational public sphere from which nations developed within the geographical expansion of these three empires gave them an ideological diversity and complexity entirely alien to what Anderson prescribes for them:

> Finally, [the nation] is imagined as a community, because, regardless of the actual inequality and exploitation that may prevail in each, the nation is always conceived as a deep, horizontal comradeship. Ultimately it is this fraternity that makes it possible, over the past two centuries, for so many millions of people, not so much to kill, as willingly to die for such limited imaginings.[15]

No nation has ever been "always conceived as a deep, horizontal comradeship" in these territories. Race, ethnicity, gender, and class have always been deeply divisive factors in the formation of national consciousness. In Iran, for sure, Kurds, Baluchis, and Arabs have always had legitimate reasons to display centrifugal tendencies. As Qajar or Pahlavi nationalism sought to bring the nation towards its monarchic centers, Islamist movements from Babism to Khomeinism drew it towards the larger Muslim world, just as socialism pulled the loyalties of Iranian Marxists far more towards the Soviet Union than towards a bourgeois nationalism. As "for so many millions of people, not so much to kill, as willingly to die for such limited imaginings," during the Iran–Iraq War of 1980–88, the rhetoric of the war on the Iranian side was

---

15   Ibid.

overwhelmingly focused on defeating Saddam Hussein on the way to liberating Jerusalem—a clear indication that the war was waged in pan-Islamist and decidedly not in a pan-Iranist or pan-socialist terms. During the heyday of the Mosaddegh era in Iran, as he was calling for the nationalization of Iranian oil, the Tudeh Party called for the nationalization of Iranian oil in southern Iran, wishing for the oil from the north to flow freely to the Soviet Union.

The origins of postcolonial nation-states like Iran, Turkey, India, and Egypt were without borders, from the purgatorial passage of Muslim post-imperial histories facing European imperial onslaughts. Muslim empires had different contested borders, and today the geopolitics of the region are also borderless—partitioned from India, Pakistan is today in Afghanistan; carved out of Qajar realms, Iran is in Iraq, Syria, Afghanistan, Lebanon, and Palestine, as Saudi Arabia is in Bahrain; while Israel is the last enduring European colonial outpost built on Palestine, and its chief sponsor, the United States, is the dominant empire laying claim on the entirety of the globe. We must thus de-fetishize these fictive frontiers and see them for the porous lines and invitations to transgress that they are. We must acknowledge the postnational politics of the region, which pays lip-service to these borders as it aggressively trespasses across them. "Syria is more important to us than Khuzestan," said one prominent Iranian cleric, referring to the southern Iranian province in the wake of the effects of the Syrian civil war. But the border-trespassing is not limited to politics. There are social movements, border-crossing poets, and the revolutions they anticipate—all liberated or becoming liberated from all fictive frontiers. The artificial barriers between Arab nations are equally fictive and nonsensical. Today, in fact, the nation-state has become the limit of domestic tranny, where the ruling regimes in Syria, Iran, Egypt, and Libya can maim, murder, and imprison their citizens with impunity, and whose alternative is military intervention in the name of "humanitarian intervention." The whole range of notions of "exile" and "liminality" are fictions of alienation and disenfranchisement, disabling people, making them dually marginal, aliens where they are, irrelevant to where they cannot be. What is crucial here is the liberating force of postnational politics. But Jürgen Habermas has a very important warning: "If not only the nation-state has run its course, but along with it all forms of political integration, then individual citizens are abandoned to a world of anonymously interconnected networks in which they must choose between systematically generated options in accordance with their preferences. In this *postpolitical* world the multinational corporation becomes the model for all conduct."[16]

For that not to happen, the sustained anticolonial history of nations remains enduring. The fate of postcolonial nation-states is written after the erasure of their origins in regional and global empires, and the rise of European and now American imperialism anticipating a globalized condition of domination, theft, and distortion. Reading the frontier fiction of nations elastically, as I have here, allows for the unit of the nation-state to resume its organic life, de-fetishized beyond its fixed borders, but falls short of dismantling the fiction for the benefit of international corporations—a process of which Habermas rightly warns. That fiction has a tenuous relationship with facts, facts of a memorial nature, and it is inherently renewable by virtue of the misery that globalized capitalism leaves behind. The systematicity of that globalized destitution needs alternative modes of transnational solidarity, rather than the dog-eat-dog reality of bourgeois ethnic nationalism wreaking havoc within and beyond its frontier fictions along racialized, gendered, and class lines.

---

16 Jürgen Habermas, *The Inclusion of the Other: Studies in Political Theory* (Cambridge, MA: MIT Press, 1998), pp. 124–5.

"It's a Vacant Clean Room"

Traveling has been a central metaphor in the Iranian literary and poetic imagination since time immemorial. Classical poets like Naser Khosrow and Sa'di are now legendary for their restless souls, roaming from one end of the earth to another. But this journey is not just territorial. It is also metaphoric. In one of his most memorable reflections on the nature of poetry, Ahmad Shamlou uses the metaphor of travel to explain what it means to be a poet.[17] The poet, in his estimation, is a person who has returned from a journey. The journey is one of *mokashefeh* ("discovery"). The first part of this journey is in pursuit of *daryaft* ("understanding"), while the second provides an opportunity for *bayan* ("expression"). Shamlou keeps the metaphor of journey active: "Behold we have returned from the lands of thinking and inspiration."[18] From the *marhaleh* ("passage") of *daryaft* until the marketplace of presentation there is but a short journey. Here Shamlou introduces the metaphor of the caravan. Upon this caravan the poets begin to clothe their ideas with proper *bayan* ("expressions"): "*va ay basa mard-e caravan* / so often it happens that a man upon this caravan continues to enjoy his sojourn and refuses to give expression to his findings. In other words, so often it happens that many a poet dies without writing any poem."[19]

Other poets have used the metaphor of a journey to navigate the contours of their reflections on where and how they were—chief among them perhaps Sohrab Sepehri, whose poetic masterpiece, "Mosafer" ("Traveler") (1966) is predicated on actual journeys transfused into an unfolding poetic metaphor:

---

17   Ahmad Shamlou, "On Poetics," *Andisheh va Honar*, Farvardin 1343/March 1964, Special Issue on Ahmad Shamlou.
18   Ibid., p. 149.
19   Ibid., p. 150.

Otaq-e khalvat-e paki-st/It's a vacant clean room:
It has such simple proportions in which to sit down and think.
I feel so sad—
I have no intention to go to sleep ...
I still am traveling.
I imagine a boat
Sailing upon the waters round the globe and in it I—
The traveler on this boat—
Have been singing for thousands of years
The living hymn of ancient mariners
Into the orifice of the seasons' ears—
And I sail—where
Will the journey take me?
Think clearly:
Where exactly is the hidden harmony
Of this mysterious hymn?
Give me some wine
We must hurry up
I am returning from the sighting of an epic
And just like water I am fluent
With the story of Sohrab and panacea
Upon my traveling path ...
A few Lebanese farmers
Were sitting under an old cedar tree
Counting their oranges in their mind ...
As a few blind Iraqi children
Were staring at the Hammurabi Tablet ...
Oh all the olive trees of Palestine
Address the generosity of all your shades to me—
To this lonely traveler
Who has just returned from a pilgrimage at Mount Sinai—
And is ablaze with the heat of Divine Speech.[20]

20 Sohrab Sepehri, *Hasht Ketab* ("Eight Books") (Tehran: 1997), pp. 310–21. My translation.

CHAPTER 6

The World Is My Home

To put it bluntly, a house that has no deeds, a house about
which I know very little, I just consider this house never existed.
[What do I need a house for?], the world is my home.

Nima Yushij (c. 1921)

The crucial decade of the 1970s marked the height of that
cosmopolitanism in prose, poetry, and cinema that ultimately
resulted in the 1977–79 Revolution. That Revolution, in its
preparatory stages, embodied all of these movements—before
it was violently hijacked by its militant Islamist faction. As
Ayatollah Khomeini and his militant lieutenants moved
quickly to claim the entirety of the Revolution for themselves,
the spirit of cosmopolitan worldliness they sought to suppress went underground and fled across fictive frontiers (as it
always does), framing and compromising the legitimacy of the
belligerent theocracy.

That worldliness from which Sepehri had been nourished
had both Iranian and non-Iranian vantage points. Chief
among its Iranian pioneers in the twentieth century was the
iconoclastic poet Nima Yushij (1895–1960). Nima radically
revolutionized Persian poetry by categorically challenging its
inherited prosody and theorizing his own poetic practices in
relation to what he considered the natural musicality of words
and phrases. From a provocative location between his rural
habitat and a worldly consciousness, Nima theorized his own
poetry in a series of letters he sent to his friends and family,
particularly his wife Aliyeh. One of the collections of these
letters is titled, *Donya Khaneh-ye Man Ast* ("The World Is

My Home"). In one of the letters it contains, addressed to his mother (the letter has no date, but it is most probably from the early 1920s), he refers to a house that had evidently been a bone of contention in his family: "To put it bluntly, a house that has no deeds, a house about which I know very little, I just consider this house never existed. [What do I need a house for?], the world is my home."[1]

What could that phrase mean?

> Poetry dwells neither in its phrases nor in its rhythmic wording, nor indeed in its rhymes ... I know of people who from the mid nineteenth century to this very day have been composing poetry, and yet their poems have disappeared even before they have. I know of others whose poetry has become famous only because other people have promoted it. The lifespan of this fame is as limited as the life of these poets. But good poetry, just like an infant, is potentially alive. It grows with a nation's thoughts, even if when it is born no one pays any attention to it. This is how time is, one must ignore it ... Poetry is the description of internal wishes and dreams. Instead of describing them, we must enact them.[2]

As is evident in this and many similar passages, Nima was convinced of two things simultaneously: first, that his poetry was in tune with the emerging realities of his homeland and the world beyond; and, second, that as his nation grew in moral and imaginative terms, so would its cognizance of the importance of his poetry. History has proved him right on both accounts. The world was Nima's home because, through his capacious poetic consciousness, he had his hands on the pulse of his time. The world was his home because, in his poetry,

---

1 See Nima Yushij, *Donya Khaneh ye Man Ast* ("The World Is My Home") (Tehran: 1350/1971), p. 6.
2 Ibid., pp. 33–4. My translation.

he had reached such an intuition of transcendence that he in effect authored and authorized that world. The world was his home because his home, which was his poetry, was worldly.

Rethinking Diaspora

In her *Writing Outside the Nation* (2000), Azade Seyhan points out the rise of a particular body of literature in what she designates as "diaspora."[3] In this constellation of creative writing she detects a "transnational poetics" in which tropes of "displacement, memory, and language" become provocative metaphors. Seyhan's book is now typical of a body of scholarship that is branded as "diasporic studies." Similar sentiments to Seyhan's are evident in another major work of the prominent scholar of Iranian cinema Hamid Naficy, *Accented Cinema* (2001).[4] Echoing Seyhan on literature, Naficy considers as "accented" the cinema of those filmmakers he thinks of as "displaced," in "exile or diaspora." On this premise, he detects certain "stylistic similarities among these exilic filmmakers." These films are located between "home" and "host" societies. He regards Hollywood cinema as the standard against which he measures the work of these filmmakers, which he considers "accented."

This entire line of argument—shared by Seyhan, Naficy, and a host of other scholars working in so-called "diaspora studies"—is predicated on an active fetishization of "home" and "mother tongue," from which writers and filmmakers are then presumed to be distanced and alienated. Produced mainly by scholars who consider themselves part of the exilic community they examine, such work categorically nativizes and isolates an artist's "home" in order to make "exile" a

3 See Azade Seyhan, *Writing Outside the Nation* (Princeton, NJ: Princeton University Press, 2000).

4 See Hamid Naficy, *An Accented Cinema: Exilic and Diasporic Filmmaking* (Princeton, NJ: Princeton University Press, 2001).

plausible, theorized category. The fabricated position of "diaspora" here becomes completely insular, fetishized into a reality *sui generis*, entirely divorced from its historic location within a larger worldly context that embraced them far beyond their home or their exile. If the cinema of Hollywood were to be used as a measure, as Naficy does, the entirety of world cinema, including films made by filmmakers who have never left their home countries, would thereby be "accented." The cinema of Hollywood itself, meanwhile, is manufactured for a decidedly global market. Another major flaw of these sorts of argument is that they cross-essentialize "home" as something nativist, limited, and insular, with no organic connection to the world beyond.

Both assumptions are categorically flawed. Filmmakers like Akira Kurosawa, Satyajit Ray, Abbas Kiarostami, Nuri Bilge Ceylan, or Theo Angelopoulos are worldly when they make films inside their homeland—just as Palestinian filmmakers like Michel Khleifi and Elia Suleiman, or Armenian filmmakers like Atom Egoyan, have no country of origin from which to be displaced and exiled, from where to make "accented" films. Their work in fact makes "Palestinian" or "Armenian" cinema possible, without their ever having lived in a country called Armenia or Palestine. Kurdish filmmakers ranging from Yılmaz Güney to Bahman Qobadi make films in the Turkish or Iranian nation-state, while their cinema remains decidedly Kurdish. For them, there is no "home"—in the fetishized sense in which scholars like Seyhan and Naficy use the term—from which to be exiled and placed in diaspora. Amir Naderi's films, produced in southern Iran, Tehran, New York, and Tokyo all bear his unmistakable stylistic signature. Which one of them is "accented?" Abbas Kiarostami makes films in Iran, Japan, Italy, and Africa—all of them evoking his distinctive cinematic style. Which one of them is "accented?" There is no home or exile for him. Salman Rushdie, Aravind Adiga, and Jhumpa

Lahiri are Indian, not British; but by no stretch of the imagination are they "diasporic" novelists in the English language. Abdellatif Kechiche is a Tunisian filmmaker (like scores of other North African Francophone artists and writers), and yet is entirely at home in France. What Naficy, Seyhan, and their colleagues disregard is the factual evidence of a coloniality that has categorically dismantled the notions of "home" and "exile."

A version of Hamid Naficy's argument about accented cinema appeared in Persian in a memorial volume for the pioneering Iranian filmmaker Sohrab Shahid-Saless.[5] Naficy's central paradigm in the Persian version was again the people from "Third World and non-Western societies moving to First World and Western societies"[6]—filmmakers whose cinema when at home was "standard," and presumably accent-less, while when they moved abroad it became peripheral and accented.[7] The cinema of Shahid-Saless, however, was worldly when he was at home, and it remained reflective of his homeland when he left home. The whole binary between "home" and "exile," or "homeland" and "diaspora," is false and falsifying of the lived experience of postcolonial nations as they have emerged, with active memories of their own imperial pasts.

"Home and Exile"

Shahid-Saless's influence would continue to be seen in the work of future generations of Iranian artists. In 2013, the Mohsen Gallery in Tehran launched a solo exhibition of Azadeh Akhlaghi's work, "By an Eyewitness," to a wide and

---

5   See Hamid Naficy, "Sinama ye Lahjeh dar" ("Accented Cinema"), in Ali Dehbashi, ed., *Yadnameh Sohrab Shahid-Saless* ("Memorial Volume for Sohrab Shahid-Saless") (Tehran: 1999).

6   Ibid., p. 165.

7   Ibid., pp. 165–6.

enthusiastic reception from the Iranian and international press. I wrote my short essay on her work in English in New York, a friend of Akhlaghi in Australia translated it into Persian, and, when the exhibition opened in Tehran, she kindly sent me not just the published catalogue and book but also pictures of mutual artist friends attending the opening of her exhibition in Tehran. An invisible studio thus extended from Tehran to Europe, Australia, and New York, from which emerged a particularly powerful visual remembrance of the most traumatic moments of modern Iranian history. That visible history was exhibited in Tehran, but predicated on an invisible, emotive "Iran" and "Iranians" far beyond the nation's fictive frontiers.

Akhlaghi's photographs had touched and rekindled the most traumatic turning points of modern Iranian history—bringing Iranian clerics, athletes, poets, filmmakers, statesmen, soldiers, and revolutionary figures together to create a pantheon of their iconic deaths. Though these were exceptionally significant events, there are no real-time images of them available anywhere, except in the minds and souls of the people who love and admire these heroic figures. It is the archival details and photographic mimicry of Akhlaghi's pictures that were most haunting. This was history in a new photographic register, effectively challenging all the dominant historical narratives—not necessarily dismantling them, but declaring itself equally authoritative.

Among Akhlaghi's stunning pictures was one addressing the sudden and tragic death of the pioneering Iranian filmmaker Sohrab Shahid-Saless in Chicago. Shahid-Saless (1944–98) was born to a middle-class family in Tehran immediately after World War II and the Allied occupation of his homeland.[8] It

---

8 For a short biographical note on Sohrab Shahid-Saless, see the entry under his name in *Encyclopædia Iranica*, "Sohrab Shahid-Saless," at iranicaonline.org. There is also an excellent database on his life and work in German available at saless.werkstattfilm.de. For a more extensive study

was after this period that the Tudeh Party—the most popular and powerful socialist party in modern Iranian history—was established. At age nineteen, when the nationalist government of Mohammad Mosaddegh had just been overthrown in a CIA coup, and Khomeini had just launched his first (unsuccessful) attempt at overthrowing the Pahlavi dynasty, Shahid-Saless left Iran for Vienna, "where he attended a film school and an acting school at the same time, but his studies were discontinued there in 1967 due to a sudden diagnosis of tuberculosis. In the midst of treatment, he left for Paris to continue his film studies at the prestigious Independent Conservatory of French Cinema, and shortly thereafter, in 1968, he returned to Iran."[9]

Both the anticolonial nationalism of Mohammad Mosaddegh and the militant Islamism of Ayatollah Khomeini having now been momentarily checked and defeated by the ruling monarchy, Shahid-Saless returned to Iran at the height of a period of literary and poetic effervescence that stood in for open political activism. By now, Forough Farrokhzad and Ebrahim Golestan, among other pioneering Iranian filmmakers, had delivered the first jolts that would inaugurate Iranian "New Wave" cinema. Soon after his return to Iran, Shahid-Saless began making short documentaries. His two masterpieces, *Yek Ettefaq-e Sadeh* ("A Simple Incident," 1973) and *Tabi'at-e Bijan* ("Still Life," 1974), shaped the foundations of Iranian cinema for generations to come. His cinema—solid, simple, daring, and imaginative—saw the mind-numbing unreal in the real. In 1974—before the 1979 Revolution that would turn his homeland upside down—he

---

of his life and work, see Mehrnaz Saeed-Vafa, "Sohrab Shahid-Saless: A Cinema of Exile," in Rose Issa and Sheila Whitaker, eds., *Life and Art: The New Iranian Cinema* (London: British Film Institute, 1999). But the most comprehensive study of his life and cinema is available only in Persian, in Dehbashi, *Yadnameh Sohrab Shahid-Saless.*

9 *Encyclopædia Iranica*, "Sohrab Shahid-Saless."

left the country for Germany, and began making one film after another for German television. Of the sixteen major films he directed, only three were made in Iran, and the rest in Europe. He was active for close to two decades in Germany—a more productive and enduring period of work than his years in Iran—and yet he carried his signature cinema across all of the borders he transgressed with his art. In 1992 he left Europe for the United States, where he died of a chronic illness (exacerbated by alcohol abuse) in Chicago, deeply frustrated not by the fact that he was not in Iran, but by the far more compelling reality that he could not finance his film projects.

Of the nineteen iconic deaths that Akhlaghi depicts in this series of her work, all except one occurred inside Iran. But the death of Sohrab Shahid-Saless, which happened in Chicago, projects the worldly character of all of the other iconic figures depicted—ranging from Mohammad Mosaddegh, who became a champion of anticolonial nationalism from India to North Africa, to Forough Farrokhzad, who revolutionized Persian poetic diction and brought it to bear beautifully on similar global events, to Ali Shari'ati, who brought the revolutionary zeal of Africa and Latin America to his homeland, to Gholamreza Takhti, who as a wrestling champion raised the

Figure 5: Azadeh Akhlaghi, "Sohrab Shahid-Saless—1 July 1998—Chicago".

Iranian flag in numerous sporting events around the world, to Bizhan Jazani, who linked Iranian Marxist revolutionary ideals to similar revolutionary causes around the globe. "The original inspiration for 'By An Eyewitness,'" according to Akhlaghi, came in the aftermath of the 2009 election: "I was so shocked by the death of Neda."[10] Who was this Neda? Neda Agha Soltan (1983–2009) was a young Iranian whose murder by the security forces of the Islamic Republic during massive anti-regime demonstrations was broadcast globally. Her death was captured on a smartphone camera and "turned into probably the most widely witnessed death in human history."[11] That brutish murder became one of the key defining moments of Iran's Green Movement—a massive social uprising that shook the Islamist regime to its foundations, retrieving the nation's repressed and denied cosmopolitan political culture. The death of Neda Agha Soltan, as inspiration for Akhlaghi's artwork, became iconic. She could not of course stage that particular iconic death in her series of artworks when they were exhibited in Iran; the censorial warlords of the Islamic Republic would not allow it. But there was a transcendental synergy between her artwork and her audience within and beyond the fictive frontiers of Iran that liberated those trapped inside those frontiers long before (and thus long beyond) they were colonially conditioned.

Relocating Culture

In the twentieth century, it has not just been artists, statesmen, merchants, and public intellectuals who have left the confines of Iran, or arrived in Iran from elsewhere, bringing their own cultures with them. The example of Sohrab Shahid-Saless is

---

10 As reported in Jason Rezaian, "Unique Photography Project Gets Strong Reception in Iran," *Washington Post*, March 7, 2013.

11 See Krista Mahr, "Neda Agha Soltan," in "Top Ten Heroes," *Time*, December 8, 2009.

by no means unique. From the late eighteenth to the early twenty-first centuries, Iranian artists, writers, filmmakers, poets, intellectuals, philosophers, jurists, mystics, and revolutionary leaders alike have crossed the fictive frontiers of their homeland to east and west, south and north, and thereby expanded the moral, imaginative, and emotive domain of what they refer to when they say "Iran." The worldly disposition of Iranian cosmopolitan culture is a byproduct of its political history in all its various dimensions and twists. The Shi'i scholastic madrasah system has two major epicenters, in Qom and Najaf. These two centers attract seminarians from around the Muslim world—from Asia, Africa, Latin America, the United States, and Europe. With massive labor migrations of Muslims around the world, these seminarian students constitute a formidable political force, cherishing a legalistic interpretation of Islam at the core of their curricular learning. With immense oil revenues now squarely at their disposal, the ruling clerical order uses and abuses this seminarian system and its Qom campus for wide-ranging political and social projects—the manifestations of which can be detected from Lebanon to Palestine and Yemen. The most spectacular charismatic political figure produced by the Qom–Najaf nexus was of course Ayatollah Khomeini, who was initially educated in Qom but came to prominence in Najaf. While Qom links Iran to the Persian-speaking east, Najaf connects it with the Arabic-speaking West—uniting a long swath of the Islamic world under the power and influence of the Islamic Republic. That power and influence were not made overnight, but are predicated on a deeply rooted historical reality that recognizes no colonial or postcolonial fictive frontier.

Shi'i scholastic learning and faith are not the only transnational traditions that locate Iran within the wider world. The equally capacious spectrum of the Persianate world extends from Central Asia to India and the Persian Gulf. This world

embraces both Islamic scholasticism and Persian humanism (both adjacent to but independent of Shi'ism) as its two
common heritages. From Central Asia to the Indian subcontinent, the northern shores of the Arabian Peninsula, and the
east coast of Africa, Muslims know their cultural heritage
not just from Arabic scripture, but also from Persian literary
and mystical exegesis and hermeneutics. There is also a vast
and rich body of travel narratives written by Indian, Arab,
and Iranian travelers within this widening world. Aspects
of Persian culture have also had a far-reaching presence in
European cultures from Antiquity through the Renaissance
and Enlightenment, and beyond.[12] Meanwhile, generations of
Iranian activists have been integral to the Palestinian cause,
which has both benefited from their solidarity and lent them
a global perspective beyond their own immediate "national
interests"—as have activists and workers who have arrived
in Iran from other countries. The combination of these facts
about Iranian history, among many others, places the nation
far beyond the limits of a colonially crafted border, rendering
it far too strong to be contained or negated by any romantic
or nostalgic conception of the nation.

Abused terms such as "exile" and "diaspora" have now
emerged as the coded master-terms of bourgeois nostalgia,
underwriting a deeply rooted ethnic nationalism against the
very grain of the lived experiences of people populating those
nations far beyond their colonial borders. Three hundred
million or more human beings roam the globe in search of
a half-decent life as migrant laborers, in a world economic
system that routinely produces hunger for close to 1 billion
people in an average year.[13] As cheap labor chases afar fleeting

---

12 For details, see Hamid Dabashi, *Persophilia: Persian Culture on
the Global Scene* (Cambridge, MA: Harvard University Press, 2015).

13 "The United Nations Food and Agriculture Organization esti-
mates," according to one report, "that nearly 870 million of the 7.1 billion

transnational capital, capital dodges and seeks out cheap labor in China, India, Dubai, Doha, and then in Africa, Asia, and Latin America. The Armenian genocide under the Ottoman Empire generated real refugees running for their lives, as did the Nakba produced by the Zionist project in Palestine. Under these circumstances, bourgeois nostalgia for one ideologically racialized "nation" or another in Los Angeles or Florida has very little claim on the facts and phenomena of lived experiences. Against such misplaced nostalgia is the factual evidence of worldly cultures from one end of the globe to another. By and large, this body of "diasporic studies" is produced by expatriate bourgeois scholars beholden to the myth of "the West" as a metaphysical metaphor from which they feel unfairly distanced. Those actually suffering under the harsh conditions of massive global labor migration in places like Doha and Dubai, the slums of Paris, the poor neighborhoods stretching from New York to Los Angeles, and those millions of internal and external refugees in Afghanistan, Palestine, Iraq, and Syria never get to write about or theorize their conditions.

The singular achievement this "diaspora studies," as its proponents call it, is the cross-essentialization of the myth of "the West" as the central metaphor of the self-centering universe systematically provincializing—by marking the "accent" of others and thus repressing its own—their own worldly cultures, and thus privileging the fiction of "the West" in which they erroneously fancy themselves to be living, but from which they feel alienated. These scholars and writers thus become integral to the self-raising/other-lowering proclivities of the

---

people in the world, or one in eight, were suffering from chronic undernourishment in 2010–2012. Almost all the hungry people, 852 million, live in developing countries, representing 15 percent of the population of developing counties. There are 16 million people undernourished in developed countries." World Hunger Education Service, "2015 World Hunger and Poverty Facts and Statistics," worldhunger.org, accessed October 2015.

European capitalist modernity that has historically coded itself as "the West." The critical task at hand is to dismantle that fantasy, puncture its remaining power, expose its ideological origin and destination, and thereby actively retrieve the repressed, denied, and denigrated worldliness of the actual lived experiences of multiple worlds around the globe.

In effect, what I am proposing here is a vision of the postcolonial nations from the remnants of Muslim empires (from the fifteenth to twentieth centuries) that lies upstream from their conceptual entrapment somewhere between anticolonial nationalism as understood by thinkers from Fanon to Said and the urge to attend to the overlapping, migratory dispositions usurped under the so-called "exilic predicaments" that have yielded to an utterly apolitical postmodernism that dwells on the fiction of "in-betweenness" and thus effectively robs nations of their transnational origins and thereby their historical agencies beyond their colonial conditions. In a key passage in his *The Location of Culture* (1994), Homi Bhabha proposes that "the move away from the singularities of 'class' or 'gender' as primary conceptual and organizational categories, has resulted in an awareness of the subject positions—of race, gender, generation, institutional location, geopolitical locale, sexual orientation—that inhabit any claim to identity in the modern world."[14] This is an entirely flawed conception of those factors of class and gender, and perforce of subject positions—first presuming them to be formed as essential singularities alien to the vagaries of "the modern world," and thus indeed of his so-called "liminal" theorization to make them more aligned with such realities. No notion or reality of class, gender, or identity has ever been formed anywhere in the world within any national limitation or cultural singularity, immune to the always already transnational operations

---

14   See Homi K. Bhabha, *The Location of Culture* (London: Routledge, 1994), p. 2.

of labor, capital, and market. They have always been predicated on the active formation of transnational public and parapublic spheres that stand in no need of any manufactured "in-betweenness," which by definition manufactures two categorical and essentialized binaries. Bhabha first fetishizes hermetically sealed conceptions of nation, and then creates entirely superfluous "interstices" between them, and thinks he has thereby liberated these nations from inherent limitations to which they were never subject. Quite to the contrary: his mode of thinking and theorization has in fact entrapped them within a fictive boundary they have never honored. I know of not a single Iranian, Arab, or Turkish poet, novelist, dramatist, essayist, artist, or public intellectual who has ever thought, worked, and produced within the colonial boundaries of the nation that Bhabha thinks need "interstices" in which to live and breathe. On the basis of this false premise, Bhabha congratulates himself as follows:

> What is theoretically innovative, and politically crucial, is the need to think beyond narratives of originary and initial subjectivities and to focus on those moments or processes that are produced in the articulation of cultural differences. These "in-between" spaces provide the terrain for elaborating strategies of selfhood—singular or communal—that initiate new signs of identity, and innovative sites of collaboration, and contestation, in the act of defining the idea of society itself.[15]

There is no theoretical innovation here. It in fact reflects theoretical regression to disregard the factual evidence of the transnational disposition of the postcolonial nations, and then falsely seek to liberate them into the phantasmagoric abyss of postmodern interstices—a vacuous proposition that has no historical occasion to reason or articulate itself for the already

15 Ibid.

transnational public sphere within which nations have historically articulated their *raison d'être*. All the initial subjectivities have in fact been decidedly trans-originary, and those "cultural differences" and alterities are categorically embedded in their fluid identities. The "new signs of identity" that Bhabha seeks and thinks he has revealed are already evident in the active historical formation of the nation and the agential cosmopolitanism of its symbolic and allegorical registers; this is true of any nation, but particularly of those formed in the aftermath of the last three Muslim empires that extended from the Indian Ocean to the Mediterranean. But Bhabha seems entirely blinded to them, taking the frontier fictions of nations too seriously and thinking he has now managed to transgress them. Upon this crooked foundation, Bhabha then proceeds to build a sandcastle:

> It is in the emergence of the interstices—the overlap and displacement of domains of difference—that the intersubjective and collective experiences of nationness, community interest, or cultural value are negotiated. How are subjects formed "in-between," or in excess of, the sum of the "parts" of difference (usually intoned as race/class/gender, etc.)? How do strategies of representation or empowerment come to be formulated in the competing claims of communities where, despite shared histories of deprivation and discrimination, the exchange of values, meanings, and priorities may not always be collaborative and dialogical, but may be profoundly antagonistic, conflictual, and even incommensurable?[16]

Those "interstices" have no place in the formation of nations that have never lived in isolation, hermetically sealed within their fictive frontiers. Such ideas about nations are entirely ahistorical, ideological, and false. The "intersubjective ...

---

16 Ibid.

experiences of nationness" are historically there from their moment of inception, from the moment they take up arms against their colonizers and claim their independence; they are not a new theoretical discovery or recommendation to be made from the banks of the Charles River. Recommending them at this stage in postcolonial national histories is in fact the supreme sign of being blinded to their (always already) existence. "Strategies of representation or empowerment" have been definitive of national agency and integral to nations' shared memories, as even a passing familiarity with the history and sociology of nations would immediately reveal, and thus do not stand in need of the wheel being reinvented for them.

Palestinian and Indian Workers in Abadan

Let me give a very specific example of one instance of such "empowerment" from the history of Iran's labor unions. In mid July 2015, Mohammad Safavi, a leading Iranian labor activist, delivered a major paper, "The Project/Seasonal Workers Union Abadan, Iran, 1979–1980" at a conference on social justice at the University of Victoria in Victoria, Canada. He subsequently shared the text of his talk with me, and over three days he and I spoke in detail about his extraordinary experiences as a labor activist in both Iran and, later, Canada. Safavi's talk began with a short history of the construction of the Abadan Oil Refinery in 1912, which marked the commencement of a significant period in the history of Iranian labor activism against systematic repression by both the Pahlavi dynasty and the security apparatus of the Islamic Republic. What I found most remarkable in his report—a rare eyewitness account by a participant observer—was the fact that the first strike in the oil refinery was organized by Indian and Palestinian workers. This was not surprising to me at all for Abadan, like other major cities on the Persian Gulf, has always attracted migrant laborers from around the region, as it continues to do. Seasonal workers would be attracted to places like Abadan from all over Iran and the wider region, to the point that we should in fact disregard the notion of porous borderlines between nation-states, and instead think of a major urban cosmopolis like Abadan as a location magnetizing labor and social movements.

The presence of both foreign workers and foreign companies within Iranian borders translated their history of labor activism onto the larger regional scene. As foreign companies continued to grow in 1960s and 1970s, employing increasing numbers of workers in the region, so did labor activism. "In 1975," Mohammad Safavi reported in his paper,

> I was hired by the Iran–Japan Petrochemical Company at one of their construction sites in a remote area near the Port of Mahshahr in Khuzestan Province. The company provided poor-quality food and unsanitary shelters, and only for a portion of its employees. It paid wages that were only slightly above the minimum wage. The working conditions were horrendous and unsafe, and there were no fringe benefits. Last but not least, we were not allowed to have any kind of trade union.[17]

Just as transnational corporations are attracted to cities like Abadan, so are laborers from around the region, as anyone visiting a city like Doha today will tell you. Massive volumes of labor come to the area not just from around the Arab world, but from as far away as India, Malaysia, and the Philippines.

Labor activism, of course, has not been easy at any time,

---

17 All my citations are from the draft of the article Mohammad Safavi delivered on this occasion in Vancouver, "The Project/Seasonal Workers Union Abadan, Iran, 1979–1980" (July 2015), and kindly shared with me. The final draft of the essay is to appear in a volume edited by the host of the conference, Professor Peyman Vahabzadeh of Victoria University. I am grateful to both Mr. Safavi and Professor Vahabzadeh for their gracious friendship and collegiality.

and the shah's secret police closely monitored and prevented it. But under the revolutionary circumstances of 1977–79, it resumed in earnest. On August 19, 1978, according to Safavi, workers organized the first mass rally against the shah's regime in Abadan. This, he believes, was the first and the largest demonstration in Abadan following the 1953 CIA-backed coup d'état. Eventually, laid-off workers gathered and began to organize their activism. The first steps towards the formation of the union, according to Safavi, took place in two locations:

> in a casual gathering in a local teahouse and in front of the local office of the Ministry of Labor, where a group of desperate unemployed workers were gathering to demand a job. This campaign was followed by a large assembly of a group of labor activists and workers in the Petroleum College of Abadan, where they formed an ad hoc or temporary Steering Committee.

What, in effect, we are witness to at this point is the presence of laborers from across the country and the region doing precisely what Marx and Engels had anticipated in their *Communist Manifesto* (1848): "Workers of the world, unite!"

The emerging Islamic Republic was no friendlier to independent labor unions, and its militant vigilantes began attacking union organizers, who in turn remained as determined as ever: "Soon, almost 14,000 project/seasonal workers with various skills signed up for membership," Safavi reports. "These skilled workers were pipefitters, millwrights, boilermakers, welders, electricians, timekeepers, crane operators, maintenance men, plumbers, scaffolding workers, carpenters, mechanics, and ironworkers." The emerging union was keenly aware of non-Iranian models: "the steering committee produced a set of by-laws based on the Iranian oil workers' union experiences during the 1940s, as well as the labor laws of post-independence Algeria and post-revolutionary Nicaragua." Labor experiences from Nicaragua to Algeria, Palestine, and India were now brought to bear on a critical moment for the Iranian labor movement. This was decades before and half a world away from anyone at Harvard or elsewhere had thought of the "emergence of the interstices" or "strategies of representation or empowerment" on their behalf.

In his paper, Safavi notes in particular the significance of the presence or absence of women in these union mobilizations. "In the post–Reza Shah period," he points out,

> until the 1953 coup, the labor movement was at its highest peak in Iran, when women activists and family members were involved in organizing the labor movement in Abadan. In 1979 ... all the members of our union, including the Steering Committee, were men. The union did not play an active role in creating space for women labor activists and female seasonal workers. Also, it did not make any attempt to find out how many women, who worked as typists, secretaries, and administrators, lost their jobs after foreign companies left Iran.

The fact that, as a leading Iranian labor activist—now living in Canada as a baker, and having organized a union for the bakers in his city—Safavi is so gender conscious is a clear indication of the significant presence of women laborers, however unrepresented.

Safavi was equally explicit about the role of racialized minorities such as Arab Iranians in these labor movements. "A large number of the members," he noted,

> were Iranian Arab workers who were victims of discrimination by the state and by the oil company, and the majority of them were assigned unskilled jobs with the lowest wage and no benefits. The union did recognize the cultural identity of its Arab

members, and both Arabic and Persian were used in administrative communications. "Speeches, slogans, and poetry readings were delivered in both Persian and Arabic. On important occasions like May Day, union members performed plays and read revolutionary or motivational poems in Arabic and Persian."

All of these developments were brought to a crushing end by the time the security and intelligence apparatus of the ruling Islamic Republic managed to establish full control. "In September 1980," Safavi notes, "the short life of the union came to an end in a tragic way. The government used both the US Hostage Crisis of 1979–81 and the Iran–Iraq war of 1980–88 as pretexts to suppress and crush all of the unions and labor movements in Iran." But the hardship of workers coming from the four corners of the world to one city or another within multiple nation-states continues apace, marking the fact that it is not just they who cross porous borders, but the borders themselves that continue to cut across their daily existence.

Arash Kamangir

Through the active circulation of labor and capital, Iran has historically been incorporated into the larger world far away from the vacuous verbiage of useless theories, as Iranians have dwelled in the lived experiences and enabling mythologies of their national experiences and ancient mythologies. Arash Kamangir (Arash the Archer) is a towering figure in Iranian mythology. According to this myth, Arash was a hero in Manuchehr's army when he was engaged in battle with the Turanians and Afrasiyab. Surrounded by the enemy, Manuchehr sent Arash as an emissary to Afrasiyab, asking for a truce. In order to humiliate the Iranians, Afrasiyab suggested that one of Manouchehr's generals shoot an arrow as far as he could, and that where the arrow landed would be the border between Iran and Touran. No other general dared to accept the challenge, but Arash did. He put all his mortal power behind that arrow, and shot it as far as he could, but died instantly after he had done so. The arrow traveled from sunrise to sunset, until it landed on a walnut tree by the Amu Darya in Central Asia.[18]

The myth of Arash is one of the most potent metaphors of the Iranian imperial past. It reflects the territorial and dynastic registers of a bygone age, when heroes were made by sacrificial gestures that would expand the domain of royal domination for the Persian Empire. Based on pre-Islamic sources, the story of Arash the Archer appears only through a reference, and without any detail, in Ferdowsi's *Shahnameh* (composed 1000), while there are corroborating references to it in other sources, such as *Athar al-Baqiyeh*, by Abu Reyhan al-Biruni (973–1048). But the story assumed renewed significance during the Constitutional Revolution (1906–11), when Hasan Pirniya Moshir al-Dowleh (1871–1935) referred to it in his pioneering book *Tarikh Iran Bastan* ("History of Ancient Iran"), as did Ali Akbar Dehkhoda (1879–1956) in his multivolume Encyclopedia. From this point forward, Arash entered the active imagination of literate Iranians growing up early in the twentieth century, in the shadow of the rise of Iran as a nation-state from the ruins of its imperial past.

Soon after the CIA coup of 1953 and the return to power of the shah, the prominent Iranian scholar Ehsan Yarshater elaborated on the story of Arash in his popular *Dastanha-ye Iran-e Bastan* ("Stories from Ancient Iran," 1957). Numerous other retellings of the Arash story soon followed—in both poetic and dramatic narratives. But all of them pale in comparison to Seyavash Kasra'i's poem of that name (1958).[19] A

---

18   For more details on the figure of Arash, see the article under "Arash" in *Encyclopædia Iranica*.

19   Other poetic and dramatic versions include those produced by Arsalan Pourya (1959), Nader Ebrahimi (1963), Mehrdad Avesta (1965), and Bahram Beiza'i (1977).

prominent leftist poet, widely loved and admired, Seyavash Kasra'i recast the figure of Arash using a potently political diction. He effectively turned the mythic figure into the central hero of a revolutionary ballad, in which Arash becomes a self-sacrificing hero who finds inspiration from his people. The theme of this rendition is not so much territorial conquest, but the popular basis of heroism—informed deeply by transnational (Third World) socialist ideals. Kasra'i's Arash emerges from the rural areas of Iran, loves his homeland, is deeply rooted in his people's sufferings, celebrates their lives, and shares their pains. Arash's story is told here to young children by Amu Noruz, who is planting in their young minds a love of decency and a joy for life. He describes the land as desolate and bereft of kindness and love, full of fear and tyranny. Arash then rises from the deepest despairs of his people:

> Children upon the roof,
> Girls looking through small windows,
> Mothers sitting sadly by their doors—
> Eventually their whispers soared:
> Like a tumultuous sea
> People soared and arose in waves
> And just like a pearl out of a shell
> Produced a man from their bosoms:
> I am Arash!
> Thus Spoke the man with the enemy ...
> Don't ask of my lineage—
> For I am born of pain and hard work[20]

Kasra'i's "Arash the Archer" emerged from the deepest despairs and highest aspirations of a revolutionary age

---

20 The poem is available in the original Persian at adabiat.rozblog. com. This translation is mine.

Figure 6: Today numerous statues of Arash the Archer appear in various spots in Iran, in which the legendary hero is shooting his arrow towards unknown, unmarked, and open-ended targets. This particular statue is in Sa'd Abad Palace in Tehran.

deeply frustrated by the descent from the highest ideals of the Constitutional Revolution of 1906–11 to the CIA coup of 1953. In August of that year, Prime Minister Mohammad Mosaddegh was overthrown in a brutal coup engineered by the British and US intelligence services, because the widely popular Iranian statesman had nationalized Iranian oil, threatening British colonial and US imperial interests in the region. A Pahlavi loyalist, General Fazlollah Zahedi, became prime minister, facilitating the return to power of the runaway shah and the commencement of his repressive authoritarian regime. From August 1953 to June 1963, the shah ruled with an iron fist, emboldened by US support, which he reciprocated by turning Iran into a reliable military base for the maintenance of US interests in the region (to the extent of becoming a solid base for its military engagements in Vietnam), and a firm ally of Israel. Internally, the shah sought to preempt any revolutionary agitation by arranging his own "White Revolution," which combined land reform and Reza Shah–style social and economic changes. His notorious secret service, SAVAK, was now in full force, detecting and crushing any resistance to his tyranny.

The June 1963 uprising led by Ayatollah Khomeini was the most serious challenge to his authoritarian rule since he was ousted and reinstalled in 1953. The shah and his military and security apparatus crushed the uprising, forcing Khomeini into exile in Iraq. But soon an equally serious challenge emerged, in the form of urban and rural guerrilla uprisings, now championed by the Cherik-ha-ye Fada'i Khalq guerilla organization. Between 1963 and the rise of the revolutionary wave of late 1970s, it was Marxist revolutionaries like Bizhan Jazani and organizations like Fada'i Khalq that posed the most serious challenge to the Pahlavi regime; the militant Islamists led by Khomeini remained entirely marginal in this period. But the revolutionary zeal of Ali Shari'ati as the leading Islamist ideologue remained critical until the resurfacing of Ayatollah Khomeini, to snatch the revolution his own way. By September 1978, these earlier developments had evolved into much wider and more open rallies against the Pahlavi regime. The Marxist, Islamist, and anticolonial nationalist forces were widely present in these early uprisings. But soon Khomeini left Najaf for the Parisian suburb of Neauphle-le-Château, and increasingly assumed a leadership position in the uprising— a phenomenon that remained seriously contested even after he returned in February 1979 to Iran, where he awaited the hostage crisis of 1979–81 in order to violently establish his theocracy.

The Arash of Kasra'i was a *cherik*—a guerilla fighter. In the hands of a gifted poet, the image embedded in itself the summation of all the heroic deeds of selfless revolutionaries from around the world—men and women, young and old—committed to an idea and devoting their very life to achieve it. From the Palestinian Fedayeen to the Vietnamese Viet Minh, the Chinese revolutionaries, and the Latin American guerillas (with Castro and Che Guevara as their archetypes), they all came together to form the image of the Iranian *cheriks*, as best embodied in the of the Cherik-ha-ye Fada'i Khalq Organization. The origins of the Sazeman-e Cherik-ha-ye Fada'i Khalq Iran ("Guerilla Organization of Fedayeen of the Iranian People") go back to the crushing of the June 1963 uprising led by Ayatollah Khomeini. After the failure of this uprising, student groups began to organize themselves around critical figures from the Cuban, Algerian, Chinese, and Vietnamese revolutionary movements, reading their texts, discussing their strategies, and seeking to adapt them to the Iranian scene. These groups were Marxist in the general and diversified sense of the term. One of these groups, led by two legendary figures, Ali Akbar Safa'i Farahani and Hamid Ashraf, eventually formed the Cherik-ha-ye Fada'i Khalq organization. This organization decided to launch its first guerilla operation from the forests of Gilan, in northern Iran—most probably inspired by the actions of the Jangali Movement of 1914–21 and the Cuban Revolution of 1953–59, launched from the Sierra Maestra mountains. Although the Siyahkal uprising (February 8, 1971), as this incident would later be celebrated, encountered a catastrophic defeat, it marked the commencement of an armed struggle against the Pahlavi regime that continued until its downfall in February 1979, after which the organization split into two groups: the Majority that had sided with the Islamist faction, and the Minority that now continued its armed struggle against the ruling Islamist regime.

The reconstruction of Arash the Archer as a revolutionary, as best captured in Kasra'i's poem, placed a heroic age in the service of a critically thought through worldly idealism. Kasra'i creatively retrieved the mythic figure of Arash for his progressive ideals, so that when people looked at the towering statue of Arash shooting his arrow beyond Iran's borders it was no longer a sign or symbol of imperial conquest, but an imposing image of ordinary people placed within a worldly context beyond their fictive frontiers: laborers abused within a global capitalist system and in solidarity with their cohorts worldwide, women drawing inspiration from the struggle of their sisters around the world, students traveling far and wide to reimagine their homeland in expanding horizons. The world was now Arash's home beyond all and every border. His arrow carried a message not of separation and boundary, but of solidarity and camaraderie. Iran had been born, and now projected, beyond its borders.

CHAPTER 7

Where Is Homeland?

Where is homeland?
What do I miss?
I ask myself sometimes—
And who is the friend?
And whom do I miss?

Esmail Kho'i (2002)

The figure of Arash the Archer I invoked in the previous chapter points to the transnational universe—emotive and empirical, moral and material—opened to Iranian political and cultural history by the collapse of the Qajar dynasty early in the twentieth century, and to the constitutional discrediting of the ruling Islamic Republic as a legitimate state apparatus with a solid popular base early in the twenty-first. Soon after the Iranian Revolution of 1977–79, during the crucial decades that were the 1980s onwards, two opposite developments began to mark the elastic frontiers of Iran: (1) regnant and triumphalist Islamism took over inside Iran, seeking to destroy that cosmopolitan culture that had initially included, but categorically denied it exclusive legitimacy; while (2) the literary, visual, and performing arts (cinema in particular) became the embodiment of that effervescent culture, carrying it around the world. Leading Iranian filmmakers like Sohrab Shahid-Saless, Amir Naderi, Bahman Farmanara, Reza Allamah Zadeh, Parviz Sayyad, and eventually Bahram Beiza'i, and prominent artists like Sia Armajani, Manouchehr Yektai, Nikzad Nodjoumi, and Ardeshir Mohassess all left Iran and opted to live outside the censorial banality of the ruling regime, as did poets like Esmail Kho'i and Majid Naficy, dramatists like Arby Ovanessian and Mohammad Ghaffari, and soon afterwards the younger generation of musicians and composers like Mohsen Namjoo and Shahin Najafi, actors like Shohreh Aghdashloo and Golshifteh Farahani, leading human rights activists like Mehrangiz Kar, Akbar Ganji, and Hadi Ghaemi, Nobel Laureate Shirin Ebadi, and leading scholars of Persian culture and literature like Ehsan Yarshater, Jalal Khaleghi-Motlagh, Mahmoud Omidsalar, the most eminent novelists, including Shahrnoush Parsipour, Goli Taraghi, Moniru Ravanipour, Mahshid Amirshahi, and Shahryar Mandanipour, prominent theologians like Mohsen Kadivar and Hasan Yousefi Eshkevari, even leading "religious intellectuals" like Abdolkarim Soroush, who had rendered his services to the ruling regime and was now discarded, widely celebrated pop singers like the late Hayedeh, Daryush, Ebi, or Googoosh, among scores of others, all left Iran to live abroad. Other globally celebrated artists like Abbas Kiarostami, Bahman Qobadi, Asghar Farhadi, and Jafar Panahi (before his arrest and incarceration), beloved vocalists like Mohammad Reza Shajarian and Shahram Nazeri, and novelists like Mahmoud Dolatabadi, among scores of others, frequently travel in and out of Iran, defying their Islamist custodians the power or authority to confine them within any fictive frontier.

Meanwhile, a new generation of Iranian artists emerged and achieved global recognition entirely outside Iran, and yet firmly rooted in its cultural heritage. Artists like Shirin Neshat became the recognized names that they now are entirely outside the fictive frontiers of their homeland. But, even beyond those among the generation of Shirin Neshat, who were born inside Iran, we are now witnessing the emergence of globally celebrated filmmakers like Ramin Bahrani, who was born in Winston-Salem, North Carolina, to Iranian parents, but traveled back to Iran to make his first film, then leaving once again to extend that inaugural experience and rite of passage into far wider domains of filmic art in the United States with a firm root in Iranian cinema.

The mission of carrying the torch of an officially denied worldliness into the wider world thus passed from one generation to another within the lifespan of the Islamic Republic. In the crafting of that worldliness, the Islamists remain entirely helpless. In order to manufacture a semblance of democratic dissent, the ruling Islamists generated their own opposition in the form of what they continue to call "religious intellectuals," and thus tried to bring the dialectical force of contestation into their own domain. But the robust body of Iranian visual and performing arts denies that fake feud, staging Iranian cosmopolitan worldliness for the whole world to see. Kiarostami directs Mozart operas in Paris, shoots his feature films in Italy, exhibits his photographs in Paris, and teaches master classes in the United States. Amir Naderi moves from New York to Japan to continue producing his distinctive cinema. Mahmoud Dolatabadi's novels are published in German, French, English, Dutch, and other languages while still awaiting permission in Iran for their original Persian editions. Meanwhile, Dolatabadi's daughter, Sara Dolatabadi, who began her career as a conceptual artist in Tehran, has moved out to continue with her artwork in Morocco, Tokyo, Paris, and New York. Jafar Panahi is forbidden from filmmaking, and remains incarcerated inside Iran. But he made a film, called it *This Is Not a Film* (2011), hid its digital copy inside a cake, and sent it out of the country to be premiered at the Berlin Film Festival. Just like its center, the fictive frontiers of the Islamic Republic cannot hold. The nation, and those who actively imagine it, are all always already transnational.

How Did the Iranian Revolution Become Islamic?

Almost four decades into the violent and systematic over-Islamization of a multifaceted revolution through the decidedly over-politicized Islamism of a sectarian Shi'i clerical order, it is imperative to recall the process through which a vastly cosmopolitan social uprising was hijacked by one of its components at the expense of all the others. The propaganda machinery at the disposal of the ruling regime in Iran has sought consistently and systematically to Islamize this revolution, and with it the entire course of Iranian history. But this Islamization takes the form of the most deadening variety of what the ruling regime says it is opposing: it represents a profound self-colonization in terms developed during the long course of Eurocentric (Orientalist) knowledge-production.[1] As the ruling regime is busy regurgitating ideas of "Orientalism" and "Postcolonialism" to sustain its revolutionary credentials, it in fact exposes its categorical failure throughout nearly four decades to produce a single substantive idea of its own.[2] Its leading ideologues are in fact the gaudy consumers of aging ideas that are not their own, and are thus entirely oblivious to the emerging sites of knowledge-production furthest removed from the delusion of "the West," whose demons they continue to battle in a fake war that cross-authenticates their false claim to legitimacy.

---

1 I argue this point in detail in the introduction and conclusion of Hamid Dabashi, *Theology of Discontent: The Ideological Foundations of the Islamic Revolution in Iran* (New Brunswick, NJ: Transaction, 1993).

2 This is best represented by Mohammad Marandi, who writes regularly about "Orientalism," "postcolonialism," and "native informants," and so on, to discredit both the Green Movement and the Arab revolutions, as if he had coined these terms. The only reason that Marandi is noteworthy is that he is highly placed within the nomenklatura of the ruling regime. For an example of his writing, see Seyed Mohammad Marandi, "Iran, Orientalism and Western Illusions about Syria," Al Jazeera, April 6, 2014, aljazeera.com.

No accurate understanding of the Iranian Revolution of 1977–79 is possible beyond the thick clouds of the ruling regime generating one wave after another smoke screen without actively remembering the historical composition of forces at the commencement of that cataclysmic event. The Revolution was aggressively Islamized and Shi'ified from one end and nativized and domesticated from another—against the very grain of its revolutionary cosmopolitanism, far beyond the sectarian degeneration to which it was soon subjected. The broad spectrum of anti-imperialist energies—including opposition to the Vietnam War, the US Civil Rights movement, the Palestinian national liberation movement, and the liberation movements in Africa, Asia, and Latin America—was firmly ingrained in the revolutionary forces of the 1977–79 uprising. Islamist forces were just one these many strands.[3] Through a succession of carefully orchestrated maneuvers, Khomeini and his followers stole the Revolution in its entirety—and yet, its multifaceted character stuck in the narrow throat of the Islamic Republic, whose custodians could not completely swallow what they had bitten off. How exactly this catastrophic development took place is a key epistemic trope in reading contemporary realities far beyond the fictive frontiers of Iran itself.

Three critical dates are definitive of Iranian history in the twentieth century, and integral to the revolutionary disposition of the nation in the decades leading to the massive uprisings in the late 1970s: (1) The CIA-sponsored military coup of 1953 that toppled the government of Mohammad Mosaddegh; (2) the June 1963 uprising led by Ayatollah Khomeini against the Pahlavi monarchy; and (3) the Siyahkal guerrilla operation against the same monarchy organized by the People's Fadaee Guerrillas, near the town of Siyahkal in the Gilan region of

---

3   I have detailed this process in the final two chapters of my *Iran: A People Interrupted* (New York: New Press, 2007).

northern Iran on February 8, 1971. Each of these iconic dates marks a particular revolutionary ideology simultaneously shared by wide segments of Iranian society, with not a single one of them having an exclusive claim on the Iranian revolutionary disposition. The official historiography of Iran favored and promoted today by the ruling regime picks and chooses the Islamist components of Iranian political culture, cherry-picking the June 1963 uprising and blowing it out of proportion, just as the contesting anticolonial nationalist narrative opts to highlight the August 1953 coup against Mosaddegh as the defining moment of Iranian history. But the fact is that the establishment of the Tudeh Party in 1941, the subsequent rise of leading Marxist revolutionaries like Bizhan Jazani, and the incident at Siyahkal were equally integral to that revolutionary spirit—as indeed were the arrest, trial, and execution of two leading Marxist revolutionaries, Keramatollah Daneshian and Khosrow Golsorkhi, in February 1974.[4]

What Iranians of my generation affectionately refer to as the "Goethe Institute Poetry Nights" (October 10–19, 1977), staged at the Tehran office of the Goethe Institute, mark a particularly poignant turning point, when the revolutionary spirit of the age assumed a decidedly public form, triumphantly declaring its arrival. The Goethe Institute poetry event marked the commencement of the crucial 1977–79 period, when the momentum against the Pahlavi monarchy assumed increasingly revolutionary dimensions. In the making of that event, the Shi'i clerical establishment had not the slightest presence. It was the zenith of Iranian Marxist and anticolonial nationalist sentiments—a fact that decades of tyrannical rule by the Islamist fanaticism that now rules Iran has failed to eradicate. This event took place while Ayatollah Khomeini was still in

---

4   For a thorough study of the Tudeh Party and its central significance in Iranian history, see Ervand Abrahamian, *Iran Between Two Revolutions* (Princeton, NJ: Princeton University Press, 1982).

Najaf. Although he was intensely popular among his limited constituency, by no stretch of imagination was he the "leader" of the revolution; indeed, even within the Islamist camp the name, reputation, and ideas of Ali Shari'ati (all developed through interaction with Iranian and non-Iranian Marxists and anticolonial nationalists) was far more appealing to the younger generation than those of Khomeini. It would be about a year after these poetry nights that Khomeini would leave Iraq, first for Kuwait and subsequently for Paris, on October 3, 1978—from where he began to attract global attention.

One of the monumental mistakes of the late Mohammad Reza Shah that eventually cost him his throne was to put pressure on Saddam Hussein to expel Khomeini from Iraq. Once Khomeini could not find any place in the Arab or Muslim world to accept Hussein, he and his Islamist handlers opted for Neauphle-le-Château, a small village near Paris—a fateful choice that catapulted him onto the front pages of leading newspapers around the globe. It was this sudden global fame on Khomeini's part among leading newspapers and journalists —each with a very sketchy awareness of Iranian politics— that turned him into a household name as the "leader" of the Iranian revolution. By the time Michel Foucault became interested in the revolution—traveling to Iran, where his Islamist handlers carefully controlled his exposure to the Iranian scene, and he began to write articles for *Corriere della Sera*—it was not just the fate of the Pahlavi monarchy that was sealed, but, far more catastrophically, the end of the non-Islamist (Marxist and nationalist) forces of the revolution, which were quickly brushed aside. Foucault visited Iran first in September 1978, almost a year after the Goethe Institute's poetry nights, and just before Khomeini left France, and then visited Khomeini in his residence in Neauphle-le-Château. He then traveled once again to Iran, in November, by which time his visit with Khomeini had completely blinded him to the non-Islamist aspects of the revolution. Although the notion that Foucault was "seduced" by Khomeinism or Islamism is entirely ludicrous,[5] the fact is that his limited knowledge of Iranian social and intellectual history had weakened his critical antenna while he was being handled by Iranian Islamists in Paris and Tehran.

In July 1979 (more than four months after the carefully orchestrated and triumphant return of Khomeini to Tehran), I traveled to Tehran from Philadelphia, during what was the summer break from my graduate studies at the University of Pennsylvania. The spirit of the Goethe Institute, which marked the heterodox disposition of the revolution, was very much in the air. Among many other signs of this fact was the courage and imagination of Mostafa Rahimi, a leading public intellectual at the time, when he wrote and published his historic essay, "Why I Oppose an Islamic Republic" (Dey 25, 1357/January 15, 1979), in which his central argument was tempered by his support for Khomeini's leadership. The general environment was still very open, though increasingly dangerous. When the first draft of the proposed constitution was introduced in June 1979, it contained no reference to the notorious notion of *Velayat-e Faqih* ("Authority of the Jurisconsult"). Tehran University, among other places, became a significant site of debate about the articles of this draft. As a young graduate student spending my summer in Tehran at the time, I was a witness to these debates at Tehran University. It was also during this fateful July that a major revolutionary gathering at the Tehran University soccer stadium was viciously attacked by militant Islamists, led by a notorious woman thug named Zahra Khanom. I was present at this rally, and saw how Islamist thugs (all supporters of Khomeini), attacked the

---

5 As suggested by Janet Afary and Kevin B. Anderson in their *Foucault and the Iranian Revolution: Gender and the Seductions of Islamism* (Chicago, IL: University of Chicago Press, 2005).

gathering with knives and clubs, targeting foreign journalists in particular. It was soon after that rally that the stadium was occupied by militant Islamists and turned into a makeshift mosque for Friday sermons. The most potent political forum for Khomeini's followers, the site has remained firmly occupied to this day, like the rest of Tehran University.

It was towards the end of that fateful summer of 1977 that Khomeini became increasingly agitated and angry at the course of events, particularly on the site of Tehran University, where liberal, leftist, and progressive intellectuals were busy debating the terms of the original draft of the constitution circulated by Khomeini's supporters. Though actively present in the course of the revolution, neither the left nor the liberals had any organized platform offering an alternative constitution. All they could do was to take issue with what was being offered to them. Even these limited criticisms were not acceptable to Khomeini. "No Westernized intellectual," he famously said, "will write our constitution for us." It was precisely at this crucial point that he introduced the item of *Velayat-e Faqih* into the constitution, reneged on his promise to leave the political scene, opposed the formation of a constitutional assembly, ordered the gathering of an "assembly of experts" of his most loyal supporters, and prepared the final draft of a calamitous theocratic constitution that turned the whole of Iranian society into a Shi'i jurisdiction presided over by Shi'i jurists.

There were of course prominent Shi'i clerics, like Ayatollah Taleqani and Ayatollah Shariatmadari, who remained on the side of a more pluralistic reading of the revolution, and opposed Khomeini's increasingly despotic polemics. But their support paradoxically intensified the grip of the clerical class on the overall character of the revolution, which was becoming more "Islamic" by the day—whether through the efforts of Khomeini and his supporters, or those of its clerical dissidents.[6] All kinds of resistance and schisms took place because of pressure from Khomeini's camp. Liberal Islamists like Mehdi Bazargan initially sided with Khomeini's tyranny, only to oppose it later. The leadership of the Tudeh Party became entirely servile in the face of Khomeini's commands. The leading Marxist guerrilla movement, Cherik-ha-ye Fada'i, split into a Majority and a Minority; its Islamist counterpart, the Mujahidin-e Khalq organization, initially sided with Khomeini, before he turned against them and sought their destruction. But perhaps the most significant sign of societal resistance to his tyranny, on March 8, 1979, on the occasion of International Women's Day, was a landmark demonstration by Iranian women against mandatory veiling. From the October 1977 Goethe Institute poetry nights to Mostafa Rahimi's essay against the formation of an Islamic Republic in January 1978, the women's demonstrations of March 1979, and the widespread discussion of the constitutional draft in the summer of 1979, among many similar events, solid historical evidence can be adduced of a systemic and widespread movement of grassroots resistance to the brutish "Islamization" of the revolution by Khomeini and his followers.

By the end of the summer of 1979, Khomeini and his followers knew that they had to move fast to consolidate their power. The US hostage crisis, lasting from November 4, 1979 to January 20, 1981, for 444 days created a much-needed smoke screen that distracted the world's attention from the moves of Khomeini's camp to rapidly entrench their power and immediately eliminate familiar rivals, while pretending to fight distant foreign foes. Although the possibility of a repetition of the US-initiated military coup of 1953 was not

---

6   For a thorough study of left-liberal strands among religious revolutionaries in Iran, see Houchang Chehabi's classic study, *Iranian Politics and Religious Modernism: The Liberation Movement of Iran under the Shah and Khomeini* (Ithaca, NY: Cornell University Press, 1990).

entirely a fearful fantasy, Khomeini's insistence on bringing the runaway shah to Iran to face trial, and the US refusal to hand him over while he was receiving cancer treatment in New York, led to the capture of the US embassy and the incarceration of a US diplomats in Tehran—an utterly catastrophic event in the course of the revolution, plotted and executed by Khomeini's supporters primarily to destroy their domestic rivals—Marxist and nationalist revolutionaries—while pretending to battle the so-called "Great Satan." Decades later, some of the leading hostage-takers publicly regretted what they had done; but by now they had done their historic service to the cause of tyranny in Iran, and their regrets were entirely meaningless.

President Carter's failed mission to rescue the US hostages, Operation Eagle Claw, on April 24, 1980, only strengthened the Islamist revolutionaries' position, and hastened Carter's political demise. Ronald Reagan succeeded Carter as US president in January 1981, and presided over eight calamitous years in which the country shifted its center of gravity consistently to the right, forging a neoliberal conservatism, in collaboration with the UK premiership of Margaret Thatcher, that would wreak havoc around the world. But the result was exceptionally favorable to Khomeini and his associates. In the fall of 1980—well before the hostage crisis was brought to an end, in January 1981—Saddam Hussein invaded Iran, thus commencing a bloody eight-year conflict pitting Iran and Iraq against each other. The Iran–Iraq War was the result of a strategic US policy in the region in the aftermath of the fall of the shah. As soon as he came to office, President Reagan sought to establish two buffer zones around post-revolutionary Iran—one to the east and the other to the west. As the United States and its regional and European allies were encouraging and arming the Iraqi invasion of Iran in September 1980, Iran's western front radically limited the reach of its revolution, turning a sizable Arab population against it and thus, in effect, nativizing and "Persianizing" it. On the eastern front, the US–Saudi–Pakistani formation of the Taliban in Afghanistan raised the flag of Sunni Wahhabism, and thus instantly "Shi'ified" the very same revolution. The United States and its allies were thus instrumental in helping Khomeini turn the Iranian Revolution of 1977–79 into a nativist, sectarian, and thereby "Islamic" revolution. Khomeini and his lieutenants welcomed the opportunities offered by both fronts of conflict. The cosmopolitan revolution thus degenerated into a militant sectarian Shi'ism confined within Iran's borders.

The Iran–Iraq War was still raging when the Israelis invaded Lebanon in 1982, with the intention of forcing the PLO out of the country. The move emboldened the Shi'is of Lebanon, who now sought and received the active endorsement and support of Khomeini, who welcomed the opportunity, creating the Lebanese Hezbollah as an arm of the Iranian Revolution in the region.[7] Years later, when Bashar Assad succeeded his father Hafez Assad in 2000, the ruling regime in Iran enacted the same strategy by incorporating Syria into its sphere of influence. Even before that, the formation of Hamas in 1988—soon after the First Intifada, which followed yet another Israeli atrocity in Palestine—gave the ruling regime a further opportunity to advance its interests and soft power in the region. A line of so-called Muqawimah ("Resistance"), as it came to be called, was thus created that stretched from Tehran to Syria, Lebanon, and Palestine. The only consistent beneficiary of this strategic formation remained the ruling regime in Iran. Thus, Iran's fictive frontiers were once again extended beyond any colonial concoction, and the regime began to flex its muscles,

---

7 For a pioneering study of Hezbollah, see Augustus Richard Norton, *Hezbollah: A Short History* (Princeton, NJ: Princeton University Press, 2014).

though this time in terms that were decidedly inflected by its militant Islamism.

From the hostage crisis of 1979–81 to the Iran–Iraq War of 1980–88, the Salman Rushdie affair of 1989, Israel's 1982 invasion of Lebanon, and the rise of the Second Intifada in 1988, all the way to the US-led invasions of Afghanistan and Iraq in 2001 and 2003, respectively, the ruling regime in the Islamic Republic consolidated its power systematically, eliminating its domestic rivals and manufacturing a vast territory of soft power far beyond Iran's borders—from Afghanistan to Lebanon, from Syria to Yemen. Under the umbrella of these regional crises, the "religious intellectuals"—the intelligentsia supporting the ruling Islamists—helped with a succession of university purges, the so-called "Islamization" of the curriculum, and the systematic silencing of the opposition, consolidated through a series of cultural revolutions. The magnificent cosmopolitan revolution of 1977–79, which had drawn inspiration from the French and Russian revolutions and was launched in active solidarity with every liberation movement in Asia, Africa, and Latin America, thus decomposed into a pathologically sectarian theocracy dominated by the Shi'i clerical class, their lay "religious intellectuals," and a praetorian guard of militants—all presiding over a garrison state.

Over the last thirty years and more, the Islamic Republic has overseen the systematic destruction of a deep-rooted cosmopolitan culture in Iran, to its own increasingly sectarian advantage. The rich and diversified culture of the late Pahlavi period included the paradoxical seeds of its own revolutionary dismantling by forces deeply rooted in progressive ideas whose origins extended from the Indian subcontinent to Europe, from Africa to Latin America. The revolution of 1977–79 was not pitched against that cosmopolitan culture; it was the very result of it. Leading Iranian artists, filmmakers, poets, literati, revolutionaries, and intellectuals worked with and through such Pahlavi-initiated institutions as the Ministry of Culture (under Pahlbod), National Television (under Reza Qotbi), and the Kanun-e Parvaresh-e Fekri Kudakan va Nojavanan (Center for the Intellectual Development of Children and Young Adults—under Leili Amir Arjomand). These leading artists and literati were in fact the key figures in preparing the course of the revolution, and in large part anticipated and supported it. Entirely against its own dynastic interests, the Pahlavi monarchy facilitated the formation of these cultural institutions, the open-ended revolutionary implications of which were not under the control of the ruling regime. The Islamic Republic has now categorically destroyed that culture, rewritten Iranian history in its own interests, and systemati-cally expanded its sphere of influence into the wider region.

The success of the revolution was thus due partly to the revolutionary, progressive, and emancipatory disposition of this rich and diversified culture. The militant Islamist takeover of this revolution (the cause of which is rooted in postcolonial Iranian history itself) must never be confused with its successful preparatory stages.[8] What the Islamic Republic systematically and consistently did was not to bring religion into the public sphere but, on the contrary, to force a robust and diversified public sphere that included religion into a Shi'i juridical straitjacket, so that Iranians categori-cally ceased to be citizens of a potentially free and democratic republic, and became exclusively subjects of the machinery of a clerical judiciary.[9] Leading ideologues of the revolution—Ali

---

8 The best study of this militant takeover is offered Said Amir Arjomand, *The Turban for the Crown: The Islamic Revolution in Iran* (Oxford: Oxford University Press, 1989).

9 The mechanism of this systematic appropriation and occupation of the public sphere by a violent Shi'i juridical takeover is very different from the terms of engagement in the European debate about "religion and the public sphere." For a pioneering essay in this area, see Jürgen Habermas,

Shari'ati, Morteza Motahhari, Jalal Al-e-Ahmad, Ayatollah Khomeini—were part of that public sphere, and thus limited and multi-significatory among their respective audiences. Violently determined in the destruction of their opposition and the total occupation of the public sphere and public discourse, the Islamists appropriated all of these thinkers into a singular narrative. Their favored religious intellectual (before he was dispensed with), Abdolkarim Soroush—the most prolific "religious intellectual" of his generation—then upped the ante, furnishing them with a teleological determinism, and putting the seal of his singular signature upon them all.

Against the grain of this militant ideological project, the catalytic touchstone of "Iran and the West," like that of "Islam and the West," has finally exhausted itself. The ruling regime in Iran is itself the product of one crisis after another, and continues to thrive on regional turmoil. It has long since lost any emotive, epistemic, or historical legitimacy—except in the form of the manufactured loyalties it generates and sustains from the depths of a depleted Shi'i martyrology. The Islamic Republic (of Iran) is as flawed a proposition as the Jewish democracy (of Israel). The two are at each other's throats precisely because they are the ideological replicas of each other. The Islamic republic is a theocracy, diluted by vacuous gestures towards democratic institutions—in effect ruled by octogenarian clerics who behave like the aging fraternity brothers of a discredited college. It is a clerical regime, taking its turn after the monarchy it supplanted, and its claim upon the totality of Iranian worldly culture is as spurious as was that of the Pahlavis. To protect its interests, it continues to produce knowledge against "the West"—against the mummy of a dead interlocutor that no longer exists except in the perturbed imagination of delusional ideologues who strain to

"Religion in the Public Sphere," *European Journal of Philosophy* 14: 1 (2006), pp. 1–25.

corroborate it to their east and west. Its leading ideologues are cannibalizing one mode of knowledge-production or another, in all of which they are secondhand consumers like everyone else. The world has long since become decentered. Places like Africa, Asia, and Latin America are the emerging locations for the production of new knowledge, about which the ruling regime of the Islamic Republic—from its nomenklatura to its apparatchiks—has no clue. Meanwhile, its so-called "opposition," cast in its own image, is drawn increasingly towards neoliberalism, its members banking on short prison terms in Iran, from which they hope to emerge in a position to put their talents at the service of US think tanks and lucrative endowments for the promotion of "democracy Gangnam Style."[10]

Iran at Large

The militant over-Islamization of the Iranian Revolution of 1977–79 paradoxically gave its cosmopolitan culture even greater global reach. The more the clerical regime resorted to ferocious violence in mobilizing its militant forces, militarizing its constituency, and seeking to silence or dismiss a multifaceted Iranian culture (the very result of its historical experiences), the more the country's underground and extraterritorial domains expanded in decidedly worldly and freshly cosmopolitan terms. The world has changed significantly since the revolution, in both material and imaginative ways, and so has the nature and disposition of Iranian cosmopolitanism. As the ruling regime has sought to sink Iran into the depths of its scholastic juridicalism, the world has lifted it into a far fuller recognition of its worldly potentials. As the governing institutions of the ruling Islamists took over the state apparatus and began the massive propaganda project of turning a multi-

---

10 For an explanation of "Democracy Gangnam Style," see my essay, "Tunisia versus Gangnam-Style Democracy, *Alaraby Aljadeed*, November 24, 2014.

faceted and pluralist uprising into an "Islamic revolution," the spirit of that suppressed cosmopolitanism went just one level underground within Iran, becoming the stuff of private discourse in the home, as it went beyond fictive frontiers and began to thrive in fresher and healthier environments. Denied permission to speak Persian, Iranian cosmopolitanism started to speak Arabic, Dutch, English, French, German, Japanese, Kurdish, Spanish, Turkish, and so on. The more multilingual Iranian cosmopolitanism became within and beyond its fictive frontiers, the more isolated and belligerent the ruling regime became—forging militant alliances across its borders by abusing the legitimate cause of the Palestinians or the Lebanese, just as it exacerbated the corruption of the sectarian regimes ruling Iraq and Syria.

Here we have to make a clear distinction between the healthy body of the robust communities of Iranians living throughout the world, giving birth anew to their worldly culture, and the corrupt, useless, and even treacherous "opposition" that brazenly sides with the United States and Israel, calling for crippling economic sanctions and even military strikes against their own homeland. Governments including those of Saudi Arabia and Israel, as well as institutions like the US-based National Endowment for Democracy, began funding these treacherous expatriates, while the US State Department provided multimillion-dollar grants for these runaway agents to establish websites, publish nonsense, and waste American taxpayers' money on a phantasmagoric project of "regime change." Human rights organizations, BBC Persian, and a whole panoply of tasteless but colorful Persian sites in Europe and the US popped up to map out the US/Israeli/Saudi soft power standing in opposition to the ruling regime in Iran, but in effect strengthened it. This "opposition" is cut from the same cloth as the regime it opposes: ideologically sectarian, politically nativist, intellectually and morally bankrupt, and violently insular in their politics. A deeply rooted hatred of Islam and Muslims began to inform their limited notion of being "secular," and thus they began to forge alliances with the most pestiferous neo-Nazi forces in Europe. They thus transformed their frustrations with an Islamic Republic they could not dismantle into an Islamophobic animus against Muslim immigrants and refugees in Europe. Their unseemly presence was and remains pitiful, and—unless used by the US or Israel and their allies for their own projects—entirely irrelevant.

Independently of this corrupt opposition, how can one measure the health of Iranian culture around the world except through their artists, scholars, literati, filmmakers, and poets? Filmmakers like Amir Naderi, Bahram Beiza'i, Parviz Sayyad, Reza Allameh-zadeh, and Ramin Bahrani; artists like Sia Armajani, Manouchehr Yektai, Hossein Zendehroudi, Nikzad Nodjoumi, Ardeshir Mohassess, and Shirin Neshat; scholars like Jalal Khaleghi-Motlaq and Mahmoud Omidsalar; poets like Esmail Kho'i and Majid Naficy—the list is endless, descending from one generation to the next. The more exclusionary and tyrannical the Iranian state becomes within its fictive frontiers, the more people leave Iran (in body or soul) to carry their homeland into the farthest corners of the globe. The custodians of the Islamic Republic are left entirely clueless as to what to do and where to draw the line—which websites to hack, which artists to ban, which scholars to ignore, which outspoken intellectuals to arrest and incarcerate.

This culture of defiance can be seen at work in a famous poem by Esmail Kho'i, "Vatan Kojast?" ("Where Is Homeland?", 2002). Kho'i, born in Mashhad in 1938, is one of the last remaining monumental figures of New Persian Poetry, a movement that began with Nima Yushij in the 1930s and, for at least half a century, remained definitive of Iranian revolutionary culture. Figures like Nima Yushij, Ahmad Shamlou, Forough Farrokhzad, Mehdi Akhavan Sales, Sohrab Sepehri, and Esmail Kho'i were much more than pioneering poets operating in a revolutionary register; they were the cultural icons of a nation defying its status quo, and articulating its vivid dreams of a liberated future. That liberation was conceived not only in political terms: it was iconoclastic, cosmic, universal, open-ended, and above all poetic. It had in fact begun with Nima's liberation of Persian poetic diction from its classical prosody, and continued apace in social, cultural, aesthetic, erotic, and then political terms. Esmail Kho'i emerged as a major national voice within this movement in the 1950s. Until he left Iran to live in the UK (following the execution in 1981 of his close friend Said Soltanpour—another major poet of this period), he had established himself as a major poetic voice, with a penchant for a lucid fusion of lyrical, erotic, philosophical, and political sensibilities. Today his poetry continues that alchemical mixture, though colored with a bitter and angry politics of defiance, and at times despair, that is kept at bay only through the force of his uncompromisingly elegiac gentility.

Kho'i's poem begins with a simple question of where exactly "homeland" is to be found, and who and what it is that one misses when not there.[11] But the poetic voice suddenly turns sour, addressing some comrades in Iran and wondering, since it was initially they who had insisted he leave their mutual homeland, why they are now admonishing him bitterly for not being in Iran. Why are they admonishing him? Are they simply stupid, or are they being sycophantic towards the ruling regime? He has taken nothing from Iran, and his suitcase has nothing in it except his books and music:

---

11   Esmail Kho'i, "Vatan Kojast?" ("Where Is Homeland?"), October 2002. Available online, in Persian, at akhbar-rooz.com. All cited passages are my own translations.

... and thus did I save
The cloud of my life
And my cloudy soul
From the hellish breathing
Of that dragon—
Having entrusted it to the clouds of the world
And left
So that in a nameless pond
I extend your ocean.

Then, referring to a poem by Ahmad Shamlou in which he had said that his "light burns in that house" (i.e. he prefers to live in Iran after having lived abroad for a while), Kho'i adds, even more bitterly:

You graciously say your lantern burns in that house—
Well, may it burn and be full of light
Forever and then more—
Your lantern and your eyes, sir!
But so what?
God Almighty, what is that supposed to mean?
What are you talking about?
And to whom are you talking?
Where and why do you think my little lamp burns?

What this poem of Kho'i's—and particularly that very last bitter and sarcastic line of this stanza—ultimately does, composed and published in Persian while he was living in Europe, is to bridge any presumed gap between home and abroad. The instant the poem is published (particularly on the Internet), it becomes integral to an abiding poetic provenance that has already transgressed the fictive frontiers between Iran and not-Iran. It is precisely that factual border-crossing beyond any frontier fiction that the fate of Mahmoud Dolatabadi's novel *The Colonel* (1979–2009) best represents. It exemplifies the nature and condition of cultural production where alternative narratives of the revolution and its aftermath have been successfully wrested from the ruling regime and staged on the global scene. Born in 1940, and arguably the most eminent novelist of his generation, Dolatabadi emerged as a towering figure in Persian fiction in the 1960s, carrying the mantle of his eminent predecessors Sadeq Hedayat, Sadegh Chubak, and Ebrahim Golestan into the next generation. His monumental epic *Kelidar*, published in ten volumes between 1978 and 1984, established him as the most widely celebrated and translated novelist of his age. Soon after the militant Islamization of the Iranian Revolution, he began working on a novel called *Zaval Kolonel* ("The Demise of the Colonel"), on which he worked for almost three decades. When he was ready to publish it, the Islamic Republic refused to give him permission. So, beginning in 2009, he allowed translations of it to appear in German, Dutch, Hebrew, English, and other languages. *The Colonel* is the story of an officer in the Pahlavi army whose five children join various factions in the immediate aftermath of the Iranian Revolution. The novel in effect becomes a potent counter-narrative to the official story of the revolution as propagated by the ruling regime. With a single novel, Dolatabadi thus managed to undermine the authority of the official account of the 1977–79 revolution. The irony of the story, indicative of the fictive frontiers that this work of fiction had transgressed, is the publication of a Persian translation of the German translation of the original Persian—much to the chagrin and anger of the author.[12]

---

12 For an English translation of this novel, see Mahmoud Dolatabadi, *The Colonel: A Novel* (Brooklyn, NY: Melville House, 2012). For an insightful review, see Larry Rohter, "An Iranian Storyteller's Personal Revolution," *New York Times*, July 1, 2012.

If the two towering figures of Esmail Kho'i and Mahmoud Dolatabadi come together to negate and defy the exclusionary claim of the ruling regime on the 1977–79 revolution, one from inside and the other from outside of that frontier fiction, the rise of a young artist like Ramin Bahrani as a globally celebrated filmmaker points to the even more potent extension of Iranian culture into uncharted territories. Born in 1975, Bahrani was raised in Winston-Salem, North Carolina, by Iranian parents. He attended Columbia University in New York (where he studied with me, and we quickly became very close friends), and it was here that he was smitten by the combined seductions of Iranian and world cinema. Soon after his graduation from Columbia, Bahrani traveled to Iran to make his first feature film, *Strangers* (2000). This film was screened in a few international film festivals, and the process of making it forever cured him of any false of falsifying nostalgia for his parental homeland. Bahrani at this point discovered ways in which his Iranian origins, North American habitat, and global thinking and vision came harmoniously and creatively together, to inform his singular cinematic signature.

It was in his second feature film, *Man Push Cart* (2005)— shot and set in post-9/11 New York, premiered at the Venice Film Festival, and later screened at the Sundance Film Festival—that Bahrani was born as a filmmaker beyond any fictive border, solidly rooted in the combined panorama of world, Iranian, and American cinemas. *Man Push Cart* took Bahrani to about a dozen film festivals around the world. His next feature, *Chop Shop* (2007), premiered at the Director's Fortnight of the Cannes International Film Festival, and traveled from there to a number of other major film festivals before it was released commercially to widespread critical acclaim. With *Goodbye Solo* (2008), *Plastic Bag* (2010), *At Any Price* (2013), and *99 Homes* (2014), Bahrani emerged as one of the most gifted filmmakers of his generation. Before his untimely death, the legendary American film critic Roger Ebert declared Ramin Bahrani "the New Great American Director."[13]

What is the emotive and aesthetic location of Ramin Bahrani as a filmmaker? Is he an Iranian or an American filmmaker? The question and the binary it presupposes instantly collapse once we realize that, as a filmmaker, he is the product of the worldly cosmopolitan culture of New York City, which is as far removed from Winston-Salem, North Carolina, where he was born and raised, as it is from Kazerun in Iran, where his father was born. Two world-class filmmakers, Amir Naderi from Iran and Werner Herzog from Germany, are Ramin Bahrani's closest friends, collaborators, and interlocutors, both of whom he has worked with throughout his career. When you get close to his cinema, you see within it the presence of the towering figures of Russian novelist Fyodor Dostoyevsky, American playwright Arthur Miller, French author Albert Camus, Iranian filmmaker Abbas Kiarostami, and scores of other world-class filmmakers from every continent on the planet. All of these could have happened in Tehran, but they happen to have come together in New York City. Bahrani is a close friend and cohort of the gifted Indian author Aravind Adiga, with whom he met when they were both students at Columbia. Adiga's magnificent first novel, *White Tiger* (2008), is dedicated to Ramin Bahrani.

Bahrani is neither a nativist Iranian nor a hyphenated American. He is a world-class filmmaker by virtue of the worldly disposition of his cinematic vision, learned and culti- vated in a major cosmopolitan city that happened to be New York, but could have been Paris, Istanbul, Cairo, Tehran, or Delhi. In this regard he is as much Iranian as Sohrab Shahid- Saless and Amir Naderi are Iranian, as much American, European, Asian, Latin American, or African as the traces of

13 For details, see Roger Ebert, "The New Great American Director," March 22, 2009, at rogerebert.com.

filmmakers, novelists, or poets from any one of these parts of the world have influenced his vision and have a presence in his cinema. To the degree that he is an Iranian, everything that Iranian cinema and literature and culture have invested in him are sublated into his cinema—a fact as true of him in New York as it has been of Sohrab Shahid-Saless in Tehran, Berlin, or Chicago. His cinema is not "accented" in the way that would be understood by a self-conscious exilic scholar watching his work. Quite to the contrary: it is one among a myriad of other measures of his singular vision of the world, rendered with audacity and authority. Ramin Bahrani did not cross any fictive borders to become what he is. He exposed them as already porous.

Cosmopolitanism Redux

Upon its pacification of the internal scene, the Islamic Republic soon began painting the region in its own image, radically Islamizing the healthy, robust, multidimensional, and transnational revolution it had kidnapped through a dispensing of sectarianism around the region. In this achievement of Ayatollah Khomeini and his followers, the Reagan administration's wish (aided and abetted by its European and regional allies) to curtail the wide-ranging appeal that the Iranian Revolution of 1977–79 had generated in the region was instrumental. Like Indian independence from British colonialism in 1947 degenerated into a Hindu–Muslim divide, resulting in the formation of an Islamic Republic in Pakistan, and like the creation of the Jewish state of Israel in 1948, the emergence of the Islamic Republic violently manufactured another form of religious fanaticism—this time founded on the emphatically sectarian banner of Shi'ism. "It was only in the aftermath of Iran's Islamic Revolution," leading Arab thinker Azmi Bishara wrote, "that these groups within the Arab countries began to join political formations based along sectarian lines, a phenomenon that reached its apex over the past fifteen years."[14] The historical fact of the moment is that it is too late for pre-colonial Islamic cosmopolitanism to generate any form of societal organicity, because European colonialism (in both moral and material terms) has forever robbed these post-Ottoman nation-states of their worldly cultures, at the same time transforming Islam into an irretrievably juridicalized ideology. The only possible cosmopolitanism, far removed from this pathetic sectarianism, is evident and possible through the postnational retrieval of the worldly cultures that exist now and with contemporary forces but with historical references to pre-modern imperial domains.

Conceiving of Iran, or any other nation-state, beyond its fictive frontiers, deep into the wider domain of its moral and imaginative habitat, so as to enable critical thinking and progressive ideas, must be distinguished from what today passes for "cosmopolitanism"—an entirely Eurocentric project, worthy and admirable perhaps in its stated intentions, but entirely irrelevant when it comes to the multiple worlds at large it categorically conceals in an endless articulation of itself. From Immanuel Kant to Martha Nussbaum, Jeremy Waldron to David Held, Jürgen Habermas to Jacques Derrida—the prolonged articulation of "cosmopolitanism" thrives on and regurgitates the terms of its own epistemic origins, producing a world that is the figment of its own imagination and categorically denies not just other but in fact alternative worlds. When non-European philosophers like Kwame Anthony Appiah and Seyla Benhabib[15] turn to the subject, they too address it from within the Kantian tradition—a perfectly legitimate

---

14　See Azmi Bishara, "Iran and the sick man of the Middle East," *Alaraby Aljadeed*, January 8, 2015.

15　See Kwame Anthony Appiah, *Cosmopolitanism: Ethics in a World of Strangers* (New York: W. W. Norton, 2007), and Seyla Benhabib, *Another Cosmopolitanism* (Oxford: Oxford University Press, 2008).

and worthy project for the European world, but through false self-universalization concealing the equally compelling worlds outside the moral and material imagination of "the West." For Appiah, "cosmopolitanism" is the global acceptance of the European world; for Benhabib, it is the incorporation of that world into the European moral universe. What they both miss is the fact of a different set of multiple cosmopolitanisms (in plural) around the world, encompassing but not limited to "the West."

Noting precisely this problem, David Miller has wondered if the link between the Stoics and the ideological foregrounding of the Roman Empire means that "cosmopolitanism [has] implications for worldly politics, and might [be] said always to lend support to (benign) forms of imperialism."[16] It is, of course, quite generous to pause for a moment and offer the world the possibility of a "benign imperialism." But, alas, in the muddy world of reality there is no such creature as "benign imperialism." Imperialism is based and predicated on dirt, blood, theft, abuse, and terror; and then, to camouflage it, leading philosophers of imperial centers might offer cosmopolitan ideas, and consider this "benign imperialism." Noting this trouble spot, Miller wishes to make a distinction "between moral and political versions of cosmopolitanism." While his "moral cosmopolitanism ... says simply that human beings are all subject to the same set of moral formulations ... political cosmopolitanism says that this can be achieved only if everyone is ultimately subject to the same authority with the power to enforce the laws."[17]

The authority with the power to enforce the law is the same authority that defies any law of decency, invading and occupying Afghanistan and Iraq, as it sends arms to Israel to steal

---

16 Garrett Wallace Brown and David Held, eds., *Cosmopolitanism Reader* (London: Polity, 2010), p. 377.

17 Ibid.

more of Palestine, and authorizes the philosophers and theorists of Eurocentric cosmopolitanism. And who exactly has the "power to enforce" any justice for such violent behaviors? These philosophers and theorists of Eurocentric cosmopolitanism seem to live on another planet; their ideas are thus predicated on entirely futile and imaginary bifurcations, and have scarcely anything to do with reality on this earth—either the ugly reality we live where the same nations that rule the world offer it cosmopolitan ideals, or the mobilizing reality that alternative worlds must emerge from the lived experiences of nations and not legislated for them from an epistemic position of power. The body of literature on cosmopolitanism that David Miller and his colleagues and predecessors represent is almost without exception a product of European and American imperial knowledge-production—liberal, open-minded, and benevolent knowledge-production, to be sure, but imperial nonetheless. That imperial knowledge-production manufactures drones and devises software to spy on people around the globe within the same epistemic power matrix that produces a nice, generous, kind, and lovely cosmopolitanism of the sort that they see as the "benign imperialist" kind—articulated by thinkers from Kant to Miller, and everyone else in between.

The issue we face is not how generous, open-minded, and benevolent might be this body of cosmopolitan knowledge they have produced, for which the world at large is undoubtedly richer. The issue is the alternative modes of worlds (both evident and possible), and the knowledge that a consciousness of such worlds can produce. Scholars like Boaventura de Sousa Santos have gone so far as to suggest the necessity of unearthing what they call "epistemologies of the South," by way of (1) deconstructing the Eurocentric roots of colonized thinking, and (2) reconstructing non-European philosophical legacies interrupted by colonialism.[18] But alternative epistemologies do

18 See Boaventura de Sousa Santos, "Public Sphere and Epistemo-

not reside in the south of any map whose northern elements rule the globe and abuse the planet and beyond. What enables pathbreaking thinking is not any particular location or reliance on any retrieved "epistemology of the South," but the material, moral, and imaginative location on a site outside the domain and under the radar of the dominant will to power, and thus the ability to sever the link between the knowledge that is useful and the reigning power that it serves.[19] The task is to discover and articulate an epistemic domain responsive to a traumatic history that produces knowledge to resist power and its varied manners of knowledge-production, and not to will it.[20] The locations of knowledge implicated by the will to resist power lie outside the purview of self-centering sites of knowledge-production that seek to rule and know the world at one and the same time. What that mode of thinking enables and discovers are new worlds, and how to be worldly in them. It draws new maps of and for a defiant will to change the world beyond its fictive frontiers and across from its current collapse into its ruling elites anywhere and its suffering masses everywhere.

In the production of this knowledge we need not fathom any "epistemologies of the South," but should seek the categorical collapse of the south and north of any dominant geography that produces either Eurocentric cosmopolitanism or Europhobic antagonism towards that cosmopolitanism. Realizing, knowing, articulating the existing worlds and their cosmopolitanism long before "the West" emerged as the *absolute metaphor* of our current history is the preparatory stage

---

logies of the South," *Africa Development* XXXVII: 1 (2012), pp. 43–67.

19 I have explored this mode of knowledge-production in some detail in relation between knowledge and trauma (instead of knowledge and power). See Hamid Dabashi, "From Guerrero to Gaza: Changing the Location of Knowledge," *Alaraby Aljadeed*, December 29, 2014.

20 Ibid.

for coming to understand multiple worlds that are capable of emerging in the aftermath of that absolute metaphor—not the anti-Western but the post-Western world. Those multiple worlds will emerge from the fragments and ruins of the world we have inherited, and certainly not from the defiant South of the existing dominant North—both of which are cross-essentialized as categorically as "the West and the Rest."

In destabilizing the stubborn residues of Eurocentricism, even (or particularly) among the most critical thinkers of our time, we need actively and persistently to retrieve the repressed, denied, or forgotten cosmopolitan worldliness of other worlds—from Asia to Africa to Latin America—all actively hidden deep beneath the violently domesticated master trope of "the West." Even a keenly critical thinker and literary critic like Pascale Casanova proposes that there was something particular about Paris that motivated Sadeq Hedayat to choose it as the site of his tragic suicide, and thus fails to see that a far wider geography—extending over his lifetime from Paris to Istanbul, Cairo, Tehran, Delhi, and Mumbai—embraced and enabled his short but intensely creative life.[21] The principal idea I have put forward in this book suggests that, when Hedayat moved east to Mumbai or west to Paris, the cosmopolitan universe of Tehran was already with him. Even without moving physically to Mumbai or Paris, both of these cosmopolitan settings were already embedded in his imaginative geography of Tehran, informing the emotive universe of his fiction.

As the master trope of our time, "the West" imprisons the captive imagination of those who use or abuse it by virtue of

---

21   See Pascale Casanova, *The World Republic of Letters* (Cambridge, MA: Harvard University Press, 2007), p. 239. For a cogent critique of Casanova and other world literature theorists, see the excellent doctoral dissertation of Amir Vafa, "Rethinking World Literature from *Moby Dick* to *Missing Soluch*" (University of Sheffield, 2014).

two competing and contradictory forces: one that insists and the other that resists it. "Islam and the West" pits European and Americans and Muslims against each other, and against the actual evidence of their lived experiences and effective histories. Muslims are already deeply inside Europe, alerting it to its own non-Christian aspects, just as Europe has been deeply embedded in the colonial underpinnings of the Muslim (and all other) worlds. Muslims do not live on the Moon, nor Europeans on Mars. They are both integral to the intertwined geographies of this one and only (and so far as we can tell lonely) planet. It is precisely on this planet that the integral calculus of colonial and imperial experiences of "the East and the West" is made to look like two genuses of humanity by the corrupting metaphor pitting "the West" against "the Rest."

Where is homeland? It is the epicenter of any and all emerging worlds that recasts the current geography of domination of one people over others. If one's home and habitat, where one was born and raised, is to have invested a person with an emotive universe of principled loyalty to some abiding ideas, then that homeland drives across borders and dismantles any disabling notion of exile. Once we expand the inviting horizons of any homeland towards its neighboring climes, *alterity* replaces *identity* as the site of consciousness—and upon that site a different mode of self-knowledge soon announces itself.

CHAPTER **8**

Geographical Indeterminacy

Why? Because you are born in Asia—and as they say:
Subject to geographical tyranny
Thus you are a vagabond—and all you have
For breakfast are just cigarettes and tea.

Mohsen Namjoo (2008)

In Chapter 7 I cited a range of artistic and cultural indices of border-crossings that have exponentially expanded and enriched the transnational public sphere within which Iranian cosmopolitanism now flourishes. As Iranians outside the fictive frontiers of their homeland carried their signature worldliness all over the globe, those living inside those frontiers staged the most spectacular social uprising of their history, in a direct line of descent from similar uprisings, from the Constitutional Revolution of 1906–11 to the Iranian Revolution of 1977–79.

As I mentioned in Chapter 4, when the Green Movement started in Iran, during the summer of 2009, in a number of essays and interviews in Persian reflecting on the political culture embedded in the uprising, I began to use the Persian expression *Jahanshahri* for "cosmopolitanism." The Persian term was not new, having a long and deeply rooted pedigree in Iranian political thinking. Soon after this series of articles I published a second component of the argument, in which I proposed the notion of *Iranshahri*, which, if the essay had been in English, would been rendered as "Persopolis." By *Iranshahri*/Persopolis, I meant the formation of a collective cultural memory cutting across ethnicized politics of identity, and incorporating generations of national resistance to domestic tyranny and foreign domination; by *Jahanshahri/* cosmopolitanism, I meant to signify the multidimensional and transregional culture that was irreducible to Islamism, socialism, or nationalism—the three ideological registers of anticolonial modernity. I then expanded the combination of these ideas into the central argument of my reading of the Green Movement, which appeared in my book on the social uprisings, *Iran, the Green Movement, and the USA: The Fox and the Paradox* (2010).[1] What I had identified as the reciprocal dynamics of *Jahanshahri* and *Iranshahri* was the dialectics of reciprocity through which Iranians had generated a shared memory beyond any ethnicized identity formation, reclaiming an imperial history for a postcolonial nation-state within the more global terms of a transnational encounter with the wider world.

In this final chapter I wish to expand on these ideas and interpret the consequences of the Green Movement of 2009 together with the dynamics of the Arab revolutions of 2011, demonstrating how these two complementary events brought that repressed and denied cosmopolitan culture back into the public sphere with unparalleled political potency, and in such a resounding way that the Islamic Republic will never recover from its aftershocks. The Green Movement and the Arab Spring, as the dual markers of a newly emerging worldly cosmopolitanism, signal the emergence of a transnational public sphere with global consequences.[2] The Green Movement and the Arab revolutions, with all their deep-rooted differences, both represented the return of the repressed, the resurrection of the denied and denigrated. My

---

1 For the details of my reading of the Green Movement, see Hamid Dabashi, *Iran, the Green Movement, and the USA: The Fox and the Paradox* (London: Zed, 2010), and Hamid Dabashi, *The Green Movement in Iran* (New Brunswick, NJ: Transaction, 2011).

2 For my reading of the Arab revolutions, see Hamid Dabashi, *The Arab Spring: The End of Postcolonialism* (London: Zed, 2012).

argument is that the combined effect of the Green Movement in Iran and the transnational Arab uprisings, taken together, point to the transformative powers of a new generation of cosmopolitan ideals that is neither beholden to the West nor strides by exhausted ideas of postcoloniality. This cosmopolitanism is rooted in both the colonial and postcolonial experiences, and is now poised to transcend them both. From the site of these uprisings from Iran and its environs to the rest of the Muslim world from Asia to Africa, we have begun the production of a new regime of knowledge that will uplift these historical expenses, decenter the world, overcome "the West" as a master trope of European modernity, and start navigating uncharted treaties of a new liberation geography.

In the aftermath of these two cataclysmic events, we need to consider Iran and the Arab world in the larger context of the Muslim world (which now extends well into western Europe and North America), as the potential sites of a new regime of self-knowledge that can potentially generate new modes of knowing, being, and acting far beyond the received limitations of ethnicized bourgeois nationalisms of one sort or another, and towards the renewal of a self-transcending, grassroots cosmopolitanism. Of the estimated 1.7 billion Muslims worldwide, millions live in Europe and North America—the cite and citation of the master trope that still calls itself "the West." A combination of factors that are native to Muslim history and endemic to European colonialism and US imperialism has now resulted in a widespread upsurge in Islamophobia in these locations. This Islamophobia is in fact an historical force that has periodically triggered and agitated the formation of a new mode of knowledge-production by and about Muslims. Muslims within and outside the Muslim world have to see themselves beyond the fictive frontiers of their homelands and abroad, and reassert and re-signify the democratic ideals of their collective struggles as they become native to countries in which they may not have been born, or where they form the first generation of an immigrant wave. Here they find themselves forced to defend and protect a categorical and unconditional freedom of expression, in the pursuit of a form of knowledge-production that, in explaining themselves to others, will explain themselves to themselves, thereby defending and enriching the free and open public debates that will be the conceptual and emotive matrix of their future ideas of themselves.

This would amount to a Muslim "renaissance" in the widest sense of the term, allowing for the most sacrosanct principles, canonical beliefs, ennobling allegories, and sacred symbols of their faith to be tested, fortified, articulated, and theorized in a free and open public sphere—an opportunity Muslims at large have never had in their colonial and postcolonial encounters. The *conditio sine qua non* of this new rise of Muslim self-awareness, as I have argued in *Islamic Liberation Theology* (2008) is the recognition of alterity as the site of Muslim self-consciousness. That means, first and foremost, that, for Muslims to be able to live in this world, they must recognize the inherit dialectics of alterity in their own midst—a fact and phenomenon denied and repressed by events such as the Islamized Iranian Revolution of 1977–79. To be able to live in a world that has a plurality of alterities, Muslims must first begin with the cosmopolitan fact of their own plurality—not just in relations between Sunnis and the Shi'is, but far more seriously and with far more substantive consequences, including the fact that Islam and Muslim identity are legitimately defined not only by Islamic law (Shari'ah), but also by Islamic philosophy, mysticism, and political thought. This insight must then be combined with the fact that there are nominal Muslims who have historically identified as socialists, as anticolonial nationalists, or as feminists before, after, or during periods in which they have identified as Muslims. This must lead to the fuller recognition that, within imperial contexts from Spain to India, Muslims have lived in cosmopolitan contexts that have included Christians, Jews, Zoroastrians, and so on. They must now expand and extend that pluralism to include Baha'is, gays and lesbians, atheists, and agnostics. In short, the cosmopolitan aspects of pre-modern Muslim empires will have to be retrieved for a postcolonial, post-imperial, and above all post-Western democratic pluralism that includes Muslims but, happily, is not limited to them.

Many of the contemporary Iranian artists I have discussed in this book, whether resident in their homeland or outside it—Ramin Bahrani, Nikzad Nodjoumi, Shirin Neshat, Ardeshir Mohassess, Amir Naderi, Abbas Kiarostami, Mohsen Makhmalbaf, Azadeh Akhlaghi, and many more—are engaging in precisely such aesthetic border-crossing. Their work is neither exclusively "Iranian," nor categorically "foreign." By retrieving Iranian cosmopolitanism, they are in effect collapsing such binaries by placing their nation back within the transnational public sphere from which it emerged in the first place. Exactly the same argument can be made about other artists in the larger Arab and Muslim world. Elia Suleiman from the Arab world, Nuri Bilge Ceylan from Turkey, Ousmane Sembène from Africa, among many more, are prime examples of this far more global scene.

Towards a Regional Cosmopolitanism

The emergence of Hassan Rouhani in the course of the Iranian presidential election of 2013 heralded a new chapter in the tumultuous relationship between Iran and the United States. On September 27, 2013, presidents Obama and Rouhani had a telephone conversation while the latter was in New York for a UN General Assembly meeting. On November 24, 2013, Iran and the P5+1 signed the interim Agreement in Geneva. In December 2013, during a meeting of the Gulf Cooperation

Council (GCC) in Kuwait, Arab countries were cautiously optimistic about this agreement. The fact that secret talks between Iran and the US were reported to have taken place much earlier than this (perhaps as early as during the Ahmadinejad administration) in the Arab country of Oman may indicate that official Arab awareness and approval of this deal predated its public acknowledgement.[3] At the commencement of Rouhani's presidency, in a development that broadened the implications of the Green Movement just before he took office, Iran was being pulled into a regional power politics that had unintended consequences for the ruling regime. The porous fictive frontiers of the state were obviously porous in both directions; the circulation of ideas was not entirely under the control of the embattled theocracy.

The sharp, critical edge to the relationship between the United States and Iran would effectively be primarily in Syria, and it is from there that the rest of the Arab world would also begin to feel the future consequences of any improved relationship between the two historic nemeses. Particularly critical to Obama's second term, given his proven reluctance to engage in more visible military operations in the region, Iran's soft power in Iraq, Syria, Lebanon, Palestine, and particularly in Yemen was enormously significant in its jostling for power in the decades to come. The course of the Arab revolutions had generated a new calculus of power in the region, and, given the vast network of its soft power, Iran was integral to the future of US interests in the region—a fact that was deeply troubling to Israel, but had mixed implications for the Arab world.[4] Iran

---

3 According to reports: Associated Press, "Secret US–Iran Talks Cleared Way for Historic Nuclear Deal: US and Iranian officials have been meeting secretly in Oman for the past year with the help of Sultan Qaboos," *Daily Telegraph*, November 24, 2013.

4 For an articulation of the idea of "soft power" from an American imperial perspective, see Joseph S. Nye Jr., *Soft Power: The Means To Success in World Politics* (New York: PublicAffairs, 2005).

itself would also be denied the singular master trope—the "Great Satan"—against which it had defined itself, and by the use of which it had brutally suppressed its opponents.

The fact that Oman was the site of initial contacts between the United States and Iran, and that the GCC had a positive attitude towards them, presaged the more recent news that Iran and Saudi Arabia are growing closer in their views on the future of the region. The common view of Iran as an unconditional supporter of Bashar Assad is patently flawed: Iran will throw Assad under the proverbial bus the instant it sees doing so as best serving its larger regional interests. But the fact that Saudi Arabia and the Islamic Republic are beginning to see eye to eye on Syria points to two fundamental facts: (1) they both fear the unraveling revolutions of the Arab world, and (2) they are both on the same page as the United States in this concern. So the rapprochement between the United States and Iran is really a rapprochement among all of the counterrevolutionary forces across the Arab world, united in their common concern over the short- and long-term consequences of the Arab Spring.[5] Irrespective of an Iranian–Saudi rapprochement, the fact that these two belligerent states could collaborate pointed to the changing dynamics of a region that requires unusual alliances towards uncommon horizons.

The ruling regimes in Iran and Saudi Arabia lead the two most powerful counterrevolutionary forces in the region, and their evident hostility against the Arab Spring has not only conspired to degrade these revolutions into a crude Sunni– Shi'i sectarianism, but, through that false consciousness, has also had an effect like that of a pair of scissors cutting through the revolutionary momentum that threatens both of their

---

5 According to some analysts: "A Saudi–Iranian rapprochement that did not seem possible a few months ago is now happening." Abdullah Hamidaddin, "Why Saudi–Iranian Rapprochment Will Succeed This Time," May 23, 2014, alarabiya.net.

regimes. It is for this reason that there is a forceful convergence of interests between Iran, Saudi Arabia, and Israel in coming together to oppose the more radical implications of these revolutions, which are still very evident, and thereby to protect their respective regional interests. The ostensible hostility between Iran and Israel, on one hand, and Iran and Saudi Arabia, on the other, does not negate but in fact exacerbates the factual force of this counterrevolutionary triumvirate. Nevertheless, those very contrapuntal dynamics end up exacerbating the defiant energies of the revolutions they seek to dismantle.

The implication for the wider Arab world of any emerging rapprochement between Iran and the United States depends on what we mean by "Arab world"—its ruling regimes, or its revolutionary uprisings and the promises they sustain. In fact none of the three forces involved—Iran, the Arab world, and the United States—are stable factors. All are in a state of flux, though in strikingly different ways. The prospect of a rapprochement between the United States and Iran has far-reaching regional implications that are far more serious than the mere lifting of economic sanctions in exchange for the assurance of a nuclear program that is transparent and does not go near weaponization. By far the most successful result of the collaboration between Saudi Arabia and Iran, through a paradoxical dialectic, is the brutal degeneration of the Syrian revolution into sectarian violence. In exchange for a satisfactory result in the nuclear deal, Iran will happily abandon Bashar Assad to his own nonexistent means. But the more Iran plays its cross-sectarian cards, the more it exposes its increasing entrapment in a non-denominational politics of liberation.

The United States presides over the regional triumvirate of Iran, Saudi Arabia, and Israel. But there are any number of other triumvirates—say, that involving Iran, the United

States, and Russia, which through the increasing effects of the Russian imperial attitude in the region has now assumed a much bolder posture in the aftermath of the Ukrainian crisis of 2014. One should not, therefore, privilege the United States as the key catalyst in the relationships between Arabs and Iranians. But so far as this particular triangulation is concerned, it is structurally designed to oppose and bring to an end (or else to absorb and corrupt) the revolutionary momentum of the Arab Spring and the Green Movement within the Arab and Iranian spheres, and indeed the rest of the Muslim world. A careful eye will have to be kept on the dynamics of such triangulations not just for their immediate counter-revolutionary effects, but also for the way in which they open up unpredictable longer-term processes.

Soft Power and Asymmetric Warfare

The way in which the potential rapprochement between Iran and the United States might affect the Arab world raises the crucial point that our critical thinking in these and similar contexts must not fetishize one or another relationship, but see the geopolitics of the region for the volatile and amorphous organism that it is. Two critical pairs of concepts are of paramount importance for any configuration of politics that might emerge in the region: the related concepts of "hard power" and "soft power," and those of "shock and awe" and "asymmetric warfare."[6] These are among the key operational concepts that reveal the unraveling of the postcolonial nation-states into wider emotive and political domains.

Joseph Nye's notion of "soft power"—first theorized in his *Bound to Lead: The Changing Nature of American Power* (1990) and subsequently developed more fully in his *Soft*

---

6   For more on the nature and function of "asymmetrical warfare," see Rod Thornton, *Asymmetric Warfare: Threat and Response in the 21st Century* (London: Polity, 2007).

Power: The Means to Success in World Politics (2004)—
outlined the range of non-military means for advancing
political goals. Strategies ranging from active diplomacy to
economic aid came together to provide a more organic frame-
work for the global advancement of American strategic and
imperial interests. But the best example of soft power (though
in precisely the opposite direction than Joseph Nye intended)
is that wielded by Iran in Iraq, Lebanon, Palestine, and perhaps
even Bahrain or Yemen, and can then be aggregated into hard
power, as in Syria, Lebanon, and Palestine. When we place
these two opposing meanings of "soft power" next to each
other, we are in the domain of "asymmetric warfare." Andrew
J. R. Mack, in his article, "Why Big Nations Lose Small Wars"
(1975), explored the question of why superpowers might
face defeat by smaller armies. But it was in the aftermath of
9/11 that the nature of asymmetric warfare became brutally
apparent, following the US-led invasion of Afghanistan. The
Hezbollah victory over Israel in 2006 and the ability of the
Taliban to mount an amorphous warfare were the clearest
indications of this asymmetric relationship. The rise of the
so-called "Islamic State" might thus be considered a counterrevolutionary stratagem to cast the balance between soft and
hard power into disequilibrium, to the advantage of the ruling
regimes. But, again, these counterrevolutionary forces in fact
serve to feed the energies of revolutionary movements.

What destabilizes the counterrevolutionary dynamics of the
ruling regimes and their interactions with the imperial forces
in the region is the revolutionary production of counter-
hegemonic formations—such as the reversal of the imperial
operation of soft power, supported by the logic and rhetoric
of asymmetric warfare. If Iran uses its soft power against the
hard power of the United States and Israel, Iranian citizens use
the same strategy against the hard power of the state, as do
Arabs, from Morocco to Syria, facing the brutalities of their

ruling regimes. The combined effects of soft power and asymmetric warfare thus spread over three layers of operation: (1) collaboration between the United States and smaller nation-states, (2) the reversal of such efforts by the resistances of smaller nations against the United States, and (3) the efforts of non-violent civil rights activists and ordinary citizens against repressive regimes such as those of Iran, Syria, Israel, and Bahrain. These harsh realities generate the emerging venues in which the region at large is giving birth to a renewed cosmopolitanism—from the ground up, from experience to ideas, from ideas to aspirations.

Years into the dramatic unfolding of the Arab revolutions, the rapprochement between Iran and the United States raises the fundamental question of where exactly we stand in relation to them. What, indeed, is left of the Arab revolutions themselves? In Tunisia and Libya, the uprisings were by and large localized, for better (Tunisia) or for worse (Libya). In Bahrain, rebellion was successfully repressed. The uprising in Yemen has degenerated into insular infighting under the hegemony of the Saudis, as militant jihadists of their own creation use it to launch transnational attacks. That leaves Egypt and Syria as the most potent crucibles of potential change in the broader region. In Egypt, a democratically elected (albeit incompetent) president was toppled by a military coup, and in Syria the Saudi–Iranian rivalry turned a by and large peaceful revolution into a proxy war falsely flagged between Sunni Wahhabis and Shi'i Alavis.

What is left of the Arab revolutions is precisely the left of those revolutions—now represented by the feeble face of Hamdeen Sabahi in Egypt: jaundiced, lacking convictions, cliché-ridden, purposeless, poorly thought through. The strategy of the left of the Arab (or for that matter Iranian) revolutions has yet to be thought through—not just in organizational terms, but far more urgently in theoretical and conceptual terms. Where does the Arab left stand on these revolutions? Where exactly is the Arab or Iranian left? And, more importantly, what role can it play in an emerging transnational politics beyond fictive national borders?

In order to reconfigure the left for the Arab and Iranian worlds, and beyond into the rest of Asia, Africa, and Latin America—and a fortiori the nature of transnational politics this reconfiguration may represent—we need to turn to Adorno and his *Negative Dialectics* (1966). This is because, in order to overcome the condition of postcoloniality we have inherited over the last two centuries and more—and in whose terms we continue to think through our revolutions—we must instead consider precisely the production of a new regime of knowledge. Adorno wrote *Negative Dialectics* at another time when the world seemed pregnant with endless possibilities— some time after the Jewish Holocaust, during the collapse of the Soviet model in the USSR, and just before the wave of European protests of the 1968.

Negative Dialectics

A dialectically negative trajectory has emerged in the aftermath of the rise of the Green Movement and the Arab revolutions, in which the stated objective of the historical actors produces the opposite effect from what they claim they desire. Iran hopes to support Assad, while Saudi Arabia desires the success of jihadist forces. The two aims seem to be, and are, in contradiction. But they result together in the dismantling of a revolutionary force that threatens both Iran and the Saudi Arabia—so much so that the evident antagonism between those two countries conspires to pursue an identical objective: the derailing of the revolutionary momentum of the Arab Spring. But will they succeed?

In *Negative Dialectics* (1966), Adorno took to task the classical understanding of the term "dialectics"—that from the contradiction between two negations a positive result will emerge. In its Hegelian rendition, the dialectic worked through contradiction and tension, whereby human history gathers the unfolding of human freedom as the expression of the overriding *Weltgeist*. From Hegel to Marx, this dialectic was presumed to disclose itself in an increasingly emancipatory direction until its final (inevitable) fulfillment. Adorno took this classical notion of the Hegelian dialectic, but dismantled the assumption of its necessarily positive, rational, progressive movement towards the Absolute. Adorno was here fully conscious of post-Holocaust Europe, and wanted to bring not just the fact of suffering but also the reality of unreason into the workings of the dialectic. Not every dialectic results in a positive outcome, he proposed, for the material unfolding of history may in fact find its way into darker territories.

Adorno's notion of "negative dialectics" is designed to account for negative outcomes of two sets of positive dialectical forces, and thereby to address lacunae in world history. "Negative dialectics" effectively frees historical materialism from the necessary inference of positive results, and also from the binding Hegelian dictum that "what is real is what is rational"—allowing (for example) for soft power through asymmetric warfare to migrate from the will to power to the will to resist power. But the operations of soft power and asymmetric warfare are not just between states: they are equally operative within states—between the state apparatus and the society it struggles vainly to rule.

The transformation of national liberation movements into civil rights movements—on the model of Palestinians in Israel and the occupied territories, or among the Kurds in Syria and Turkey—provides the best model of this dialectical sublation. There is a structural affinity, for revolutionary soft power, between sub-nationalized categories like the Kurds and the Palestinians, and the realm of revolutionary mimesis, from one mode of resistance to another. Adorno believed that "the need to let suffering speak is a condition of all truth. For suffering is objectivity that weighs upon the subject ..."[7] The expression of that suffering is not just political, in the way the Palestinians and the Kurds have endured it, one by occupation and the other by disintegration. The emerging regimes of knowledge will need to heed Adorno's prognosis that the mimetic potentials of language can be conflated with its narrative semantics. To achieve that liberation of the object from its endemic fetishization, Adorno offered the formation of a new "constellation" of concepts whereby liberating objects from their legislated semantics into unforeseen and yet viable offshoots of their received classifications, legislation, and codification, into a deterministic history.

Through the intermediary functions of the United States, Russia, the European Union, or China, we need to collectively observe the state of flux of our revolutionary age, in both the Iranian and Arab worlds. In this respect, we would all be better off if we were to turn to critical thinkers like Adorno and Benjamin, writing as they were in response to (Adorno) or in anticipation of (Benjamin) the catastrophe that their European homeland was subjected to during the Jewish Holocaust, for that cataclysmic catastrophe was just a heavy dose of precisely the same medicine that European imperialism and colonialism had been administrating to the world at large. From the ashes of the Jewish Holocaust and the Armenian Genocide to the unfathomable misery that European colonialism has visited upon the globe, we may thus surmise the uplifting—the Hegelian *Aufheben*—of a world beyond its fallacious collapsing into "the West and the Rest."

In *Negative Dialectics*, Adorno was still reacting to the horrors of the Jewish Holocaust when he effectively suspended the course of the Marxist reaction to the European

7 Theodor W. Adorno, *Negative Dialectics* (London: Bloomsbury Academic, 1981), pp. 17–18.

uprising of 1968 by proposing that the whole conception of political praxis had to await the production of a new theory of action that would transform consciousness. Adorno insisted on an urgent interpretation of experience. This is no easy task, for habitually we assimilate new experiences (such as a revolutionary uprising, the toppling of a regime, the flight of a dictator) backwards into things we already know—whereas that task, for Adorno, was always pending. What Adorno considered a fetishized relationship between the subject and the object amounts—for us, at the colonial edges of a now-decentered capital—to the alienated world that we assimilate retrospectively into colonial terms of operation, ranging from those like "democracy" and "human rights" to the relations of power not so successfully hidden by terms such as "referendum" and "election." Regimes such as the Islamic Republic of Iran, Egypt under Sisi, or Syria under Assad have so successfully eviscerated these terms of any meaning that the political objective can no longer be expressed in terms domestic and familiar to these vacuous words. The task that Adorno stipulated back in the 1960s is even more daunting today for humanity as a whole. I insist (as I have since 9/11) that the expedited speed of US militarism and the violent Islamism that accompanies it are the final (not the first) signs of the ending of the world of "the West and the Rest"—and thus the task of a liberated subject detached from its imperial, colonial, or even postcolonial matrix is ever more urgent.

Adorno charged the concepts he had inherited with being philosophically hypostatized—their relationship to the particularities they intended to universalize frozen in abstraction. His proposal was to reestablish a link between concepts and nonconceptuality they had effectively silenced. His ambition was to create a critical consciousness in which concepts are preempted from succumbing to this hypostatization by way of a tense conversation (or even a contestation) between what they have silenced and what they wish to conceptualize. Adorno drives this line of thought towards the ambitious proposition of a rapprochement between reified universals and meandering and amorphous particulars, thus dismantling the oppressively alienated relationship between the two. One can clearly read the guilt-ridden disposition of the mind of a German Jewish philosopher who had not foreseen the horrors of the Holocaust on the horizon (as Walter Benjamin did), targeting him and who he was as the particular that the Hegelian universal had refused to incorporate into the European subject. In the wake of the catastrophe of the Holocaust, he was coming to terms with the disruption of his European (Hegelian) claim to universality by his Jewish particularity.

Along those lines, what precisely is the new regime of knowledge we need to develop? It is to allow for the particularities of our emerging world to challenge the universals we have inherited. These particularities are now beyond the conditions of postcoloniality we have inherited. These particularities are no longer evident in denominational divisions between Jews, Muslims, Christians, Hindus, atheists, and so on. These are all categorical absolutes, vacuous universals emptied of all meaning. What are needed instead are the material encounters between collapsing universals, and the ruins that they leave, in the process producing the allegories that Walter Benjamin saw as the fertile soil of any meaningful presence in the world.

Material Triangulations against False Binaries

The triumvirate of Iran, the Arab World, and the United States is not composed of stable entities, but animated by volatile and changing dynamics. It thus points to a wider spectrum of dialectical changes in the world to come—with no single player in total control. The United States wishes to stabilize the region in pursuit of its immediate and long-term interests of imperial domination and neoliberal economics, in the process globalizing the condition of constitutional injustice rampant in the United States and around the world. The ruling regime in Iran has violently suppressed the democratic aspirations of its own citizens, and continues to direct the dynamics of its politics into the geopolitics and indeed astropolitics of the region, so that it can use its facility with soft power to secure an enduring location of power and significance for itself.[8] The Arab world continues to be ruled by regimes inimical to the social justice and economic equanimity that, like anywhere else, it urgently needs. Whenever we consider any such triangulation of power, we need to consider how it can be turned against the interests of the dominant regimes and to the benefit of the revolutionary forces. But, in order to do so, we first need to reconfigure a world beyond the condition of postcoloniality, with its fictive borders, so that we can mobilize our untapped forces that lie beyond the sterile binaries of secular–religious, Arab–Iranian, Sunni–Shi'i, and indeed "the West and the Rest."

The geopolitics of the region today operate entirely outside postcolonial fictive frontiers. Iran is present today far beyond its political borders. In every troubled spot in the region, Iran has an insidiously influential presence. From Afghanistan to Bahrain to Yemen, from Iraq to Syria, from Central Asia to North Africa, even as far as Latin America (and not just in the late Hugo Chávez's Venezuela), Iran has spread the tentacles of its soft power. Iran has modeled itself on its chief nemesis: the United States. Demystifying the myth of the nation, recognizing its postcolonial origins and inevitable extensions beyond its borders, are the preconditions for coming to terms with the realities lived by many millions of human beings. Making the nation conscious of its porous borders—retrieving its cos-

---

8   For more details of Iranian astropolitics, see my essay, "From Russia with Love: An Iranian Space Odyssey," Al Jazeera, June 2, 2014, aljazeera.com.

mopolitan character by remapping its transnational origins in Istanbul, Calcutta, Delhi, Cairo, London, Paris, Berlin, and now anywhere from Mexico City to New York to Tokyo— restores the nation to its postnational consciousness. On this map, major cities become the loci of culture—just as London Istanbul, New York, and Cairo are today—and absorb the myth of the sovereign nation-state into a far more compelling map. Tehran is integral to that map, which is superimposed over the cultural landscape of Tehran. The terms of our future liberties are framed not by the fictive frontiers of the nation-state, but by the factual evidence of megacities and the active circulation of labor, capital, culture, and industry. Consider the population of cities like Tehran (10 million), Istanbul (14 million), Cairo (8 million), New Delhi (11 million), Mexico City (9 million), and so on—these megacities are larger and more populous than many Scandinavian countries, and the nature of the circulation of labor and capital has made them entirely multilingual and multicultural.[9]

Cities are now concentrations of political power, migrant labor, transnational capital, rambunctious markets, and of the varied cultures they all come together to generate. Countries are just the extended shadows of these major cities. Ten minutes by train out of New York, we are in wilderness. On an overnight flight to London, Istanbul, Tehran, Cairo, or Seoul, you will scarcely notice any difference past the immigration officers. Cities have now become extensions of the Internet, and vice versa—an active fusion of the public and cyber spheres. The transnational public sphere within which the fictive frontiers of nations are erased have now been extended far and wide into cyberspace and outer space. On one side is the security apparatus that maps cyberspace, on the other the actively

---

9 Saskia Sassen has studied this phenomenon in detail. See her *The Global City: New York, London, Tokyo* (Princeton, NJ: Princeton Paperbacks, 2001).

militarized outer space, and in between are the atomized individuals—as much victims of this security-state digitization and surveillance as they are capable of mobilization, resistance, and solidarity. Edward Snowden, the American security analyst who leaked classified information from the National Security Agency, and Julian Assange, the Australian editor-in-chief of WikiLeaks, have shown how the tables can be turned against abusive power in the service of a more responsible citizenship. Changing the locations of cultural production away from the self-centering myth of "the West," replicating the polylocality of real transnational public spheres, exploring and theorizing alternative epistemologies of knowledge-production—these are among varied strategies of mobilization against abusive power, and are now evident more than ever before. Only in the materially rooted epistemologies that will emerge from these sites will Europeans and non-Europeans begin to overcome their received and perceived alterities, and think together upon the debris of their manufactured identities. Thus will new sites of knowledge emerge from crises and traumas that today define the fate of postnational nations—not from the corrupting will to power.

Today, millions of Iranians live beyond the fictive frontiers of Iran but within the emotive universe of their homeland. They live, study, work, and raise a new generation of Iranians outside their place of birth. They are taken beyond their political borders by the force of labor migration, for higher education, for trade and commerce, or else to escape the absurdities and tyrannies of the ruling regime in their own country. They give their newborn children Persian names, use their mother tongue in the home, and seek out pre-school facilities to deposit their children in a cultural environment familiar to their grandparents. More and more Iranians are being raised multilingual, adding English, French, Spanish, or German to the Arabic, Kurdish, or Azeri they know, in addition to their common Persian. They make regular visits to Iran, where grandparents are charged with speaking Kurdish, Arabic, Azeri, or Persian to their grandchildren. Whether they are born within or outside Iran, the identity of Iranians has become increasingly elastic in terms of its territorial claims.

An Intuition of Transcendence

Wherever they go—whether they remain at home in Iran or carry that home anywhere else with them—to be Iranian means to be born in a state of mind extending from its most ancient imperial pedigree to its latest postcolonial remnants, a homeland located beyond any frontier fiction. The transnational history of the nation exposes the layered pedigree of its people's consciousness. Beneath any extroverted worldliness dwells an inner sanctum of the person, where the intuition of transcendence that this worldliness has occasioned best manifests itself. The very character of the person, even (or especially) in its most isolated and insular being, still exudes the historicity of that worldliness that enables personhood. To show you the way in which this intuition of transcendence works through the inner sanctum of a person's solitude, let me guide you through a masterpiece of Iranian cinema.

Among such masterpieces, very few have achieved the status of Amir Naderi's *Davandeh* (released in the English-speaking world as *The Runner*, 1984) as a landmark event that defined much that happened after it caught the attention of the world cinema. Although it appeared halfway through Naderi's extraordinary career as a filmmaker, *The Runner* marks the initial moment in the global attention that came to be focused on Iranian cinema in general. Much has happened in Iranian cinema and its global reception since the mid 1980s, when *The Runner* took the Three Continents Festival by storm. Today, the names of Abbas Kiarostami, Mohsen Makhmalbaf, Jafar Panahi, and Bahman Qobadi have overshadowed that of Amir

Naderi. Naderi himself moved to New York some time ago, from where his continuing work has achieved considerable global success. Whether or not he should now even be considered an "Iranian filmmaker" is subject to debate. But the central significance of *The Runner* in defining much that has since happened in Iranian cinema still endures. His move to the United States might in fact be considered a logical extension of his worldly presence in Iran long before he left his homeland.

By far the most globally celebrated of Naderi's films, *The Runner* is an autobiographical film in more than one sense—and precisely in its autobiographical capacity, it contains a critical component of what has now flourished in Iranian cinema more generally.[10] When Naderi was six years old, he was accidentally stranded on a ship and taken to a faraway land whose location, to this day, he has no idea. The story of this mysterious voyage is very simple. The husband of his aunt, who adopted him after the death of his mother, used to work on a ship in Abadan as a painter. Amir was assigned to bring this uncle his lunch every day. After giving him his lunch, Amir would roam through the ship and play on its various decks and floors. One day, as he found his way to the lowest level, where the engines were, he fell asleep on top of some potato sacks. Soon after he fell asleep, the ship pulled up its anchor and left Abadan port, carrying the six-year-old Amir to its next destination. He woke up frightened out of his wits, and was soon discovered by the ship's crew and put into quarantine for about ten days. He could not see anything but the sea, until they reached a destination where he remembers seeing some sort of traffic policeman with white gloves, controlling sparse traffic on a coastal street where the ship had

---

10 An earlier version of this reflection on Amir Naderi's *Runner* appeared in Gönül Dönmez-Colin, ed., *The Cinema of North Africa and the Middle East* (London: Wallflower, 2007), pp. 81–8.

come ashore. The ship then returned to Abadan, and Amir returned to his aunt—by now obviously frightened out of her wits. Naderi reports that, according to his aunt, he remained unable to speak a word for about six months after the incident, but that the first thing he said after his long silence was that he wanted to leave for a faraway land on a ship.

What happened to Naderi during this strange, ambiguous, outlandish journey? He speaks of it in terms that are perfectly realistic, simply as a matter of biographical fact. But did it really happen? Did he dream it? Or, when he related it to me, was he just telling me a story he wished to turn into a film? All the indications of his recollections are that it did really happen. He also reports that, a few years after this incident, when he was eleven years old, he again tried to run away to Kuwait—this time intentionally. But he did not make it beyond a couple of islands off the coast of Abadan. That there has always been a restless disposition about Naderi, a desire to be somewhere else, is evident in practically all his films. But the story he narrates about his first (accidental?) journey on board a cargo ship is saturated with imagery of a lonely child, a solitary *mosafer* ("sojourner"), lost on a wandering ship, leaving a familiar island for an unknown destination, of which Naderi has only a visual memory, captured through the small window of a cabin, where he was stranded. That small window has mutated into the lens of his camera for the rest of his life. Imagine: Amir Naderi, solitary inside a cabin, standing on top of a potato sack, peeping through a small window, at the unfamiliar world outside, trying to make sense of where it was and how it had come about. This image effectively sums up his cinema.

The abandoned ship in *The Runner*, on which Amiru lives, is the miasmatic memory of a ship on which Naderi has always dreamed of departing for a faraway land. In the most enduring sense of the term, he still lives on that ship. His small cubical apartment in downtown Manhattan has a remarkable similarity to a cabin aboard an abandoned ship—precisely where Amiru lives. Central to this ship, the abode of both Amir and Amiru, is the solitary disposition of its whereabouts—a space removed from society, suspended in midair between his dreams and his visions as a filmmaker. It is as if Naderi, as perhaps the preeminent Iranian filmmaker, still lives and dreams and travels on that ship: from Iran to Europe, the United States, and Japan, to all the major film festivals around the world.

Who is Amiru? A poor orphaned boy growing up on the shores of a nameless land, fascinated with every moving object—huge ships, small boats, speeding cars, lazy bicycles, noisy motorcycles, rambunctious trucks, slumbering trains, flying airplanes: anything and everything that moves by itself and can carry him away from where he is. The terror of his life occurs when he sees a one-legged man or an aging woman—people who cannot run away from there. Lacking access to any vehicle, he runs, faster and faster, until he runs out of breath. When a man drinks a glass of water from a bucket of ice water that he carries around to make a meager living, he chases after him—not only to secure payment for the water but for the simple challenge of catching up with him on foot (the man is on a bicycle). When another man steals a piece of his ice, he runs after him, grabs hold of the ice and runs away—both for the triumphant joy of outpacing the much more muscular man and so as to reach his destination before the ice melts.

Running has become definitive to Amiru. What is he running from? What is he running to? Nothing. Everything. Running is his state of being. Something somewhere calls on him, something that is always somewhere else. Amiru is mesmerized by moving objects, anything and everything that moves, that can carry him away from where he is, to somewhere else. Because they are not taking him anywhere, he runs. He runs after the indeterminacy of not being-there. Being where? Anywhere that is not where Amiru is. There is a scene early in the film where, while he and his friends are collecting empty bottles that foreigners have thrown into the sea, they are suddenly attacked by a shark. A fisherman alerts the children, and they run furiously out of the sea. Amiru comes out frightened out of his wits—frightened not by the possibility that he might have been killed, but by the terror that the shark could have chopped off his limbs, his solitary claim to mobility, to running away from here, to somewhere else—somewhere that is not here, or anywhere else.

It is wrong to read Amiru as running away from poverty. Amiru is poor, but his life is not desolate or joyless. He has the jubilant company of a band of young, equally poor boys, with whom he plays soccer, rides bikes, chases after running trains, and shares joyous songs on top of speeding wagons. His relationship with his friends is not free of quarrels. Poverty reigns supreme. But there is a serenity about Amiru, a gentility about his manners, a solidity to his friendship. While trying to run away (from nothing and everything), Amiru lives a rich and fulfilling life—rich in the dimensions of his solitude that he explores, fulfilling in the company of his friends. There is a scene where Amiru is washing his shirt in the abandoned ship (his home), in which Naderi brings his camera close (ever so gently) to the diverted gaze on the face of this poor, orphaned, solitary soul. This look on the face of Amiru is the look of humanity at a loss, facing an abyss beyond recognition. There and then, *The Runner* is no longer the story of a lonely boy, and Amiru is no longer a poor, orphaned child—there and then, Naderi is picturing humanity at large, at a loss. What is this? This thing: The world? Whence, why, how, for what purpose? Sometimes Naderi is capable of the cruelest insights. He holds the hand of his audience, moves ever so imperceptibly, gently even—but where he is taking you is no party. He has seen something terrorizing, a nightmare perhaps, a meta-physical cruelty beyond human measure. He has seen the absurdity at the root of the cruelty that all lives seek to suppress. He has seen it, and he has mastered a way to show and tell it—ever so softly, gently even, for the vision he wishes to reveal is frightful.

Amiru is unable to read or write. He collects pictures of airplanes and hangs them on the wall of his cabin/room in his ship. He goes to a magazine seller, buying more magazines to look at their pictures. He soon discovers that he cannot read or write, and that bothers him. He registers his name at a school to learn how to read and write. His teacher begins to teach him the letters of the Persian alphabet: Alef, Beh, Peh, Teh, Seh, Jim, Cheh, Heh, Kheh, Dal, Zal, and so on. The result is not that Amiru now learns how to read and write, but something quite else. Amiru does not learn the letters of the Persian alphabet; his creator, Naderi, teaches them to un-learn themselves. Amiru takes the letters to the seaside so that Naderi can teach them truth. The alphabet sequence of *The Runner* will endure as the most glorious lesson in a literacy beyond words. This sequence is one of the most spectacular achievements of Naderi in his legendary virtuoso performances as a sound designer: sounds of water, wind, fire, and dust gather momentum in syncope with Amiru's recitations of the Persian alphabet.

Amiru is illiterate. But what does that mean? Naderi himself is not a very literate person. He dropped out of school early in his life. He had no formal education of any sort. To him, the letters of the alphabet are strange creatures—not just Persian letters (as we see them in *The Runner*), but also English letters, as we will soon see in *Marathon* (2003). The letters of the alphabet are strange creatures. What are they? And who, by the way, gave them this authority to sound, seem, and suggest one thing or another? Amiru takes the letters of the Persian alphabet to the seaside, for Naderi to teach them to behave. Amiru memorizes them to the rhythm of the waves crashing upon the rocks; he memorizes them to the sound of wind, water, fire, and dust—a theme Naderi will pick up in his next film, *Water, Wind, Dust* (1989). Amiru is elemental, elementary, figurative, phenomenal. In the alphabet sequence of *The Runner*, humanity is reduced to literacy, literacy to words, words to letters, letters to alphabets, alphabets to sounds, sounds to noises, and noises given back to earth—to its water, wind, fire, and dust, to its four elemental irreducibilities, back—off you go, go back where you came from, to earth, to life, to the world, to existence, to being. There: off you go, stay there and do not come back. Leave the world alone. What Abbas Kiarostami would later do in his mature cinema, by deploying an ingenious fictive transparency of the real, Naderi achieves in *The Runner* through his trademark visual realism.

The final sequence of *The Runner* will endure forever. Amiru and his buddies have made yet another wager for nothing, just for the fun of it, and for the challenge that it occasions—to see who wins. But who wins what? The game begins. A huge block of ice is placed near a thunderous fire. What do people see when they see this block of ice near that roaring fire? A universe. Those two items are insignia of a universe—ice, the soul of salvation from the ungodly heat of summer, placed next to a fire whose raging flames exude an elemental violence at once life-affirming and deadly. More than anything else, the visual contrast between the block of ice and the raging fire commands the camera's attention. Again, accumulated here are fire, wind, water, and dust—and, racing towards them, a bunch of children desperately running from a fate they cannot articulate; a useless flight, yet temporarily made meaningful by virtue of the significance of the act itself—which it will lose as soon as the game is over.

Gathered in the anonymity of this elemental space is a cosmic moment, when history has no longer much of a claim over reality, where reality has become evidence *sui generis*. Naderi is a master at crafting such moments, in which time and space vacate the site of their articulation of all signs of historicity. These are metaphysical moments, in which Naderi has brought humanity at large for a quick look, a cursory visit. We are no longer in Iran, or Asia, or Africa, or planet Earth, or anywhere in that vicinity. Here we have entered the miasmatic zone of what medieval Persian philosophers would call *sarmad*—"the everlasting." Time is suspended here, space morphed into a cinematic site of visual contemplation. There is no sign of society here—solitude is all-encompassing. We are inside Naderi's creative intelligence. All signifiers have metamorphosed into their originary signs.

The marathon begins. Amiru and his friends start running towards the fire. The challenge is dual: to be the first to get there, and to get there before the ice has completely melted. On the way, between the origin of that match and its destination, a brutal banality becomes evident. If you cannot get there, then you must also prevent others from getting there.

Figure 7: Majid Niroumand (Amiru), in a scene from Amir Naderi's *Davandeh* (*The Runner*, 1984).

In this match Naderi has discovered and displayed a barbarity of unsurpassed terror in the very heart of our innocence. Amiru and his friends start sabotaging each other's progress, getting in each other's way, as they run towards the fire and try to be the first to get to the ice before it is melted. In no other film in the history of Iranian cinema has such a banality been so vividly and honestly captured. The children run, roll, bump, bounce, throw, hit, strike, jolt, jerk, jump, punt, push, pull, drag, and yank—doing anything and everything to be the first to get to the melting ice by the subterranean fire (coming up from the heart of a hidden terror), or at the very least to prevent anyone else from getting there. Amiru gets there, against all odds, against everything that was meant to prevent him. He gets to the ice by the fire, reaches for the barrel on which the piece of ice was placed. He begins a triumphant, joyous, jubilant beat of victory. He begins to beat on the drum, victoriously. He has won. "Barandeh shodom!" you can see him say, if you watch his lips carefully, "Barandeh shodom!": "I won!" Beating on the drum, on the melted ice, rhythmically, splashing the water, joy, pure, undiluted, ecstatic joy. He picks up the last remaining piece of ice, lifts it to his head and starts a triumphant dance to the rhythm and the tune of his victory, holding the piece of ice victoriously over his head—the goblet of his victory. This is no ice, no frozen water: this is a trophy, held triumphantly over the struggle for his existence. He is. He lives. He is triumphant. Hope. He brings the piece of ice to his lips, drinking his victory, water—the fruit of his exultant achievement—by the furious fire. That is not a minute or a second or an instant—when this lasts. That is an eternity and it lasts forever. The eternity finally breaks. Amiru comes to his senses. He turns around, looks at his fallen friends—his comrades-turned-rivals. They are approaching but all dying of thirst, one after the other begging for a drop of water. Amir turns, extends the piece of ice. This is no longer a trophy. The moment of myth has passed, the magic ended. Reality roams, fire is back. Boys, men, dying of thirst. Generous, Amiru extends the ice, gives it to the first boy in his reach. The boy drinks from the ice and passes it on, sharing, and then on to the next, and then the next. The boys unite in the last drop of life that the melting ice can give. Life is restored. Amiru is victorious. Naderi, meanwhile, commands with confidence: cut.

Amiru is the soul of Iranian self and society in dialectical incarnation. He is itinerant, misplaced, dislocated—never happy where he is, always looking to go somewhere else. The film was shot at multiple locations during the Iran–Iraq War (1980–88), but it could have been shot anywhere—in Europe, in Asia, in Africa, Latin America. Its location is dislocated, its time is untimely. It is perennial, omnipresent. It is the best film to see to gauge the omnipresence of Iranian visual culture in a place beyond its geographical location. Geography in fact disappears in this film into a cinematic landscape that is far truer to the lived experiences of Iranians. It is impossible for a filmmaker to achieve that landscape if in his mind and soul he has not already traversed far beyond his physical place of birth and upbringing.

Amir Naderi's is a cinema of solitude rooted in the round-about society of his birth and upbringing—solitude not merely as the autobiography of a filmmaker, but solitude as the aesthetic articulation of social alienation and cultural anomie. Yet this sense of anomie is not ailing and fraught, for it is predicated on an enabling solitude, pregnant with all of its own opposites. As an artistic space, Naderi's cinema is the site of a creative transformation of alienation and anomie, for cinema is where society comes together in soli-tude—we always watch a film in the company of strangers, in the social presence of our shared singular solitude. The result is a creative entry into the social function of solitude, constitutional to a creative space that is no longer culture-specific, that smells and looks local and yet is global by virtue of the creative space it has cultivated in solitude—a socially significant, communally enabling, and emotively charged solitude.

A Microcosm of the Universe

Amir Naderi's cinema is a microcosm of that cosmopolis that has given birth to a visionary imagination far beyond the domain of his birth and upbringing. As a filmmaker, Naderi becomes an allegory of a world he inhabits far beyond his homeland—a landscape rooted in one geography but spread across the topography of a far vaster universe. That cinema is the *Alam-e Saghir* ("microcosm") of the *Alam-e Kabir* ("macrocosm") of the world beyond his homeland but embedded in his homeland. Just like the idea of *Insan-e Kamil* ("the Perfect Person"), in thirteenth-century Persian mystic Aziz Nasafi's famous book by that name, Amir Naderi and his cinema represent and instantiate a far more planetary claim on the world.[11] In this book, Nasafi extensively theorized the notion of the Perfect Person—a notion that had originally been articulated by the Andalusian mystic Ibn Arabi (1165–1240), and had sought to perceive a picture of a human being who had mastered the varied forms of doctrinal authenticity in law, reason, and love, and yet had overcome them all, and in the solitude of his person had perfected their scattering among humanity at large. That person is Iranian by virtue of being universal, and universal by virtue of being Iranian. The fusion of the particular and the universal is here site-specific and pitch-perfect.

---

11 Aziz Nasafi, *Insan-e Kamil* ("The Perfect Person"), ed. Marijan Mole (Tehran: 1960).

Geographical Indeterminacy

The Tyranny of Geography

When, from his Brooklyn studio, Mohsen Namjoo, a leading Iranian singer-songwriter popular among the urban youth, sings in one of his most celebrated songs about "Jabr-e Joghrafiya" ("The Tyranny of Geography"), about the evidently inherent limitations of a person being born in Iran or Asia, he is already liberated, in body and soul, from that fictive tyranny. That very pronouncement of the "tyranny of geography" is the luxury afforded by a liberation geography. Namjoo (b. 1976) emerged as perhaps the most popular (and yet most vehemently contested) singer, composer, and songwriter of his generation—for he was at once widely appealing to a new generation, and yet also broke many classical taboos. He broke loose from, made fun of, and playfully experimented with classical Persian music, with its tyrannical rules and demanding modulations. The result was and remains widely intriguing to Namjoo's own generation of admirers and yet quite jarring and troublesome for the classicists. But the overriding fact about Namjoo's music is that it is informed by musical traditions from all over the world—happily and melodiously fusing Jazz and Blues with Persian classical music. Namjoo's music was formed entirely while he lived in Iran, and it began to find an even wider audience when he moved to Europe, and then the United States. So when he sings of the "tyranny of geography," he is himself in fact entirely liberated from any such presumed tyranny.

Namjoo is not alone. He is representative of a decidedly subversive culture of defiance, breaking the tyranny of the ruling political regime by forcing his received national habitat outside and beyond its manufactured borders. He is now at home in the world, the way his forebears over the last three hundred years or more have been at home—definitive of the structural transformation of the bourgeois public sphere that has enabled them all. His diction resonates with the world at large; his music shakes the foundations of a jealously guarded Persian classicism; his poetry is iconoclastic; his appeal reaches far beyond his homeland, now relocated on the reimagined global map, where it has always belonged, and where he and his generation have already turned "the tyranny of geography" against itself.

> One day you wake up and you see all is lost
> You are left all alone, lonely, and forlorn—
> A few more strands of your hair have turned gray,
> You wishy-washy man!
> Your wedding party has turned to mourning,
> You are beyond any hope.
> Your hunched back is even more crooked,
> Your shoulders more dropped—
> Look around yourself carefully,
> Sinners and innocents are burning alike.
> Why? Because you are born in Asia—and as they say:
> Subject to geographical tyranny.
> Thus you are a vagabond—and all you have
> For breakfast are just tea and cigarettes.
> Oh God Almighty what do you really have in mind?
> Tell me when will you be kinder to us,
> Swear on your mother's grave? ...
> Why? Because you are born in Asia—and as they say:
> Subject to geographical tyranny.
> Thus you are a vagabond—and all you have
> For breakfast are just tea and cigarettes.[12]

---

12 The original Persian lyrics (of which I have made this partial English translation) are available online at iransong.com/song/28789.htm. For a video clip of the song, see youtube.com/watch?v=EHo5Hjhw1S8.

Conclusion

His elephant misses India.

A Persian proverb

Let me conclude by reminding you of that famous Persian merchant and his proverbial parrot. The merchant was about to leave for India for business and asked his family and other household members what he could bring them as gifts when he returned home. Everyone asked for one thing or another— a pair of shoes, a nice garment, a necklace, a book, some dried fruit, or else medicinal herbs. Then, in jest, he turned to his eloquent parrot and asked what he could bring for him from India. "Nothing," the parrot said. "Nothing?" The merchant asked. "Well," the bird said, "when you see my fellow parrots in India, ask them if it is fair for them to fly freely and sing and dance in the woods while I am here in this cage in Persia." "No problem, I'll give them the message," he assured the parrot.

The merchant traveled to India, did his business, and on his way back bought all the gifts he had promised the members of his household. Remembering the message his parrot had made him promise to convey back in Persia, he searched and asked around, and finally found a thick jungle nearby. He moved to its edges and saw a whole flock of parrots flying around, singing and frolicking busily. He went straight to the parrots and gave them his parrot's message. No sooner had he delivered the message than all the birds suddenly dropped dead right in front of his eyes. The merchant was utterly bewildered by what he saw, and wondered what exactly was in that simple message that caused this calamity. But he continued with his journey until he returned home to Persia.

"Did you deliver my message to the Indian parrots," his parrot asked upon his return. "Yes, I did," the merchant replied, "and what a bizarre message it was, for upon hearing it they all dropped dead." No sooner had the merchant finished this sentence than his own parrot dropped dead. "What madness was this?" he wondered. Heartbroken and confused, he took the parrot out of his cage and dropped it by a tree. As soon as the parrot was left alone, it jumped and flew up to a branch of that very same tree. The merchant was saddened, frightened, puzzled, and looked up in bewilderment wondering what had happened. "Nothing," the bird replied, "my comrades sent me a secret message from India. Stop talking, singing, and complaining, and pretend you are dead so you will be set free—and that is what I did, and now I will fly back to my friends in India."

Though this story might be much older in origin, the most famous account of it comes from Rumi's *Mathnavi*. Molana Jalal al-Din Rumi (1207–73), perhaps the most widely loved and admired Muslim mystic of the Persianate world, was born in what is now Afghanistan. He traveled through Iran in his youth, and settled until the end of his life in Anatolia, in modern Turkey. With perfect legitimacy, you can call Rumi an Afghan, Iranian, Turkish, or Muslim mystic, without being able to claim him categorically for any one of these postcolonial identitarian groups. A much different geography informed Rumi's period and poetry. The imperial geography of the Seljuq dynasty, soon to succumb to the Mongols, embraced Rumi's spirit of the age. That geography implicated the worldliness of a different world, of varied and multiple worlds, held together and torn asunder by successive empires and worldly experiences. The story of the Persian merchant and his Indian parrot is a simulacrum of bygone days, now hidden and yet dreamt of in our midst.

Conclusion

Imagining Iran Otherwise

It is impossible to imagine Iran except in its immediate and distant environments. On the surface, Iran looks just like one among many other countries: one people, one nation, gathered around a flag. But a closer look reveals multiple peoples, sharing histories with other nations gathered around them. Iranian Arabs living on the northern shores of the Persian Gulf are connected to the larger Arab world; Iranian Kurds are part of a people divided into five adjacent countries; Iranian Baluchis have South Asian connections; Khurasanis are integral to Central Asia; and Azaris have a claim on the social and intellectual movements of the Caucasus. The empowering fact of these historic cross-currents of various cosmopolitanisms can in turn be broken up into separatist movements of Arabs, Kurds, Turks, and Baluchis, precisely because they have been systematically disenfranchised under both the Pahlavis and the Islamic Republic (the first monarchical Persianist, and the second sectarian Islamist, and both categorically in denial of the cosmopolitan reality that overcame them both). A distorted history of the nation has yielded to lopsided subnational sentiments and a prevalence of false consciousness, and thus produced dwarfed ideological positioning, robbing people of the enabling fact of their historical cosmopolitanism.

Given the transnational origin and disposition of all postcolonial nation-states, including but by no means limited to Iran or any other similar national formations in Asia, Africa, or Latin America, it is today imperative to retrieve and rearticulate the regional, and in fact global, consequences of a creative defiance of all the current frontier fictions that hold the fate of peoples imprisoned within frames of reference that confine and control their liberation movements. From Palestinians to Kurds, Baluchis, Azaris, and so on, people who have been historically denied their national formations can in fact overcome and dismantle the frontier fictions that have foreclosed their future, and offer alternative modalities of postnational solidarity and alliance.

Overcoming such frontier fictions, we discover that the rise of *territorial nationalism* is in fact squarely rooted in the prior formation of *aterritorial public spheres*. Upon the political potency of such frontier fictions, then, a *national economy* is presumed, and in turn a *national history* is imagined, giving rise to a *national polity*, from which a *national culture* then springs. The more ethnic and territorial nationalism insists on its veracity, longevity, and authenticity, the more clearly it exposes its anxiety of origin. The presence of Turkish, Kurdish, Arab, Baluch, Turkmen, and other components of Iran as a multifaceted nation destabilizes ethnic "Persian nationalism" just as much as it enriches and enables its transnational origins. The idea of Iran beyond its current borders that I propose here embraces the imperial pedigree of the nation as such, and remaps it within a transnational public sphere that embraces and enables all these people within an interpolated conception of the nation beyond its colonial concoction and postcolonial fetishization.

Early in the nineteenth century, Iran was emerging from its imperial age—from the splendor of the Safavids down to the long and languorous decline of the Qajars, incapable of dealing with the vastly changing world around them—weakened as it was by the Babi Movement, which had emerged from within its own Shi'i political culture. The pervasive reform movements of Mirza Hossein Khan Sepahsalar and Amir Kabir were not sufficient to enable the outdated Qajar monarchy to deal with the newly empowered European empires. Thus the best and most potent young minds left their homelands for adjacent realms, to breathe in the fresher air of the emerging world. As the Ottomans, the Qajars, and the Mughals had commenced their decline, Europe was rising, and in between these two colossal processes a new generation of thinkers emerged as now decidedly "public" intellectuals, forming a transnational public sphere within which they thrived. When they invented the term *vatan* ("homeland") to designate their nation-state, they were in effect giving that public sphere a code name, and lending it its transnational character. They were the most potent force in the emerging world, and what they produced in effect lay outside the fictive frontiers of the colonially conditioned nation-state—so much so that it would not be an exaggeration to suggest that the origin of "Iran" as a national identity in fact lies in the transnational activities of expatriate intellectuals.

One might also argue that the metaphysical force of Persian ethnic nationalism, so potent and powerful throughout the nineteenth century, is precisely a product of its germination among expatriate intellectuals who protested too much: the intensity of their Persianate nationalism was a camouflage for their anxiety of origin. Having left a village or small town for the cosmopolitan setting of Istanbul, Cairo, Calcutta, London, Paris, or Berlin, from where they imagined an entirely fictive homeland to which they were giving territorial, geopolitical, historical, and especially metaphysical reality. In this regard Frederick Jackson Turner's famous frontier thesis, *The Frontier in American History* (1893), assumes an unexpected significance, for it is in fact quite a potent argument for all postcolonial nation-states and their myths of origin. In this famous text, Turner advanced the provocative idea that American political culture was deeply informed by its roots in the rugged realities and open-endedness of frontier life. In the Iranian case, and those of other postcolonial nation-states in its vicinity, the frontier fiction assumes a monarchic character, and a simultaneous Shi'i disposition with an Islamic provenance—to which the Shi'i clerics had in turn added their own minority complex. In its monarchic disposition, the frontier fiction invokes the ancient frontiers of the old empires, from the Achaemenids to the Sassanids, while in its Shi'i-Islamic disposition it recalls the medieval Muslim empires, from the Abbasids down to the Safavids. Overcoming that frontier fiction, of both Pahlavi and the Shi'i gestation, is definitive in the discovery of a liberation geography that is open-ended and inviting.

Retrieving Hidden and Thriving Worlds

The central task in retrieving the cosmopolitan worldliness that surfaced historically in Asia, Africa, and Latin America is to overcome the cul-de-sac of European modernity, with all of the "alternative" or "multiple" modernities it has generated —all of them epistemically and culturally contingent on their decidedly colonial progenitor. Postmodernity and postcoloniality are both politically compromised and epistemically exhausted themes. They have nothing to offer the world at large. The issue has never been *modernity versus tradition*, or *modernity versus antimodernists*. Both colonizing and colonized minds have come together to manufacture this false binary. Factor out the whole colonial project of modernity, and the whole system collapses: the fake binary fades away. The question is, rather, between historical agency and subjection. As the European subject has come to its crisis in the aftermath of the Jewish Holocaust, the critical path for the articulation of a post-European subject is wide open, for now it is not just the terror European colonialism has visited throughout the globe that is the issue; it is the internal implosion of European modernity, at the site of Auschwitz, that has ended the project for good, for Europe itself. The enunciation and assertion of that agency beyond a Eurocentric world is predicated on (1) the articulation of an alternative cosmopolitan worldliness that has long existed, but camouflaged in such a way that it has yet to be mapped out; (2) retrieving modalities of subjection and historical agency embedded in those denied worlds.

From Kant and Hegel to Marx, Freud, Habermas, and Foucault, almost the entire gamut of the social sciences and humanities is exclusively articulated in terms of a self-universalizing European experience. Neither those experiences nor indeed those philosophical articulations hold any brief for the rest of the world, which at best has functioned as the anthropological field in which to corroborate Europe's civilizational alterities. The entire field of European and American anthropology is a domain in which the self-centering superiority of the location of knowledge-production is narratively constituted and systematically institutionalized. Long before the horrors of the Jewish Holocaust had frightened Adorno and Horkheimer out of their Eurocentric wits, the violence structural to the colonial corners of that selfsame Enlightenment modernity had wreaked havoc around the world. The theorization of non-European sites eventually gave rise to the generic field of "postcoloniality," which paradoxically only corroborated and consolidated the primacy of the "Western" world. We need, against the grain of that world, to rediscover those worlds that were glossed over by the overriding myth of "the West."

Paradoxically—or perhaps not—the retrieval of Iranian cosmopolitan culture is taking place in the language of the towering hegemony. Thus, the dismantling of the dominant hegemony is rightly and appropriately taking place in the dominant language—but so is the search for alternative worlds and worldviews that seek to disassemble the overriding *Weltanschauung* that today defines the world. The retrieval of that cosmopolitan worldliness requires not a totalizing narrative resembling the myth of "the West," but one in which history and metahistory come together organically to reveal alternative (emancipatory) worlds. While the historical narratives geared towards the constitution of a knowing subject can rely only on lived experiences, in art and literature we may detect the ruins of an allegorical constellation of dismantled worlds that Walter Benjamin saw as the fertile ground of our emerging agency. In contemporary Iranian art, particularly in its cinema and other visual arts, we sense the transcendent endurance of an intuition that cosmopolitan worldliness has generated and sustained in this living culture.

The task at hand is no longer the sudden discovery or forced articulation of alternative modernities. They are useless, ultimately only confirming and consolidating European Enlightenment modernity, long after Adorno and Horkheimer exposed their fundamental paradox. Instead, what is required is the specific articulation of historical agency and authorial subjecthood outside the normative, imaginative, and epistemic matrices of European (or, from the perspective of the world beyond Europe, categorical) colonial modernity. When you look at a picture by Abbas Kiarostami you have two options: either to assimilate it retrospectively to its presumed "Western" antecedents, or alternatively allow it to breathe and live within its own pictorial, aesthetic, and ontological idiomaticity, rooted in the Iranian and non-Iranian visual, performing, literary, and poetic arts. The location of these pictures in Iran, and their staging in European galleries or biennales, generates the forced *mise-en-scène* of self-alienation for these works of art. If imagined and seen in their own emotive universe, within the sphere of an Iran without borders, that world and worldliness are restored to these pictures, and allowed to reveal themselves. The work of art will then speak and teach its world in a contrapuntal semiotic lexicon that acknowledges other possible worlds and worldlinesses, but does not yield its specific aesthetic space to them. Any other way of looking at such a picture instantly turns it into an anthological curiosity, or an instance of "Western modernity." To be sure, very few artists have in fact achieved that visual intuition of transcendence. But those, like Kiarostami, who have achieved it have opened a whole new window onto the vista of aesthetic registers of worlds otherwise hidden and denied.

The project Europeans call Enlightenment modernity, as Adorno and Horkheimer realized only too painfully, ended up in the death camps of Auschwitz and Buchenwald, and the unsurpassed evil of the Holocaust. Before Adorno and Horkheimer, in his dissection of technological modernity and European humanism, Heidegger had articulated his critique of instrumental reason and technological modernity. But long before even Heidegger, it was Max Weber who had detected the end of enchantment in the beginning of instrumental reason and the commencement of European rational modernity, which he surmised would end up in an Iron Cage occupied by "specialists without spirit, sensualists without heart; this nullity imagines that it has attained a level of civilization never before achieved."[1]

Adorno, Horkheimer, Heidegger, and Weber were all Europeans, and Germans in particular, and so is the critical philosopher Jürgen Habermas, who, against the grain of his postmodern age, has tried to salvage the project of modernity by branding it still "unfinished." It is this particular pedigree of the European radical critique of modernity, long before it exploded into the monumental work of Michel Foucault and beyond him gave rise to the postmodern movement, that deeply colonized minds like those of Daryoush Ashuri and Aramesh Dustdar, and a whole banal band of nativist modernists (all of them unknown entities outside Iran, and yet alas widely read and regarded by monolingual Iranians trapped inside their own language), disregard when they attribute the critique of European modernity to anticolonial and postcolonial thinkers ranging from Aimé Césaire and Frantz Fanon to Edward Said and Gayatri Spivak, whom they dismiss as suffer-

---

[1] See Max Weber, *The Protestant Ethic and the Spirit of Capitalism* (New York: 1905), p. 182.

ing from a *ressentiment* against "the West." In them, a visceral hatred of the Islamic Republic has replaced any legitimate critique of that state; seduced by their wholesale purchase of the thing called "the West," they drag a particular brand of nativist Iranian intellectual into a deadening quagmire.

The equally significant critique of colonial modernity, and the long and forceful pedigree of postcolonial thinking it has enabled, had pondered the ravages of European modernity from the vantage point of the site of colonialism. Between the two of them, the postmodern and postcolonial critiques of instrumental reason have exposed the bourgeois disposition of the project of colonial modernity and the calamity it has visited upon the world. The rich and robust heritage of this critique of European modernity extends from the heart of Europe to the farthest reaches of the colonial world in Asia, Africa, and Latin America. But, subjected to an astonishing degree to their nativist limitations—for which one can only account by the fact that these mostly nativist intellectuals are trapped inside a troublingly monolingual world—these mostly expatriate Iranian thinkers, and the unfortunate younger generation that follows them, continue to present themselves as champions of an outdated and nonexistent "modernity," and thus represent their nemesis as recalcitrant and backward "traditionalists." The reach of expatriate intellectuals of this type is, to be sure, fairly limited. They operate within a cliquish club, and command a minimum of attention only to the degree that they represent the decaying relics of colonized minds at the tether end of the project.

This false and falsifying binary between the modernists (like Daryush Ashuri) and the traditionalists (like Seyyed Hossein Nasr) was further exacerbated soon after the Islamist takeover of the Iranian Revolution of 1979, when the ruling regime began to market its brutish elimination of its ideological nemesis in terms of "Islam" versus "secularism"—or, worse, "Westernization." A terrifying jargon of authenticity took over, and Muslims were sent on the wild-goose chase of finding their "true self." Instrumental in the consolidation of this binary was the rise of a particular brand of public intellectual who now called themselves *Roshanfekr-e Dini* ("religious intellectuals"). These intellectuals were at first wholeheartedly supportive of the ruling Islamist regime, aiding and abetting it in purging the universities of their intellectual rivals, and helping the reigning Shi'i clerics to conduct a succession of cultural revolutions. But eventually, as the brute and vicious disposition of the ruling regime became evident—especially from the actions of its security and military apparatus—these "religious intellectuals" parted ways with the regime, and were forced into silence at home or subjected to the indignity of living abroad, outside their manufactured habitat. But whether they coalesced with the circumstances and stayed in the country or opposed the regime and left, these religious intellectuals continued to think and write precisely in those binary terms of "religious" versus "secular," and thus joined forces with the self-declared "secularists" and "modernists" to plunge the cosmopolitan fact of Iranian political culture into the abyss of a false and falsifying consciousness.

The propagation of this false consciousness continues apace in Persian, because much of this outlandish debate between the ossified "secularists" and their recalcitrant "religious" adversaries takes place in Persian—both sides trapped in an astonishingly impoverished intellectual vacuum, isolated from the rest of the world. Why? Because the universities suffer inside, the public sphere is brutalized by censorship, and expatriate intellectuals spend most of their days driving cabs in Germany, or receiving undeserved pensions from their European host countries; or else they sign up for lucrative grants from neoconservative outfits in Washington DC, and continue to produce gibberish that hardly anyone reads.

Dominated by an ideologically insecure and thus vulgar regime, the Persian-speaking world remains aloof from the rest of the world, since much of the scholarship on modern Iranian history—the product of various groundbreaking theoretical and philosophical debates—is necessarily published in English, or to a much lesser degree in other European languages. Against the grain of this mothballed nativism, a direct link connects Iranian artists, poets, filmmakers, and literati, both within and outside Iran, to meet the active theorization of a postnational consciousness that from Asia to Africa to Europe and the Americas altogether posits an entirely different and entirely liberating historical emplotment for anyone who still cares to call herself or himself Iranian.

Towards a Critique of the Postcolonial Nation

What are the terms of that liberation? In the introduction to this book, I pointed out how today the idea of the "nation" is trapped within its manufactured postcolonial borders, and unduly coupled with the systematic function of violence in any conception of the state. Today the notorious gang known as "Islamic State" is precisely what it says it is: it is "Islamic" and it is a "state." It is "Islamic" precisely in the combative sense manufactured by the Islamist ideologues in the aftermath of their colonial encounter with European capitalist modernity; and it is a pure "state" in its brutish monopoly on naked violence, without any claim on any nation. It is a fiction, rooted in reality. Its naked violence is its means of conquering lands that it rules with a brutish juridicalism bereft of any trace of Islamic culture or civility. The "Jewish state" in Israel, the "Islamic Republic" in Iran, "Hindu fundamentalism" in India, "Buddhist nationalism" in Burma—and the "Christian empire" of the United States, which seeks to rule them all—were all preconditions for the emergence of this "Islamic state." The "Islamic State" thus represents the return of the repressed of all states, the fact of their decoupling from any nation they might claim as theirs, and the fictional carving out of a "caliphate" against the fact and phenomenon of the formation of all postcolonial nations within a transnational public sphere.

The central argument and the defining leitmotif of this book point to a new and liberating reading of Iran as a postcolonial nation-state imagined beyond its current manufactured frontiers. I have sought to map out a topography of the nation beyond its colonially imposed frontiers—a conception of the very idea of the nation that actively remembers and reauthorizes its transnational, cosmopolitan origins, and thereby seeks to defy the self-enclosed banality of domestic tyranny and imperial domination, which have fed on each other to perpetuate a cycle of state violence and national disenfranchisement. The result is a theoretically ambitious contemplation on the larger frame of reference I have explored over the years and named *liberation geography*. The idea of a nation without borders liberates the nation from its fixed cartography of domination, in which domestic tyranny feeds on a fear of foreign domination. The idea of the nation I put forward here dismantles this vicious circle.

To take a necessary distance from the rapidity of current events, so as to enable us to read them more accurately, this book is a considered act of remembrance—a defiant invocation of origins consistently repressed, here actively recollected and articulated in pursuit of an emancipatory destination, overcoming the trauma of a colonial birth to renew a pact with a postcolonial history no longer trapped in the gridlock of coloniality. This book will reset the course of the postcolonial study of nation-states by demonstrating how today the fate of nations is determined by turbulent forces entirely outside the purview of any national consciousness, to the degree that this consciousness remains decidedly nativist, domestic, and falsely localized, against the grain of its transnational, trans-regional, and global origins. Remembering and expanding the transnational disposition of the nation, as I show in this book, is a defiant epistemic act that relocates the political idea of citizenship back on the track of societal sovereignty beyond a retrograde monarchy then or even a more backward nativist and sectarian theocracy now—neither of which has ever had a legitimate claim on the integrity, totality, and entirety of that transnational origin or its thriving postnational consciousness.

From its imperial origins, Iran eventually emerged as a postcolonial nation-state deeply conscious of its far wider, much richer, and more diversified cultural and territorial heritage. Today Iran, Afghanistan, and Tajikistan are three distinct postcolonial nation-states with a common claim on the Iranian cultural legacy. That legacy is precolonial, and thus postnational. The collective consciousness predicated on that heritage was neither falsely placed at the service of an outdated monarchy (the Pahlavis) nor denied by an even more retrograde theocracy. But the greater the absence of that enabling cosmopolitan legacy within the political apparatus of any ruling regime, the more it extends its multifarious roots into the collective consciousness of the nation at large.

My contention has been that the historical consciousness necessary for us to understand momentous events such as the fall of the Qajar and Pahlavi dynasties, as well as the rise of the Islamic Republic and the profound crisis of legitimacy it now faces, must be located where it belongs: in the painstakingly cultivated transnational public sphere claimed and reproduced by a *public reason* that is both its parent and offspring. The enduring fact and the historical phenomenon of that transnational public sphere and its contingent public reason, and all their revolutionary and transformative potential, constitute the springboard of any future politics of liberation. This book is a sustained account of the details of that emancipatory politics.

Hidden Messages of Nations Beyond Borders

In Rumi's allegory, the merchant is the carrier of a message of whose substance he is unaware. The message remains embedded in the gesture of the Indian parrots, and carries itself symbiotically mutated until the parrot in Persia decodes and interprets it. Rumi gives the message a meaning within the context of his own mysticism beyond what the Indian parrots could have intended, or beyond what the Persian parrot interpreted, and certainly beyond what the merchant could comprehend. But the link between the parrots in India and the parrot in Persia remains still coded, loaded, subject to further readings, decoding, unloading. Rumi told this story in the thirteenth century, but its origins must be much older. By the fifteenth century the link between the Indian subcontinent and Rumi's home in Asia Minor became more real, when generations of Iranian and Indian poets came together to give a new meaning and momentum to Persian poetry. Rumi reads the story of the parrots as containing advice not to be too verbose or plaintive, not to sing, not to articulate, from separation, but to remain silent—in fact, to pretend you are dead so that you are set free. Therefore, he firmly recommends, one ought to remain silent; and yet, paradoxically perhaps, Rumi himself was far from silent, despite his nom de plume: Khamush ("Silent"). He was exceptionally articulate—eloquence was the very definition of his legacy, his poetry urging others into silence so that they could hear. But what exactly is it to hear when we stop talking and writing in a familiar language, stop reading the dominant prose, demanding and exacting something else?

The contemporary history of postcolonial nations like Iran, Afghanistan, Tajikistan, and Iraq is like a body of coded messages—messages from their own repressed history, from the imperial to the colonized, used, abused, left to rot, stillborn to the hegemony of the world that calls itself "the West." However, when we place Iran in its environment, that deadly, encoded message starts decoding itself, recovering repressed memories, retrieving hidden messages. The task is to recover those hidden geographies of emotions, connections, of having been in the world.

In an attempt to retrieve that hidden history, the idea of Iran without borders maps a daring topography of the nation beyond its colonially manufactured fictive frontiers, as it stipulates a conception of the very idea of the nation that actively remembers and reauthorizes its transnational, cosmopolitan origins, and thereby seeks to defy the self-enclosed circularity of domestic tyranny and imperial domination that feed one another. Iran without borders is located within the larger frame of reference I have already identified, in my book *The Arab Spring* (2012), as "liberation geography," a remapping of the world beyond its colonial contortions. This idea liberates the nation from its fixed cartography of domination by *domestic* tyranny fearing (and feeding on this fear of) *foreign* domination. Iran without borders is decidedly an act of remembrance, a defiant vision of an origin consistently repressed, now actively recollected and articulated towards an emancipatory destination, overcoming the trauma of a colonial birth for a renewed pact with a postcolonial history no longer trapped in the gridlock of coloniality. The fate of the nation is today determined by forces and ferocities entirely outside the purview of a national consciousness, to the degree that this consciousness remains decidedly domestic, nativist, and localized, against the very grain of its transnational origins. Between the monarchic delusions of an imperial past and the theocratic sectarianism of a postcolonial present, the idea of Iran without borders cuts through two compounding political banalities to retrieve an emancipatory atlas of lived experiences.

Remembering and expanding the transnational disposition of the nation is a defiant epistemic act to relocate the very idea of citizenship back on the site of societal sovereignty and beyond a retrograde monarchy or an even more backward theocracy—neither of which has ever had a legitimate claim on the integrity of that transnational origin or its thriving postnational consciousness. My contention in this book is that historical consciousness must be placed where it belongs: on the transnational public sphere claimed and cultivated by a *public reason* that is both the parent and the offspring of that public sphere. The geographical fact and the historical phenomenon of that transnational public sphere and public reason, and all their revolutionary and transformative potentials, are the springboard of any future politics of liberation.

That liberation is already taking place in the realm of ideas and arts, in anticipation of their wider realization beyond the politics of corruption and despair that now rules nations. In a beautifully nostalgic melody, Mohsen Namjoo's widely popular song, "Khat Bekesh" ("Draw a Line")—which in colloquial Persian means something like "forget about it, let it go!" The song is meditative, melancholic, self-referential. Staging the song, you see Namjoo sitting alone playing his tar, singing in a subdued tone.[2] Two female backup singers then join him, and with the famous melody of Dean Martin's "Sway," they are joined by a pianist and sing:

> *Ma keh Rah-e Rafteh-im Bad ast keh Migozarad …*
> We are the road all traveled,
> It's the wind that will pass over us—
> We are broken-hearted,
> It is the memory that will have emigrated—
> Draw a line around Iran, draw a line man, draw a line!
> Cursed be this fate, spit it on it, I say!

---

2 For a clip of this performance, see youtube.com/watch?v=IOz4 VSEqXN4.

Dean Martin's playful "dance with me" has now fused sway-ingly with Namjoo's melancholic lyrics, jointly generating a mellifluous dissonance. The fusion of joy and melancholy that ensues is jarring, liberating, defiant, and subversive of the ruling banality in Namjoo's homeland—now musically expanded to the emotive universe he generates from his studio in Brooklyn, or in concert halls around the world. In his lyrics Namjoo combines sense and nonsense, as in his music he combines local and global, native and national, domestic and regional, to sing songs of a decidedly metromelodic reach. The result is a harmonious liminality that expands and over-comes both sides of any cultural divide. So, paradoxically, he in fact erases any fictive line around the nation precisely at the moment when he says "draw a line around Iran," remember-ing and singing it far more loudly exactly when he says "forget about Iran."

Iran without borders is the liberation geography of various peoples cross-identified and thrown out of an imperial past, embedded in a postcolonial frontier fiction, overriding the factual evidence of a transnational public sphere that has enabled and empowered them throughout their contempo-rary history. Deeply dialogized into a glorified monarchism on one side, mesmerized by a triumphalist Islamism on the other, the historical agency of an entire citizenry is held hostage to its own complacency, its imagination held captive. The ruling regime competes with an "opposition" it has begotten through the banality of its brute power. In between them lurks what calls itself *Farhang* ("culture")—a miasmatic specter of things soaring to become sublime and beautiful, and yet spinning around itself in a quagmire of self-deception. It is that very *Farhang* that relies on the indeterminacy of its varied func-tions as a *pharmakon*. It is through this *Farhang* that what is today the dying soul of the culture can become its invigorat-ing body, what is staged as good exposed as evil, whereupon a hidden, inner history becomes manifest—its memory disappearing into forgetfulness, and what is forgotten remembered with vigor.

To retrieve and reclaim the forgotten worldliness of the idea of Iran—born somewhere beyond its imperial past and its frontier fictions—requires a bold and brave defiance of the ruling fanaticism of clerical Shi'ism and all its manufactured alterities, from the mighty myth of "the West" to the jejune chicaneries of its "opposition." The agent of that change is no ordinary revolution, and certainly no chimeric reform. Like the dawning of a new historic consciousness, it will have to surface from the deepest recesses of a people's history, their awareness of a not-so-glorious imperial past and not so trapped a postcolonial frontier fiction. Iran without borders is the manifesto of that history yet to be remembered and lived, now to be written and laid bare. The fluidity of peoples and their lived experiences negotiates the gravitational pull of the two poles of *identity* and *alterity*. Neither of these two poles is fixed, essential, or predicated on any metaphysical certainty. All metaphysical certainties have melted, dissolved, and disappeared into thin air. The current political crises of Islamism and Islamophobia, Persianism and Iranophobia, Eurocentricism and Europhobia, are simply the final flames of various dying candles. The sun is rising from an entirely different horizon, and will set on a planet yet to be mapped.

Acknowledgments

I developed the idea of this book in many fruitful conversations with Audrea Lim at Verso. She initially proposed the idea of writing a new book for Verso, and always had sound advice and a perfectly pitched pair of ears to listen to my ideas as I embarked on writing the book in one swoop, from A to Z. She then went through a first draft and offered sound advice, critical comments, and some very helpful suggestions. To her and to the entire Verso editorial team goes my enduring gratitude. My research assistant at Columbia University, Hawa Ansari, was exceptionally helpful in the course of writing the book—finding resources on and off the Internet, and chasing after high-resolution images and permission to use them as illustrations. The final draft of this book was carefully proofread by Dina Khatib to find typographical mistakes. I am grateful to her. My good friend and colleague, the distinguished contemporary art historian Hamid Keshmirshekan, was equally helpful in securing a high-resolution image of the magnificent Abbas Kiarostami photograph that now graces the cover, and permission to use it. I am equally grateful to good friends Nicky Nodjoumi and Azadeh Akhlaghi for allowing me to use their artwork. Carlos Stuart of Flood Gallery kindly extended both permission and high-resolution copies for the Iranian posters in their possession. Generations of my graduate students, some of them now leading scholars and academic professionals in their own right, have been my most immediate interlocutors. My colleagues at Columbia have provided a network of trust and confidence, support and solidarity, that enables me to try to be worthy of their enduring friendship and camaraderie. Columbia, like any other major university, is indeed an ivory tower, and I dwell in that tower blissfully confident that I have an angle on the world worth sharing. I dedicate this book to two dear friends, Alejandra Gómez Colorado and Moisés Garduño García, whose unending kindness, enduring solidarity, and generous hospitality during my many trips to Mexico City have mapped the immediate contours of the emotive universe I occupied when writing the book. I thank you all, friends—beyond all borders.

Index

Index

Index

Index

Index